AF695971

FIRE@40!

(Applied Personal Finance)

P. Leerberg

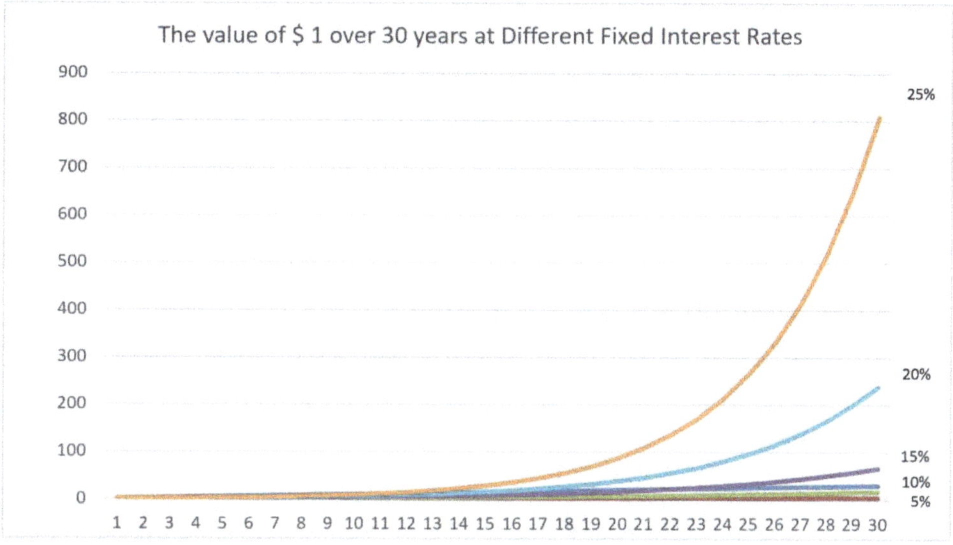

© Executive Business Consulting Ltd

Disclaimer:
Neither the author nor the company is responsible for any errors or omissions, or for the results obtained from the use of the information contained in this publication. All information in this book is provided "as is", without any guarantee of completeness, accuracy, timeliness or the results obtained from the use of this information.

The material in this publication is subject to the provisions of the Copyright Act. Without a separate agreement with the copyright holders, any reproduction and making available is only permitted to the extent permitted by law or permitted through an agreement with Kopinor, an interest organization for copyright holders. Exploitation in violation of law or agreement may result in liability for damages and confiscation and may be punished with fines or imprisonment. Inquiries about this course can be directed to the publisher.

Automated analysis of the work to obtain information, in particular about patterns, trends and relationships ("text and data mining"), is prohibited.

FiRE@40! (Applied Personal Finance). © 2002, 2003, 2024 P. Leerberg

Automated analysis of the work to obtain information, in particular about patterns, trends and relationships ("text and data mining"), is prohibited.

Copyright © 3.rd. ed. 2024 Per Leerberg. All rights reserved.
Cover Design: © Executive Business Consulting Ltd.
Published 2025 by Ikkyo Publishing, a part of Executive Business Consulting Ltd.

Ikkyo Publishing books may be purchased for educational, business, or sales promotional use. Online editions are also available for most titles. For more information, contact our corporate/institutional sales department at ask@fireat40.com or ask@executivewayto.com

See https://fireat40.com or https://executivewayto.com for any release details.

The Ikkyo Publishing logo, and the Mastering Business Management logo are registered trademarks of Executive Business Consulting Ltd.

Many of the designations used by manufacturers and sellers to distinguish their products are claimed as trademarks. Where those designations appear in this book, and Ikkyo Publishing was aware of a trademark claim, the designations have been printed in caps or initial caps.

Although the publisher and author have used reasonable care in preparing this book, the information it contains is distributed "as is" and without warranties of any kind. This book is not intended as legal or financial advice, and not all of the recommendations may be suitable for your situation. Professional legal and financial advisors should be consulted, as needed. Neither the publisher nor the author shall be liable for any costs, expenses, or damages resulting from use of or reliance on the information contained in this book.

Paperback ISBN: 978-82-94176-04-5
Digital ISBN: 978-82-94176-05-2

"It is impossible for man to learn what he thinks he already knows"
Epictetus (60-120A.C.) Roman philosopher.

Why do some people succeed over time while others don`t?

FiRE@40! *(Applied Personal Finance)* is a book equally suitable for practitioners who do not have higher formal education, and for those who have higher education but want an up-to-date, research-based refresher. Just like all my other books in the ***Mastering Business Management*** series.

To my best friend Hilde!

My best friend, the love of my life, and the mother of our wonderful son!

To my very best bestfriend Knuta!

Numbers are in themselves not interesting!
But the information they give us is.

You are as always the spreader of joy and happiness,
and you use the knowledge I gave you back then.

I couldn't be prouder of either you or your call!

To everyone and anyone.

I think the biggest mistake everyone makes in the western world is to think that I`m so unique that no one else is as smart as me. This is arrogance.

Likewise, I think an equally big mistake is to think that no one else thinks like me, which leads to loneliness.

In this lies the understanding that many people have relatively similar thoughts and are not at all more unique than that they lead to relatively similar patterns of action.

In all other cultures, this results in the needs of the group being put before those of the individuals, regardless of the human or material cost.

Preface

This book contains the most applicable part of economics and finance for non-economists from the business school educations, whether we are talking about Master of Economics and Administration-MEA or Master of Business and Administration-MBA. This book has two parts. The first part, "Part I: Exogenous Conditions", contains one chapter each on macroeconomics, microeconomics, behavioral economics, and cost and operating accounting. The lion's share of this book, "Part II: Endogenous Conditions" is all about personal finance. First of all applicable for non-economists in mind.

Why start the book with these four chapters on what someone would call "business thinking" in a book on personal finance? Some of the arguments in the discission with my MEA son and a couple of professors, is that first of all, it is difficult to make well-considered decisions without having deeper than superficial knowledge of how everything affects you. To understand this you need to know why things happen, and therefor how this again is going to affect you personally. So, the simple answer to the question is that you need to have a broader view on why global economy affects you. How does a war affect your personal finances? Why does one industry react one way, and another opposite to the same situation? What happens with your job? Why doesn't you salary increase as much as the prices in general, and why and how does inflation occur? Why do the government do the opposite of the Fed? How's that affecting general employment, and is the "promise of lower rates" something you can rely on? How does the companies increase the prices, often more than the inflation index? What will happen next?

These are questions I think young adults need to understand about the economy of the world around themselves to be able to make good, sensible and well-thought-out financial choices based on serious knowledge. Also, a lion's share of this book , the section *"Part II: Endogenous condition"* is about applied personal finance, the same chapters you'll find in that book. So you don't need both. However, that book was written with high school level in mind. These four chapters of Exogenous conditions is much more demanding to grasp, so I've written those chapters for non-economists maybe with a program in personal economy at high school. It should work well in a class as a colloquium, perhaps at college, and absolutely for young adults in search for literature on personal economy and finance.

Being an economist does actually not mean you have a formal economic education or diploma. Being a *good* economist means that you have trained what you've studied and keep thinking in an analytical about economy, using your understanding in a practical manner. However, one of the most important things to remember about the economical subjects is that they in themselves are founded in logics. And that most of the financial subjects you need in your personal everyday life are algebra you learned before you entered high school. Even though some professional elements are very advanced! The financial part is put in the section *"Part II: Endogenous condition"*. This is the part you influences and controls directly itself.

So why didn't you learn it at middle school? However, you learned to calculate how fast a ball rolls down a slope at a 45 degrees angle, and when two trains with different speed meet on a railway. But not everyone wants to become a physicist, engineer, doctor or astronaut. On the other hand, *absolutely everyone has to deal with their personal finances*!

I have used my most practical glasses writing this book. So, in this book, I'll show you how MBAs and MEAs think about personal finance, both the knowledge from economics, and from finance. Because as a regular wage slave, like 8 billion other people, you can actually retire when you are around forty if you start early and apply the knowledge from this book. Anyway, regardless of your age, you will be much better off financially if you follow the principles and actively use the examples from the book.

This easy to read book is should suit anyone interested in mastering their private economy in simple but effective way. From high school level and onwards.

BEST OF LUCK ON YOUR PERSONAL FINANCE JOURNEY!

Table of content

Introduction

At the time of writing this, a lot of Millennials and Gen-X have identified themselves with the FIRE (*Financial Independent, Retire Early*) trend. Their goal is no more mysterious than to gain control over their personal finances, save the "daily surplus", and invest this in order to be able to drop out of the working life at the age of about 40. To achieve this, they follow many of the same principles you will find in this book, which again is the principles that the Masters of Economy (MEA) or MBA`s are using to tackle everyday situations in daily life themselves. Because it is both simple and yet so incredible effective.

The lion's share of this book, ***"FIRE@40!"***, is about *financial economics*. You will find this part in my book *"Applied Personal Finance (What You Just have to Master!)"* intended for high school readers and onwards. It was originally written to my own son 23 years ago so he could be financially independent no matter what life path he chose as an adult. I say it`s simple, because that part (Part II: The endogenous conditions) is just algebra we all learned in middle school, but which the average student never learned to apply in everyday life. I will therefore systematically review how you can use and use this knowledge in your own applied personal finances.

There are four elements that make you financially independent, or FIRE@40:

1. It`s knowledge,

2. It`s will,

3. It's savings,

4. It's investment

Through these elements, we learn to see how we can manage our cash flow (our income and expenses) and that we always can save some of it. This gives us an interest in gaining control of our finances, what we call *cost control*, so that we can invest some of what we save. That's how you become *FIRE@40!*. If you start early in your work life. *But no matter what your age is, you too can come much better off!* Because reduced consumption today leads to increased consumption tomorrow and vica versa: The more you spend today, the more sorry you`ll be tomorrow.

However, in this book, ***"FiRE@40!",*** the point of everything is that in part 1, I want to show you how you can understand how the world around you affects your life. And part 2 *(same as the book "Applied Personal Finance" What You Just have to Master!)* how you yourself can take control of your daily life's need to adapt to personal financial challenges. The material is presented in an everyday way, however scientific grounded. Because part II was initial intended for students and wage earners from the level of high school onwards, and for those who are not going to take a master's degree in finance themselves. Although it can be difficult to imagine that this will be necessary so early in life as, for example, high school: The sooner you get access to this knowledge and understand how to use it, the better the end result. And the less financial problems you will experience in life. This knowledge was just as relevant 20 years ago as it is today and as it will be in the next 20, 30, 40 or 50 years. If the world hasn't ended in the meantime. So I'll help you get started here.

This is not an AI product! Behind this book there is a lot of hard work! Because AI cannot help anyone to think for themselves. The apps I have built in Excel, and the explanations of the financial mathematics used here in the book, are also my own. These are apps that I use even today. I explain to you the financial mathematics (it's not as difficult as you think!) it's simple algebra we learned from middle school: Fraction calculus, percentage calculus and simple equations with one unknown. Thus, you can do the calculations yourself with pen, paper and a small table calculator. Or you can build the models in Excel yourself and test whether they are correct, as I have done. By the way, it would fit well as a work project for a family, a study group, or in a class in high school and onwards. Then the knowledge and understanding will increase even more in groups.

References to this book can be found in Appendix A. Suggestions for further reading at college/university level can be found in Appendix B.

You can find more information about me and my books on:
executivewayto.com or at fireat40.com

Chapter 1. The General Idea

"You can become a multi-millionaire as an ordinary wage earner. Yes, actually! Without winning in Lottery, and without doing anything criminal. You just need a bit of knowledge to be able to use it. So I'll help you get started here." (Cicco, A., 2002)

1.1 What this book is about

However, as I was not talking about *dollar-millionaire* in my first book. It was figuratively speaking. Because that is a question of what currency we are talking about. Pesos? Easy. Scandinavian Krones? Harder. Dollars or Euros? Even tougher. Nevertheless, numbers in themselves are not interesting, but that is certainly the information they can give us! You can also achieve the dream of becoming financially independent and retiring from working life already from the age of 40 if that is the goal. Just like the goal is for the F.I.R.E - movement today no matter what currency we're talking about.

How?

In middle school, or junior high school, we learn arithmetic and algebra, and it is a very useful knowledge. So we learn to calculate how fast an object moves from A to B, when two vehicles meet on a railway line when they have different speed or how fast a ball rolls down a slope at a 45 degree angle. But not everyone wants to become a physicist, doctor or astronaut. On the other hand, *absolutely everyone has to deal with personal finances*!

But we don't learn much about that when we should have. The basic idea of this book is to show you all the economic topics that you, as a student, or ordinary wage earner, are interested in knowing something about in relation to getting more benefit from your salary. To become financially independent or becoming a true FIRE if you wish. Because all people want to get the most out of the money they already have, but most don't understand how. I`ll show you all the powerful but easy techniques and explain the theories on how to gain personal financial control or become a ***FIRE@40!*** if you like. So you understand how you can apply them to your own life if you wish. Maybe you won`t let yourself be fooled by cheap tricks from financial institutions. Included, you'll find 37 *"Test-yourself-questions"* and summary answers, so you can develop your understanding of how to adapt to different financial situations that you encounter in your future life.

1.2 Who this book is for.

This is not meant as a playbook for professional programs, nor is it a math book. ***FiRE@40!(Applied Personal Finance)*** *is equally suitable for any practitioner from senior high school level and onwards but will work well in a study group. For those who do not have higher formal education as for those who have higher education but want an up-to-date, research-based refresher. Just like any books in the* ***Mastering Business Management*** *series.*

I don't know of any other books that cover these personal finance topics the way I do here. I have simply written a book I wish I had myself in the early professional life. There are, of course, various other books on these subjects, and far more advanced ones, but written for the professional MEAs and MBAs. I have given you a couple of tips for such books in Appendix A and B. But they are very advanced and are not about personal finance but on business finance. It is not easy to familiarize yourself with beta-values and other advanced mathematical topics as a private individual, so we leave the very advanced stuff here. My approach is the opposite because in the first place I wrote the lion's share of this book for my newborn son thinking: *"How can a subject I know a lot about fit into his life, regardless of what he wants as a profession as an adult?"*

This book is for all kinds of visionary people, from the youngest, most eager with allowance, or without parental support, to wage workers who wonder how the economic future can be improved despite the conditions around them. Or for those who made some wrong choices and ended up in debt, but who wants to get back in the saddle again in order to cope financially and have a much better financial everyday life from today on.

The language and pedagogy in this book is made for anyone who may be interested in these subject. For everyone who can read every day English, starting with ordinary students in high school or college. It`s for those who want to understand these important connections and want to be able to use it themselves. That is, for everyone who didn`t go to the university or business school just to improve their personal financial stands. So, all technical terms that are used are explained and hopefully it is in an understandable way to everyone interested.

1.3 What this book contains.

You actually learned all the easy basic financial formulas already at middle school; however no one showed you how to apply it on everyday matters that absolutely *everyone* must face in their life: *Applied Personal Finance. Why not?* Because neither you teacher nor your parents learned it themselves, unless they've studied economics and finance. Only professional economists have learned these topics. But their formal education involves handling complex business-related situations where the pace is completely different from that in private life. Of course, they deal with a lot of this simple algebra on a personal daily basis, but most of what they use as professionals is far more advanced. But they don't focus on most of the basics I show you here.

I will not tell you what to do, but I will certainly show you how economists thinks of finance in our personal life. I`ll show you all the important techniques you can benefit from as an ordinary wage earner and *explain how and why* it all fits together. I will show you the simple, most important, effectful, and actually the most powerful part of financial economics as Master of Economics and Administration (MEA) or Master of Business Administration (MBA) study at business schools and uses as civilians themselves. Simultaneously you can train on 37 *test yourself questions with summary answers* to understand how to apply the theories in practical life, so you can make it work for yourself.

So, Part I of the book contains four chapters from the exogenous conditions, i.e. how the conditions you hardly thinks of in society around you affects you. Like how and why prices are rising, or why governmental spending can increase GDP more than tax reductions or that not losing is more important than winning is making humans compete at all levels. The idea is to give you a larger, 360-degree view of the exogenous conditions, before we dive into the endogenous conditions of practical financial economy that you can act on and can control yourself. It can be a little more difficult to get to grapple with the first two exogenous chapters on macro- and microeconomics, than the rest of the book. But I advise you to read it anyway. If you find it hard to grasp; then after finishing the book, turn back and read it again, because that part needs to mature, so second time it will be much more comprehensible!

The lion's share of the book, Part II, is on applied personal finance. In this part of the book, you'll find all the everyday examples I have told you about, which most of the chapters have the *test-yourself-questions with summary answers* I spoke of earlier. If you use them without checking the answer before you have pondered your way to the solution, you will hopefully have become a racer on personal finance by the time you finish this book! Please do remember that the size of the numbers in the examples are there just as examples, the scale of everything does not alter the point of the theories!

So, whether you want to become an engineer, a supermarket clerk, a teacher, a health worker, a firefighter, an electrician, a police officer, a doctor or already are one of the aforementioned, to name just a few professions: Keep this book close to your heart in life! Because it never gets out of style.

1.4 How to Use this Book

The goal of this book is *not* that you should become a financial acrobat. *The goal* is for you to be better equipped to make more qualified personal choices for your own life and get more out of the financial means you have at your disposal. In other words, to manage *your cash flow*, as we economists call it, *in the best possible way for you.* Before you start taking on a loan, lease a car, use credit cards in the bars, or maybe give up trying to buy a home all together. Thus we arrive at what the lion's share of the book is all about; How you can relate to the society around you, how you can plan, save, invest and finance your life as a student or ordinary wage earner for yourself or your family. Just like the MEAs or the MBAs do themselves. Without undertaking

5 years of heavy financial and personal sacrifices as a student to find this interesting fraction of it all.

I know of no other book that treat these subjects the way I do. There are of course many different books of these topics, but my idea is that you should read one chapter at a time. I`ll explain and show you how the professional MEAs or MBAs think of all these situations in our private life. From first paragraph of macroeconomics to the last one on infinite growth series. The idea is that you should progress in a reflective way on how it can fit into your project, in your situations, your life, in your world. If learning math, or economics was not a success in your previous school careers, I have created Excel apps/models for you to download from our website. You will find directions in the first chapter we are going to use them, so read on!

When you have worked through the whole book on ***FiRE@40*** *Applied Personal Finance,* then what? I`ll give you only one piece of advice: Keep this book close at heart, because everything in it is relevant as long as we have an economy based on exchanging all kinds of commodities for a value of any kind of money. When you come to think *"Where did I read..."* or *"How was that again?",* pick up my book (just as I still do), and look up what you have read earlier to be reminded. Like your personal financial encyclopedia.

A warning before you continue: I am not responsible for what you get out of what I write, but you are indeed yourself.

BEST OF LUCK IN YOUR IMPROVED PERSONAL FINANCIAL LIFE!

You can find more information about me and my books on:
executivewayto.com or at fireat40.com

Part I: Exogenous Conditions

Chapter 2. Macroeconomics

"The central concerns of macroeconomics are (1) the short-term business cycle and (2) the long-term economic growth". (Schiller, B., 2016)

We start with economics, which is one of the three "pillars" of all business management, a large subject that permeates everything. In other words, it means home economics or housekeeping. In other words, economics is about distributing scarce resources as sensibly as possible, *not* about grabbing as much as possible yourself. Economic thinking is based on the premise that there is a scarcity of resources, i.e. that there are not enough resources to satisfy all needs that exist. Today, we divide economics into various specialized disciplines, such as social economics, which we in turn divide into macroeconomics (society) and microeconomics (industries), and business economics (companies), which in turn includes the branches of accounting and financial subjects.

In relation to running a business, it is very important to have insight into all five disciplines in the economics subjects. But here too, we will take the practical short version, because every single one of the five disciplines contains thousands of syllabus pages, and we do not have room for that. It is also far beyond the purpose of this book. From a purely pedagogical point of view, I therefore think that we start with the major economic conditions, i.e. (international) trade economy, (national) macroeconomics, then zoom in on (industry-specific) microeconomic conditions, before we flick into behavioral economics. Then we look at business economics' focus on internal business issues such as internal management data and understand different calculation models. We skip accounting and business financial challenges, but we steer straight into private financial matters that you can control yourself.

2.1. Eight important factors in macroeconomics

In these first four chapters, I will try to be brief, I hope that it will not be too short. So we start with macroeconomics, which is the overall picture, the major global and national conditions. First, some global conditions, i.e. trade theory. Few other topics in economic theory have attracted as much interest as trade theory. From around the 1500s, the first representations were prepared by philosophers and politicians. Their view was that the state's task was to increase the nation's wealth by stimulating exports and preventing imports, we call them mercantilists. The trade surplus was to be invested in precious metals such as gold. Opponents of mercantilism found their support in the philosopher Adam Smith's 1776 treatise *"An Inquiry into the Nature and Causes of the Wealth of Nations",* which we like to refer to as *"The Wealth of Nations".* In it, he emphasized division of labor and specialization. We like to call Adam Smith "the father of economics".

These principles were worked on by David Ricardo, who contributed to our understanding that a country always has a comparative advantage, even if other countries have an absolute advantage in producing all goods. The principle is that two countries that both produce the same commodity, A and B will one be more efficient in the production of, for example, one commodity A compared to commodity B, and vice versa in the other country. Then both countries can benefit from production specialization and trade with each other, even if one country is absolutely superior in the production of both goods. This is Ricardo's *"principle of comparative advantage."*

Another important turn in trade theory came with the two Swedes behind the Heckscher-Ohlin theory, which explained *why* a country was comparatively inferior in the production of certain goods, but comparatively superior in the production of other goods. Capital-strong countries will therefore concentrate their production on capital-intensive goods and export these, while labor-intensive goods will be produced and exported from poor countries with a lot of cheap labor. Their point was that trade is really about the exchange of factors of production and that the prices of the individual factors of production between these countries will tend to equal to some extent over time.

2.2. The national product and the various concepts of "... flation"

We stick to the national conditions in this chapter, so we take the initiative and start by defining the concept of Domestic Product. By this we mean a relatively complete overview of the entire national economy in a way that makes it easy to grasp the contexts in which we are particularly interested. We start with Gross Domestic Product (GDP), which is the total value of the goods and services generated in a country's economy during a specific period of time, typically a calendar year. This term is often defined as follows; *«The total market value of all final goods and services produced within a nation's borders in a given time period.»*. (Schiller, B., 2016).

In the same way that we distinguish between nominal interest rates (R_{nom}) and real interest rates (R_r) (we discuss this in more detail in Chapter 14), we distinguish between nominal GDP and real GDP. Schiller formulates real GDP, or GDP_r, with this formula

$$BNPr = \frac{\text{Nominal (GDP) in year } t}{\text{Price index}}$$

The main difference between GDP_r and GDP_{nom} is that GDP_{nom} does not take into account how inflation (or deflation) affects the price of goods over time. GDP_r is *the increase* in goods and services produced. The price is as a consequence of inflation or deflation in the economy. If a country has higher GDP_r growth than GDP_{nom} growth, it means that the country is experiencing deflation. Let us therefore go through the various *"... the concepts of flation"* right away:

- *Deflation* means that the price of goods and services falls steadily in the economy over time. In other words, you get more bang for your buck the longer it goes on, or the higher the deflation. This can typically happen if you are afraid that the prices of goods and services will fall. The consequences are that households become hesitant, the unemployed do not get a job and no one therefore wants to spend money. Companies do not want to invest or hire employees, unemployment rises and then wage, and price inflation falls. Inflation is also falling because companies have to compete for fewer customers, and then prices fall gradually. Unemployment is not good at all, and mass unemployment is catastrophic for society. Not only psychosocially for the individual unemployed, but purely nationally. Deflation is fortunately an unusual problem.

- *Inflation* is the opposite of deflation and far more common. This means that the prices of goods and services are constantly increasing, so you get less and less for your money. That is not good either, because prices can run wild without wages keeping up. When we have an inflation-driven economy, central banks must raise interest rates to curb inflation, and both create problems for households. Another fact about inflation is that if you believe that "now there will be inflation", then you turn up the prices yourself (demand more wages) to be ahead of the price increase you yourself believe in. And so do others you talk to. Then the price increase has started.

- *Hyperinflation* is what we call it when inflation gets out of control and gets out of control; you get less and less bang for your buck with each passing day. The salary is simply not enough for loans, interest, heat, light and not least food. A common definition of hyperinflation is that inflation is in double digits for more than 3 months in a row.

- *Stagflation* is both that the economy stagnates, at the same time as we have inflation. Stagflation results in high unemployment, stagnation in output growth and inflation at the same time.

- *Shrinkflation* is a completely new concept that has spread in the last couple of years. This is one explanation for the fact that the suppliers of goods (e.g. in the grocery market) both deliver a smaller (shrunk) quantity of goods in the same package, and at the same time the price (inflation) increases compared to before. In other words, less content at an increased price. Even President Joe Biden has criticized the food industry for this "trick" and asked them to stop doing it.

2.3. The general or real equation

It is now time to take a closer look at the socio-economic cycle. To help us, we have an equation. We call this the *general or real equation.* Schiller distinguishes between Gross Domestic Product (GDP) and Net Domestic Product (NNP), and we use the latter which only includes domestic production. (Schiller, B., 2016). Gross domestic product (GDP) is found by taking total private consumption (C) and public consumption or consumption (G), plus enterprises' total investments (I), plus exports (X) minus imports (M), during a calendar year. Schiller writes the general equation in this way:

BNP = (C+G) + I + (X-M)

Where:
C = Consume (private consumption)
G = Governmental expenditures
I = Investments (gross fixed capital investments)
X = Export
M = Import

2.4. The current account

We can use this real equation for various purposes, such as explaining how a country can save. A country saves (CA) when it has a surplus on its current account, i.e. the CA > 0. In other words, it means that CA is net financial investment (X-M) + fixed investment (I). The savings can be shown in the equation in this way; CA = (X-M) + I.

The question then becomes: What does the current account (CA) describe in relation to the central government accounts, i.e. the central government budget? Well, the state budget is what describes the government's estimated total revenues and expenditures in a calendar year. We describe this as tax revenues (T) minus public expenditure (G), i.e.:

T – G = CA.

The current account (CA) consists of the balance of trade with other countries (exports - imports) and return on foreign investment, as well as aid. We write this in the equation

CA = (S-I) + (T-G)

If a surplus in the central government budget occurs at the same time as a current account deficit, this must mean little saving and high investment.

Household saving declines and business investment increases in periods when the central government budget is in surplus and the trade balance is in deficit. In other words, there is a high degree of optimism and little concern among both companies and households.

2.5. Competitiveness

There are various factors that can make the industry in a country less competitive. For example, we can mention high wages, high inflation, high borrowing rates and high commodity prices. Let's think a little about what happens in relation to other countries, for example NOK (Norwegian Crowns) in relation to the USD (US Dollars). First, we introduce two terms that we use in forex trading:

Appreciate – strengthen

Depreciate – weakens

Let's take an example of two currencies: Does the exchange rate of 8 NOK/USD (8 Norwegian kroner per 1 dollar) go up or down if the Norwegian krone appreciates nominally? If the NOK appreciates, it means that it strengthens against the dollar, i.e. that the exchange rate in NOK goes down. The dollars thus becomes cheaper for us, so that we pay less for each dollar we buy, for example 7 NOK/USD.

Let's look at what has happened in a country if the currency depreciates (nominal depreciation) while the competitiveness of manufacturing deteriorates because the real exchange rate appreciates. If the country's currency is nominally depreciated, the exchange rate will be more expensive (e.g. increased to 9 NOK/USD) and then the imported goods will be more expensive. In other words, we can import less grain or other goods for the same amount of money or pay more for the same amount of grain. This in turn leads to less private consumption (decreases), there is increased inflationary pressure because imported goods have now become more expensive. This, in turn, reduces the country's foreign exchange reserves. This is of course good for the export industry, as domestic products are cheaper compared to foreign countries in relative terms. Foreigners get more goods for their money. Schiller shows that we can set up the relationship in this way:

$$\text{Real Exchange Rate} = \frac{\text{Nominal exchange rate * price level abroad}}{\text{Price level at home}}$$

Change Exchange Rate = Change in nominal exchange rate + inflation abroad - inflation at home

If inflation at home is higher than inflation abroad, the real exchange rate will have appreciated (real appreciation) and this worsens the competitiveness of manufacturing

2.6. Supply and demand

To understand the relationships in the broad lines of the economy, we must go through the AS/AD model. This also gives us insight to understand three important things in relation to economic thinking: Supply - (AS), demand (AD) and equilibrium (E). The AS/AD model is a simple graphical representation where AD stands for Aggregate Demand. AD is expressed by a descending line from left to right. AS stands for Aggregate Supply and is expressed in a curved growing line from left to right. We represent the equilibrium (Equilibrium E) graphically by drawing price along the y-axis, and gross domestic product (GDP) along the x-axis in this way:

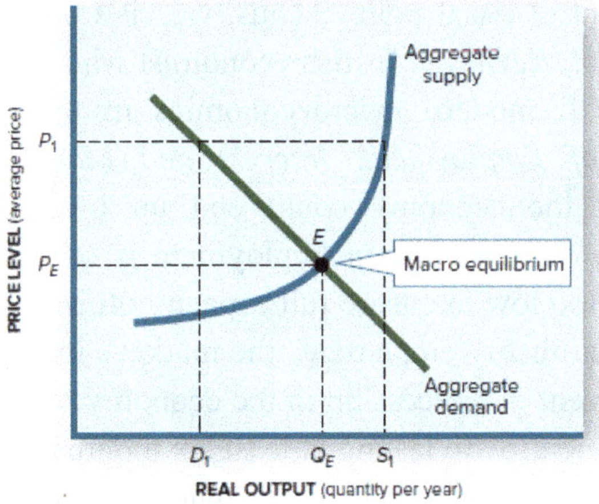

(***Fig***: Schiller, B., 2016)

A prerequisite for this model is that there is spare capacity in domestic production. *The point* of presenting this graphically is because it is easier to understand how supply and demand affect price and quantity by showing where the balance occurs in the market. This is what we call the equilibrium point Macro Equilibrium (E). Where price P1 crosses the aggregate demand line AD, we see that you and I are not willing to buy more than the amount of D1, which is fewer units than when the price drops to price PE. If the price decreases further, we will also buy even more goods, as we can see from the aggregate supply line (AS) at the intersection with S1 and P1. If we are at point E, and move to the left towards point D1, we say that we have a recession, while if we move to the right of point E, we say that we have a boom. When we compare this model with the general equation in the first point of this chapter, we can see the connections much more clearly:

AS *(GDP)*	=	**AD** *(C+G)+I+(X-M)*
(T-G) + (S-I)	=	(C+G)+I+(X-M)
(Aggregate Supply)	|	*(Aggregate Demand)*
(Monetary policy)	|	**(Fiscal Policy)**

2.7. Fiscal policy

Our politicians control fiscal policy. Thus, we visit one of the most famous economists, *John M. Keynes*, a British economist who laid the foundation for what we today call modern macroeconomics in the famous work *"The General Theory of Employment, Interest and Money."* (1936). Keynes' concern was that the economy could end up in a permanent state of imbalance with low output and unemployment if overall effective demand over time became too low to ensure full capacity utilization and employment. Classical Keynesian theory emphasizes the market's inability to self-regulate, especially in the event of a recession in the economy. An economic recession is negative economic growth lasting at least six months, which in turn usually means a decline in a country's GDP. If the market does not adjust itself as the monetarists like to claim it will, the authorities typically have to intervene, i.e. to intervene and influence by various means.

According to Keynesian theory, the recession gap between Equilibrium (E) and full GDP can be solved by stimulating consumption, i.e. making the AD line shift outwards to the right. The authorities can , for example, stimulate (expansionary policy), or reduce (contractionary policy) private consumption (C) by increasing or decreasing taxes (T), public consumption (G) by, for example, building roads, hospitals or schools. The opposite way is to tighten public services. But they can also affect the companies' overall willingness and ability to invest (I) in new production and equipment, which in turn stimulates exports (X) or reduces imports (M) during the calendar year.

The basic real equation is as described where the AS line (describes GDP), while the AD line is described by (C+G+I+X-M). The correlation can be graphically displayed in this way:

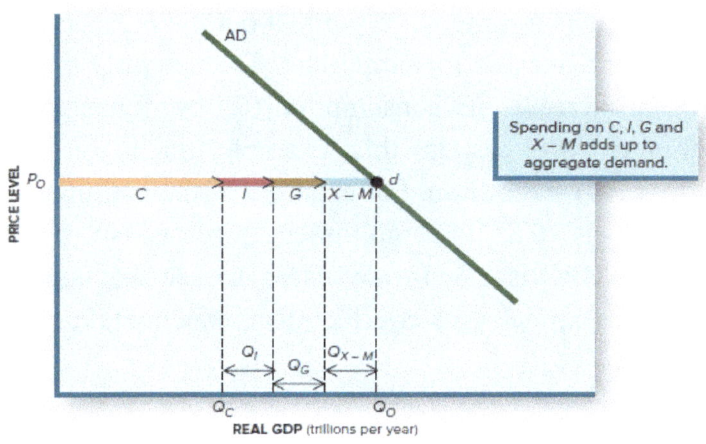

(*Fig*: Schiller, B., 2016)

Here, AS and AD meet in Equilibrium in point *d*.

As the model shows, politicians' choices will have ripple effects in the economy beyond their initial intervention. And the ripple effects are greater than the authorities' initial efforts. This is due to the multiplier effect and the marginal propensity to consume (MPC). We can take a closer look at how these ripple effects occur using the Keynesian in the equation set with the multiplier effect. The prerequisites for this are short-term, fixed prices and a demand-based equilibrium model. We set up the equation set:

GDP = C+G+I+X-M, given C = a+bYd, og (Yd = Y-T) der b = 0,75

When filling in the formulas, we get that : I = 4 times (multiplier) at b=0.75 (because 1/(1-0.75) = 4G = 4 times (multiplier) at b=0.75T = 3 times (multiplier) at b=0.75

The effect can be shown as follows:

1) When G increases by 100 => GDP increases by 100
2) When G increases by 100 => C increases by 75
1) When C increases by 75 => GDP increases by 75
2) When GDP increases by 75 => C increases by 56.25 etc (75% of 75)

As we can see from the equation, increased public consumption (G) has *a greater effect* than by reducing taxes and duties (T). It is also the case that the greater the marginal propensity to consume, the greater the ripple effects of any change made by the authorities on total gross domestic product GDP.

Maybe you think this is advanced, or pointed out unnecessary, but my point comes every moment, because it is important. To exemplify the theory better, if the government increases its consumption (*G*) by, for example, 2 billion and the multiplier is 4 as in this example, then total consumption (*C*) increases by (2*4) = 8 billion. For example, if the marginal consumption propensity (*MPC*) is 0.8, the multiplier increases to 5. Or reduced correspondingly if MPC is 0.6. In any case, we see that increasing public consumption (G) has a much greater effect than reducing taxes (T).

2.8. Monetary policy

When it comes to *monetary policy*, we are primarily thinking of the American professor of economics *Milton Friedman*, who was awarded the Nobel Memorial Prize in Economics in 1976. He was the strongest proponent of a monetarist view, according to which the money supply better explains the changes in nominal national revenue (GDP) than the changes that occur through fiscal policy instruments.

Monetary policy is controlled by the *central bank*. Now, you may be wondering how a central bank can influence the Money Supply via the

Money Multiplier. Then we start with what this money multiplier is. First, let's look at the formula for the money supply multiplier which is defined like this (Schiller, B., 2016):

$$\text{Money Multiplier} = \frac{1}{\text{Required reserve (money)}}$$

The relationship with the money supply multiplier is such that the required reserve requirement is necessarily less than 1. This means that not all of the deposit you put in the bank has to be in reserve in case you want to withdraw it again tomorrow. The rest can therefore be lent out (circulated) again. Let's say that the reserve requirement is 0.6 per krone. Then the bank can lend again 0.4 per krone, or 40%. In this way, *the money supply is increased* by the banks in a way "producing" their own money can then lend, the aforementioned 0.4, on which they can in turn earn interest. The central bank can thus increase the money supply in the country by reducing the requirements for banks' reserve reserves. The central bank can also raise or lower interest rates, and it can also buy bonds in the markets. Or they can do the opposite to reduce the money supply.

We look again at the general equation, which is expressed as follows:

GDP = C+I+G+(X-M), where C+I is the demand channel (total consumption and investment), and (X-M) is the currency channel (exports minus imports).

We change the equation a bit and get that

BNP + M = AS, and C+I+G+X = AD.

In other words, production + imports = consumption + investment + public consumption + exports. The central bank controls monetary policy with its instruments, which are the money supply and interest rates to adjust aggregate output, i.e. GDP. An expansionary monetary policy means bringing down interest rates by increasing the money supply. Schiller shows us what's going on:

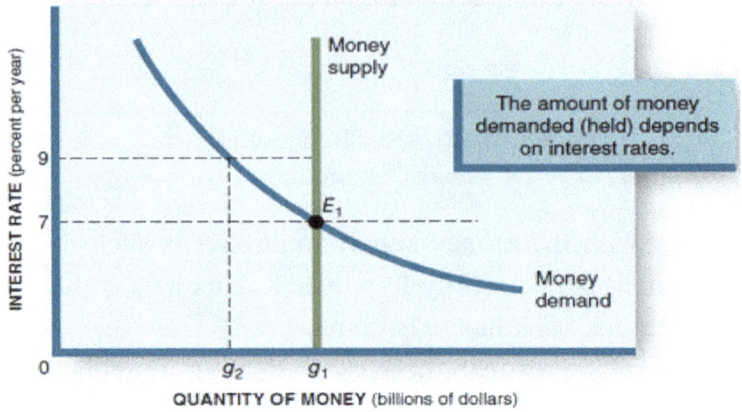

(***Fig***: Schiller, B., 2016)

The demand for money (loans) decreases the higher the interest rate. However, the monetarists themselves emphasize that there is a *lag effect* in managing the money supply, i.e. that the changes take place over time. Thus, it can quickly become the case that the effect of monetary policy has an impact at the wrong time. The central banks' management problem is therefore often criticized as: *"Too late and too little, or too early and too much"*.

2.9. Unemployment, Inflation, and Tax Burden

" Insistence on carving the pie into equal slices would shrink the size of the pie. The fact poses the trade-off between economic equality and economic efficiency". (Arthur M. Okun).

After familiarizing ourselves with what inflation is, how it arises and is combated, how the fiscal policy of the politicians, and the monetary policy of the central banks work both separately and together, we take a look at something that everyone is concerned about, namely unemployment, inflation and the tax burden. Economists, workers, business leaders and politicians alike worry loudly: Regardless of the level of taxation, unemployment and inflation, it will never be quite right for anyone. What everyone agrees on is that the more unemployed, the worse it is for the country, not only because of the economy. But both GDP and tax revenues T decrease when fewer people work, while G increases due to social benefits during unemployment, etc. This has major negative ripple effects, and the longer this lasts, the longer it will take for the nation to recover. But what is the connection here? Several people have tried to find the different conncctions, so we look at three of them:

The Phillips curve:

The New Zealand economist *Alban W. Phillips* developed a graph that summarized the inverse (inverse) relationship between unemployment and inflation in England for the years 1826 – 1957. The curve showed that the higher the inflation, the lower the unemployment rate. *«Phillips curve: A historical (inverse) relationship between the rate of unemployment and the rate of inflation; Commonly expresses a trade-off between the two.».* (Schiller, B., 2016). Later, P. Samuelson and R. Solow from MIT found that the curve showed a reasonable correlation for the American economy for the years 1900-1960. Now, in retrospect, it turns out that the Phillips curve cannot be completely correct. I have tested it myself and found that it is at least not true in the medium and long term. But we will not go further into that here. He shows the Phillips curve as follows:

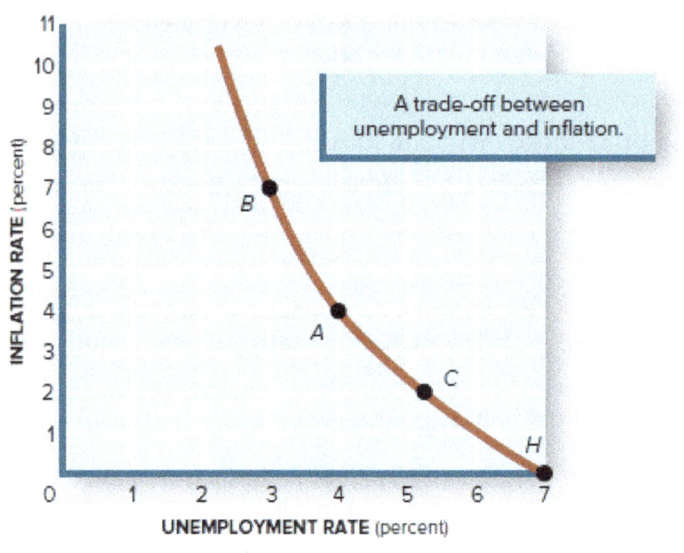

(***Fig***: Schiller, B., 2016)

Okun's law:

Let's look at another context. One that is actually true, namely the relationship between unemployment and gross domestic product GDP. The American professor Artur M. Okun from Yale found a relationship between unemployment and GDP. He quantified (quantified) the relationship between unemployment and the production potential curve. The correlation he found was that for every 1% increase in unemployment, it led to a 3% reduction in GDP. But during the turbulent 1970s, when stagflation (a stagnant economy with inflation) hit the United States, this rule turned out to no longer hold. The correlation is 1% increase in unemployment leads to 2% reduction in GDP. So *"full employment"* is not just a socially accepted slogan. It is financially very important.

<u>Reasons for growth in the economy can often be due to:</u>

a) Employment growth > population growth
b) Productivity growth is increasing due to:
    (i) Capital intensity
    ii) Factor productivity due to
        * New technology
        * Higher competence
        * Better management
        * New industries/markets are opened

<u>Political instruments can be:</u>

1) Education/investment in human capital
2) Highly educated immigrants
3) Facilitate more efficient companies, stimulate investment in industries (Tax policy, Infrastructure, Fiscal stability, etc.)

The Laffer curve:

The problem for the politicians who control fiscal policy is to adapt and optimize tax revenues (T) to public spending (G) without *"suffocating"* the entire economy (GDP). One of the most basic understandings in modern economics is that the tax rate affects your willingness to work, produce, and invest. What economists may disagree on is how much the AS curve shifts to the right or to the left in relation to changes in the tax burden.

In any case, the business community is crying out for lower taxes to increase investment in order to create jobs and government revenues in turn, while politicians are constantly crying out for higher tax revenues to solve the tasks that politicians impose on the state to solve. So we therefore end the macro chapter with a simple and basic food for thought that most people have not heard of, and not least a good number of politicians do not understand, namely *the relationship* between the tax burden (in %) and the state's total tax revenues in money.

In this connection, we are also introducing a new concept of elasticity that explains this mathematically: *"Tax Elasticity of supply.* This correlation is the percentage change in the quantity offered, divided by the percentage change in the tax rate. We calculate this like this:

$$\text{Supply-side tax elasticity} = \frac{\text{\% change in supply quantity}}{\text{\% change in tax rate}}$$

Now it's time to pull out *"the world's most referenced napkin"* from your sleeve. *The Laffer curve* refers to the theory that the increase in the tax level above a certain level will lead to *a reduction* in the state's total tax revenues and is therefore used as an argument in neoclassical supply-side economics for why *tax revenues* will increase, if the government reduces *tax rates*. *The Wall Street Journal* named the basket the Laffer curve after the American economist *Arthur Laffer,* who during a dinner in 1974 drew this curve on a napkin as a counterargument in the discussion of President Gerald Ford's tax increases. However, the connection is intuitive and ancient, known as early as the 1300s. Keynes also formulated how taxation above a certain level will actually lead to reduced tax revenues for the state.

As we can see (next page), a 0% rate gives no tax revenue, while a 100% rate gives just as little because the incentive to work is then gone. However, we saw in the section on fiscal policy that increased public consumption (*G*) actually has a greater effect than by reducing taxes and duties (*T*). It is also the case that the greater the marginal propensity to consume, the greater the ripple effects of any change made by the authorities on total gross domestic product GDP. The Laffer curve is both very intuitive and enlightening in this respect, it is a single graph that shows the relationship between the government's total *tax revenues* (the y-axis), and the total *tax rate* (x-axis) in this way:

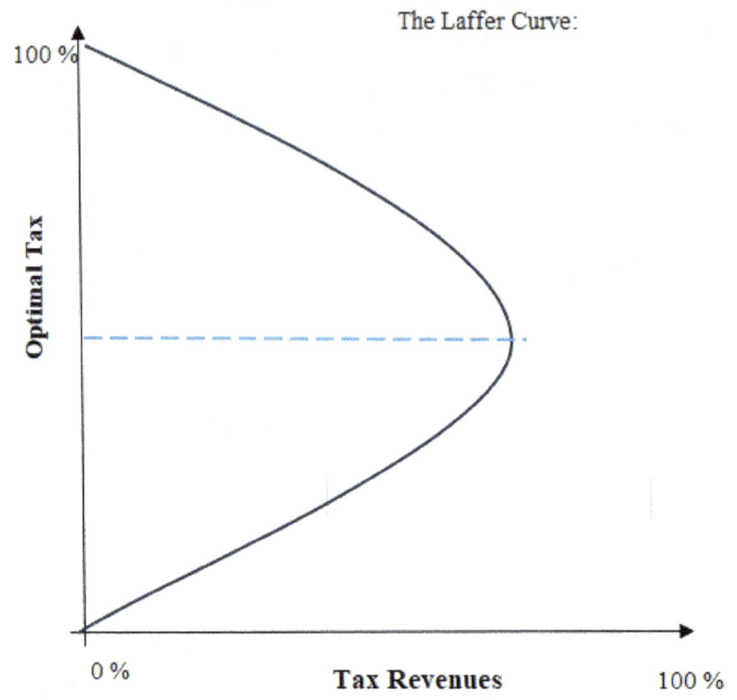

Fig: Laffer curve. (Laffer, Arthur B. 2004.)

Too high a domestic tax burden will sooner or later lead to capital flight and thus reduced tax revenues for the state, which in turn will lead to politicians increasing the tax burden again. Until they understand the connections of the Laffer curve.

You can find more information about me and my other books here:

executivewayto.com

Chapter 3. Microeconomics

"The essence of market power is the ability to alter the price of a product.". (Schiller, 2016)

Microeconomics is about the details of the economy, or marginal considerations as we say, so now we zoom in on the connections in a market or for a product. Different market forms exist, from no competition at one end, to perfect competition at the other end. Most providers are somewhere on this scale, very rarely at the extremes at either end. Let's therefore start with a quick overview of these market forms before going through the main points of each individual market form as Schiller briefly summarizes it (2016):

Monopoly: One provider supplies the entire market supply of a particular good or service.

Duopoly: Two providers supply the entire market offer of a product or service.

Oligopoly: A few firms supply all or most of a particular good or service. More or less a shared monopoly.

Monopolistic competition: Many firms offer similar goods or services, but where each firm has some independent control over its own price.

Perfect competition: Lots of companies offer the same good or service, and the providers have to adapt to the product prices that are "given" by the market.

3.1. Seven important aspects of microeconomics

For example, what is the "right price" and why is it so? It can be a price when we think socio-economically, but something completely different when we talk about a business price. As we know, a picture is worth a thousand words, and once again it is the economists' secret weapon, the graphs, that we use to show and explain the various relationships. Therefore, we must first go through some abbreviations and basic relationships so that we can more easily interpret the graphs and understand the points.

3.2. Basic theory, abbreviations, and assumptions

It may come as a shock to some, but the goal of anyone who offers a good or service is *profit maximization*. The word profit comes from the English word *profit* and is simply the difference between total revenue (TR) and total cost (TC), in other words, the profit. This is necessary for the company, or society, to be able to survive and continue to produce goods and services in the future, and thus not a bad word.

A very important principle in all economic thinking is *the opportunity cost,* and we keep that in mind all the time. The difference between a cost and an expense is that a cost is something that we have agreed will be paid at some point in the future, while an expense is something that has been paid or is being paid now. For a product, the opportunity cost can be measured against *another alternative product* that could have been produced with the same resources. A common definition for opportunity cost is: *"The most desired goods or services that are forgone in order to obtain something else."*. (Schiller, B., 2016). Otherwise, you can just put the money in the bank and get a secure return there instead of producing socially useful jobs, products and services. *The models* in this chapter are not technical, but *explanatory*. Moreover, they are typical, because we have to make reasonable assumptions in order to understand the theories in relation to the practice. It is important to keep this in mind in the future.

If we draw a graph of profit, it is not a straight upward line because it decreases after a certain amount produced. The explanation is that even if we sow more grain, employ more workers or buy more raw materials, production or profits *do not increase* successively. There is always one or more constraints somewhere in the production line. Thus, we understand an important economic principle, namely that there are limits to how much we produce, not only physically, but that is economically profitable.

In microeconomics, marginal *considerations* are in focus. According to Schiller, the basic rule for maximizing profits is as follows; «*Produce at that rate of output where marginal revenue equals marginal cost.*». That is, to produce one more unit, to where the marginal revenue (MR) is equal to the marginal cost (MC), which is MR = MC.

Thus, the law of diminishing returns, *which means that the return is not steadily increasing with the increase in the input factors, suddenly makes* sense. So we now introduce the concept of *marginal physical product* (MPP), which we calculate as follows:

$$\textit{Marginal Physical Product (MPP)} = \frac{\text{Change in totalt Output}}{\text{Change in input Quantity}}$$

Marginal revenue (MR) is about *the change* in total revenue that occurs when we produce an extra unit. The formula is as follows:

$$\textit{Marginal revenue (MR)} = \frac{\text{Change in total revenue}}{\text{Change in production quantity}}$$

If we calculate the MR and draw it into a graph, the line takes on a descending shape. The best rule of thumb is that we "... *never produce a unit that costs more than it gives back in revenue.*" (Schiller, B., 2016). Otherwise, we will lose.

The marginal cost (MC) is the change, or additional cost, that accrues in our total cost when we produce an additional unit. If we draw MC into a graph, it has an ascending, curved shape.

The rule of *profit maximization* in the short run is when the marginal revenue (MR) is equal to the price (p): MR = p

Average total costs (ATC) are found by taking all variable costs and dividing by the total amount produced in a given period.

Average fixed costs (AFC) are found by taking all fixed costs and dividing by the total amount produced in a given period.

3.3. Elasticity

Keep in mind the demand line AD from AS/AD - the model from the previous chapter on macroeconomics (chapter 2.1), which explains the principle of the relationship between supply and demand, when we now look at price elasticity. *Price elasticity* is a ratio that shows the relationship between price and quantity changes. As a supplier, we are interested in this because we want to know if it is profitable for us to set the price of a product up or down, or if it does not affect sales at all.

Price elasticity (Ep) is also a basic principle, and very useful to understand. In technical terms: "*Price elasticity is a percentage change in the demand for a product, when the price changes by 1%.*" (Schiller, B., 2016). We describe *the price elasticity* (Ep), what you have been willing to pay for a given item, in the formula as follows:

$$\textit{Price elasticity (Ep)} = \frac{\%\text{ - change in } \textit{volume requested}}{\%\text{ - change in } \textit{price}}$$

This means that:
E > 1: Demand is *elastic* (consumption change is relatively larger than price change)
E = 1: Demand is *neutrally elastic* (consumption change equals price change because 1/1 = 1)
E < 1: Demand is *inelastic* (consumption change is less than price change)

The law of *demand* implies that *the elasticity of demand* will always be greater than 1, because we do not demand negative quantities. Now, let's take a closer look at demand elasticity. First, we look at how much the price fell between two points on the demand line, so that we find the average price for that area, i.e.:

$$\frac{\text{Price1} + \text{Price2}}{2}$$

Then we do the same with the change in quantity between the same two price points, and then we can answer the question: How much does the average demand change in relation to the change in the average price? In other words, how many percent more sales do we get for every percent we lower the price? Or vice versa, how much do sales fall in the event of a price increase? We can calculate this according to this formula:

$$\textit{Volume elasticity } (E) = \frac{\text{\% - change in } \textit{requested volume}}{\text{\% - change in } \textit{price}}$$

We use this, for example, to set the price of a product in relation to how much we are going to produce of a good or service. In some industries, this can be used as a competitive tool. The connections are described as follows:

E > 1 : Elastic demand: Price change affects the quantity *to a large extent* (Luxury goods, air travel)

E = 1 : Neutral elastic: Price change affects the quantity change *to the same extent*

E < 1 : Inelastic demand: Price change affects the quantity *to a small extent* (Bread, milk, petrol, electricity)

Neutral elastic is shown as an oblique, falling line at 45 degrees from the X axis towards the Y axis.

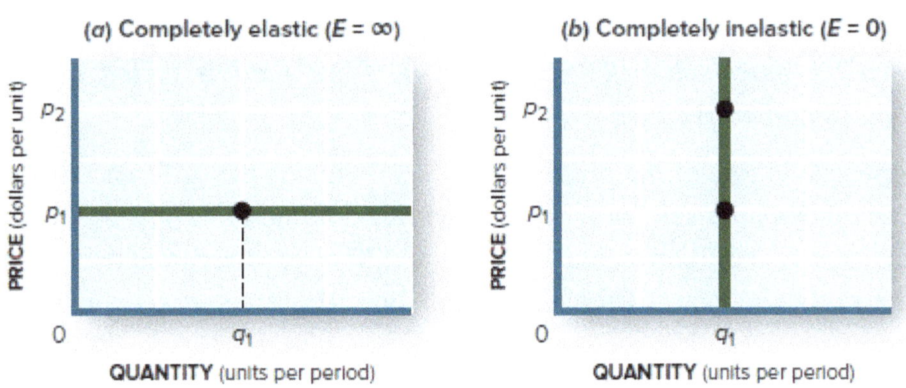

*(**Fig**: Schiller, B., 2016)*

3.4. Price discrimination, consumer and producer surpluses

Let's start with the concept *of marginal utility*: It is essentially a measure of how much we want from a particular good. Schiller points out that the price of the good is often an important factor in what we choose. *"The more marginal utility a product delivers, the more the consumer is willing to pay for the product."* (Schiller, B. 2016)

But the marginal utility value is diminishing. Let's illustrate with this example: If you walk in the desert for a whole day without carrying food and water, you will be completely dehydrated, thirsty, and hungry after a few hours. The further into the day you get, the higher the price you will be willing to pay for a glass of cold water. Maybe just as much for glass number two, while glass number three you are probably not willing to pay quite as much for. And for glass number four, five and six, both interest and willingness to pay are declining successively. In other words, your demand and willingness to pay falls like the AD line we showed in the AS/AD model. This is because your *marginal utility decreases*, you are only willing to buy additional quantities of a commodity only if the price falls.

The consumer surplus is *the difference* between the maximum price you are willing to pay for a good or service, and the price you actually pay. *"A person will buy a product or service only if the price is equal to, or below the maximum price that the person is willing and able to pay. The difference between the maximum price limit and the price paid is called consumer surplus*." (Schiller, B., 2016).

The opposite is true of *the producer surplus,* which is the difference between the price they *could* sell for a good or service and the price you actually pay for the item. They can achieve this through price discrimination, in that different people pay different prices for the same good or service. *"Manufacturers can extract some or all of the consumer surplus by charging different prices to individuals, based on their willingness to pay – a practice known as 'price discrimination'.* (Schiller, B., 2016).

Thus, we got an answer to what *price discrimination* is at the same time, and here the car salespeople are completely "raw": Their success lies in negotiating prices for the same product to different customers at different prices. In other words, they sell a car with the same specifications to different customers for different prices because the different customers have different "pain thresholds" for how much they want to pay for the same car.

3.5. Monopoly

We have now come to different market forms, starting by explaining the *"perfect market form for producers"*, namely monopoly.

Monopolies are bad news for consumers, and we will now look at why. A monopoly is a business that produces *the total quantity* of the product or products offered to the market. Thus, we understand the statement with which we began the chapter: *"The essence of market power is the ability to change the price of a product."*. (Schiller, B., 2016)

A monopoly means that there is only one producer because there are obstacles to establishing themselves in the market. There can be various reasons for this. Examples of barriers to entry may be conditions such as competence requirements (authorization requirements, license requirements, technologies), legal requirements (police, military, patents), political requirements (infrastructure, alcohol, drugs, etc.), or particularly high costs (infrastructure such as airports, railways, etc.).

A monopolist can *almost* set the price they want without losing their customers, and that is bad news for society. However, they are far more scientific when it comes to pricing policy. The monopolist's demand curve is also falling. The marginal revenue (MR) is always less than demand (AD), and the MR curve always falls twice as fast as the demand curve. Since profit maximization is the point, we will produce and sell so many units that *the last unit* covers the cost of production. The monopolist then finds *the optimal quantity of production X* where MR = MC and *the optimal profit-maximizing price P* at the set of equations:

(1) MR = MC to find the amount X

(2) Inserting X into the demand curve to find the price *P*

The graph below shows MC (ascending curve), MR (descending curve), E (descending curve) and the average total cost ATC (u-shaped curve). We can read from the monopolist's optimal price and quantity, where the quantity *d* can be read from just below where MR = MC on the x-line. But since the price elasticity E = AD (Aggregated Demand) falls half as fast as the MR line and is therefore *much higher* than price *d*, we find the monopolist's new price for this set at point *D* by drawing a *straight line upwards* from set *X (4).*, i.e. past point *d* up until it hits *a point (D)* on the demand curve.

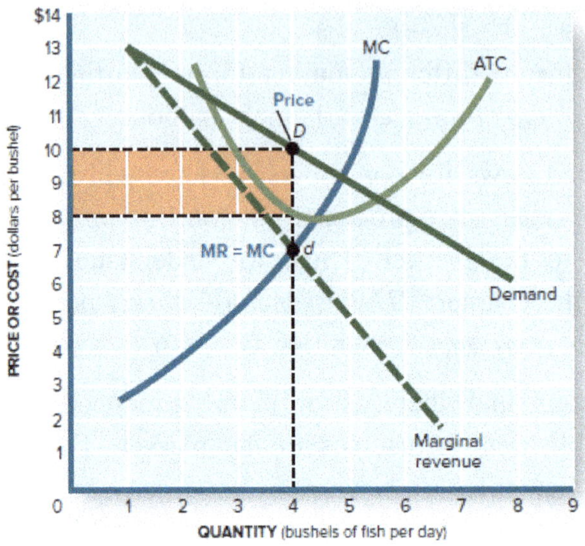

(***Fig***: Schiller, B., 2016)

The shaded square shows a monopoly profit equal to the price increase (here $10-8) * 4 pcs = 8. In other words, monopoly entails both a higher price and a smaller quantity for consumers, who lose the shaded field because the monopolist grabs a part of our consumer surplus.

3.6. Oligopoly

"People of the same trade seldom meet together, but the conversation ends in a conspiracy against the public, or in some diversion to raise prices". (Smith, Adam, 1776)

Between the extremes of monopoly and perfect competition, we find most market forms. *Oligopoly* is characterized by the fact that the market is dominated by a few producers supplying virtually all of the supply of a good to the market. In other words, this is also an imperfect form of marketing.

There are some common denominators for such market power: That there are few providers, that the providers are large, that there are barriers to establishment such as patents, laws, etc., and that there is little availability of substitute products. We can find examples of oligopolies in consumer electronics markets with dominant players such as Apple, Samsung, Lenovo, LG, Microsoft and Sony, or often in the credit card market with dominant players such as Mastercard, Eurocard, American Express and VISA.

The market structure naturally affects how the providers act in their market, and hence the revenue they get from their business. In a monopoly, all this profit goes to a provider (monopolist). An oligopoly will seek to make the same profit. We can look at an oligopoly as a monopoly that shares the excess profits between a few actors. But the total market can never be larger than 100%, and thus an oligopoly is characterized by intense competition between the players to achieve dominance, and hence all the profits that the market provides. The oligopolists will thus also strive to achieve a monopoly, and a well-known way to try to achieve this is by acquiring competitors. That is why states create competition authorities to prevent this. One may ask how successful the authorities have been. The industry's profit is maximized in the same way where the industry's production volume *MC = MR,* here in point *J.* However, since market demand, and hence willingness to pay, is significantly higher than point *J*, the price at which the quantity hits the willingness to pay (MD) is found on the demand curve. The oligopolists thus obtain an extra profit, which is marked as *"Industrial profit"* in the graphic representation:

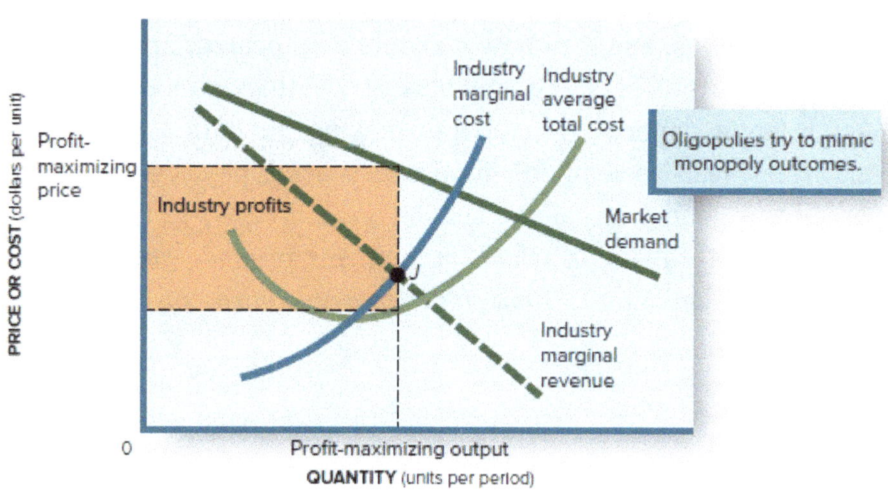

(***Fig***: Schiller, B., 2016)

3.7. Monopolistic competition

A provider that is in a market that has low barriers to entry and simple and homogeneous products or services, etc., will very quickly face competition if it is possible to achieve additional profits. This creates *monopolistic competition,* which occurs when we have a market with low barriers to entry and enough suppliers to ensure competition. So let's now look at profit maximization under monopolistic competition.

The market is characterized by many providers, *heterogeneous* (uniform) products and low barriers to entry, as well as relatively simple technology. Examples could be grocery stores, clothing stores, fast food chains, coffee shops, beer or wine producers, fuel stations and various franchises, or what we call brand chains. These providers must therefore *differentiate* themselves to increase their margins, and they do this through branding. Examples of product differentiation can be the jeans market with its brands such as Levis, Wrangler, and Lois jeans, fast food chains such as Burger King or MC Donald, soft drinks such as Coca-Cola, Pepsi Cola and Jolly Cola. Another example is the coffee shops that have popped up everywhere. If you walk into a coffee shop and ask for *"a cup of coffee please!»* it is no longer a simple matter: You are faced with a wealth of counter-questions about Cafe Latte or Cafe au Lait (yes, there is a difference!), different milk substitutes, different flavorings (syrups) whether it should be cold or hot coffee. And if you're so boring that you ruin *the barista*'s day by repeating *"Black coffee please!"* you have to go through all the world's coffee-producing countries, different coffee roasts, and then how it should be prepared. From steaming to hand pulling. The coffee shops are thus innovating with different coffee products, different flavorings or ways of making the coffee, and often with additional sales such as tempting food and snacks, physical design of the premises such as good armchairs or seating areas, free Wi-Fi and the like. As Schiller writes: *"A market in which many firms produce similar goods or services, but each maintains some independent control of its own price."* (Schiller, B., 2016).

A supplier in monopolistic competition also finds its starting point in the equilibrium MR = MC. The greater the excess profit that is discovered in a market, the more competitors will establish themselves.

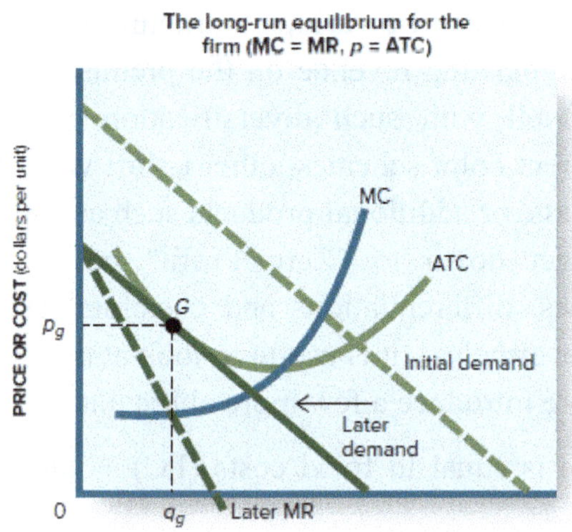

(*Fig*: Schiller, B., 2016)

This in turn leads to a shift in the demand curve, from the dotted line *"Initial demand"* towards the left to "*Later demand*" in the chart. This in turn leads to a new price level where demand *E* and average total costs *ATC* are tangent to each other at point *G*. It gives a new amount of q_g and a new price *Pg* in the figure above. In the long run, *the surplus profit = 0* for all providers in monopolistic competition.

3.8. Perfect competition

We will now explain the "perfect form of competition", at least for us as consumers. Keep in mind that we are now going to explain the point of maximum *profit*, not maximum revenue. A *perfect market* is characterized by many providers, identical products, that everyone has perfect information all the time, and that there are no or very low barriers to trade, that MC = *p*, and that no one achieves so-called excess profit or extra profit. We can look at the T-shirt market as an example, hamburger bars, or coffee shops. The point is that the technologies do not require any long education, the products are relatively uniform, and that there are little or no trade barriers. If your price is too high, customers will therefore cross the street to the next provider and leave you bankrupt.

In other words, price competition is fierce, and providers resort to various innovations as I explained in the section above on monopolistic competition. As you understand, this can be various marketing tricks to create customer loyalty, increase the existing revenue on the premises and hopefully a little on the prices as well with such diversification. The t-shirt shops may innovate with different color schemes, other t-shirt variants or maybe cooler, or more political texts, or additional products such as caps, etc. So, in reality, you never quite get down to "Zero Profit" because new innovations, production processes, differentiations and customer tastes change more or less all the time. Nevertheless, it is useful to look at the theory behind the free market. We therefore introduce a few more abbreviations:

The total cost (TC) is equal to fixed costs (FC) + variable costs (VC). We write

$$TC=FC+VC$$

The marginal cost (MC) is the change, or additional cost, that accrues in our total costs when we produce an extra unit. In a perfect market, there are only three adjustments to the marginal cost:

$p >$ MC which means that we will produce more (or enter the market)
$p =$ MC which means that we have maximized the amount of production and the surplus
$p <$ MC which means that we have to reduce production (or go out of the market)

The average cost (ATC) is equal to the average fixed costs (AFC) plus the average variable costs (AVC). We write

$$ATC=AFC+AVC$$

The profit maximization is such for the free-competition provider that MR = MC, p = ATC

So when do we enter the market, or when do we shut down production? Where is the specific point where we do not find it profitable to continue production? Fixed costs must be paid anyway; they are independent of production. Thus, the question becomes whether we lose more by continuing production than if we shut down the business completely? *"A firm should shut down only if the losses from continuing production exceeds fixed cost."*. (Schiller, B., 2016). He shows it graphically like this:

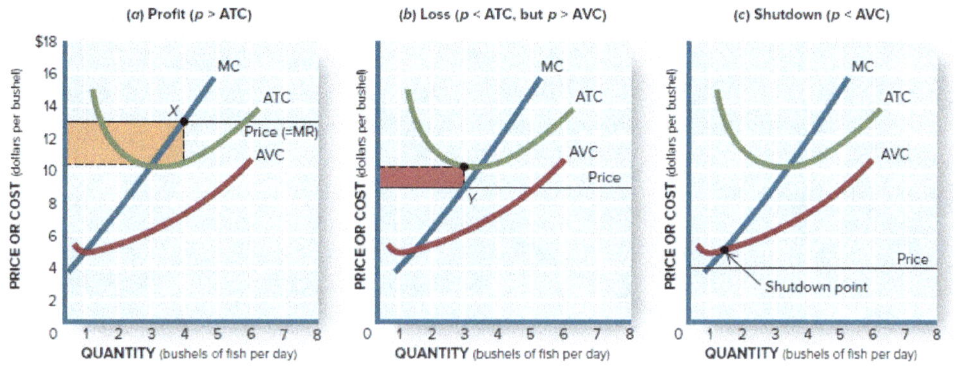

(*Fig*: Schiller, B., 2016)

We see here in figure *a)* that where MC = ATC at point x (10, 3) there are market potentials to increase (in the orange field *x*) to price *p* = 13 and quantity = 4. Figure *b)* shows a loss because the price *p* is lower (10, 3) than at the intersection MC = ATC at point *y* (11, 3).

In figure *c)* we see that the price p has dropped to an unacceptable combination of price and quantity where MC = AVC (4, 1) which tells us that it is time to close the store.

In other words, when the *marginal cost* (MC) crosses *the average total cost* (ATC) or the average variable cost (AVC), we find the Entry and Exit points as follows:

Entry Market the area where MC = ATC = *p*
Exit Market the area where MC = AVC = *p*

The merciless squeeze of profit in the perfect market revolves around the fact that:

- High prices mean that consumers want more goods
- Higher prices result in economic profits that lead to new establishments and increased competition
- The AS curve then makes a shift to the right and the price drops downwards along the AD lineThe graphical representation of p = MC can be displayed like this (Schiller, B., 2016):

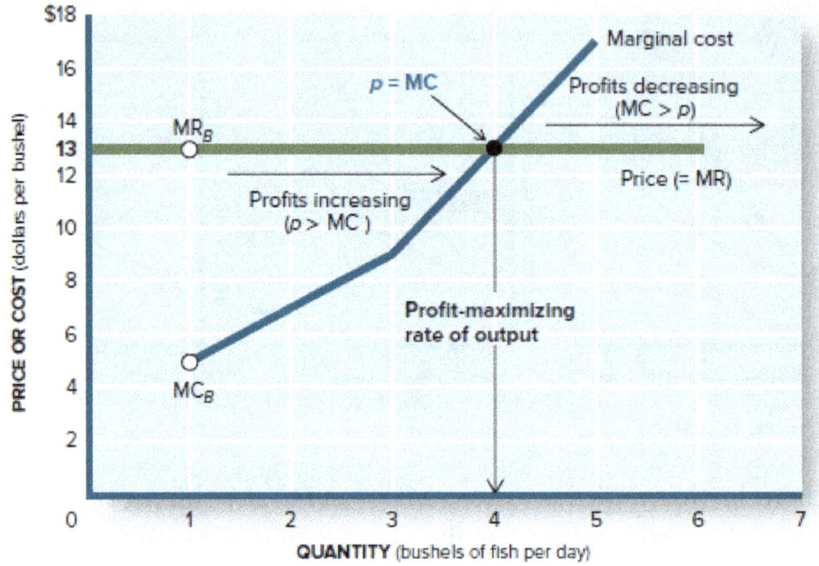

(*Fig*: Schiller, B., 2016)

The graph shows that when the price p is 13 and the marginal cost MCB is 1, we will want to *increase the* production quantity all the way up to quantity 4, which is the intersection MC = p. It occurs at the intersection of p = 13 and MC = 4. If the marginal cost MC is higher, for example = 16, we will either reduce production to quantity 4 to price 13 or choose to exit the market because we are unable to match the price given by the market.

In a perfect market, suppliers have two adaptations, *short-term* or *long-term* adaptation:

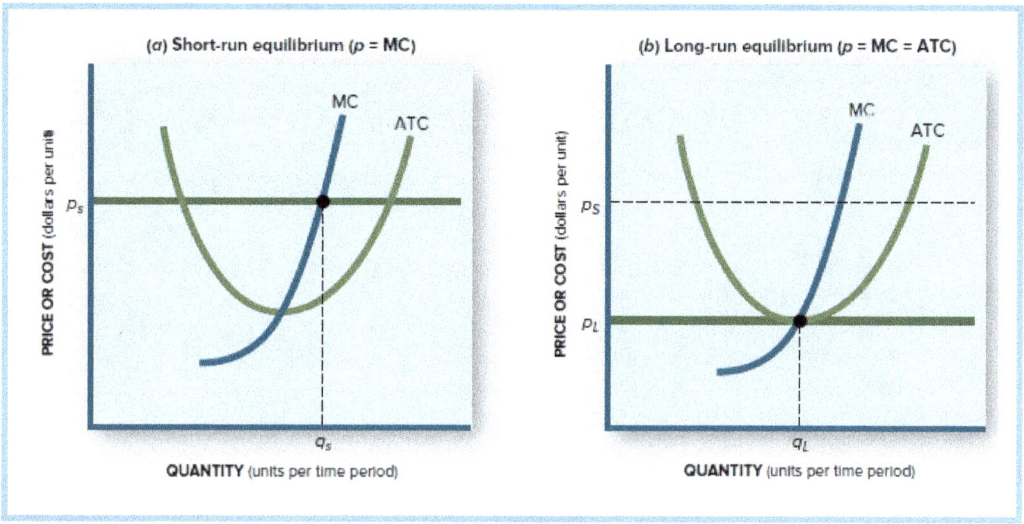

Short-term competitive equilibrium price is where P = MC

Long-term competitive equilibrium price is where P = MC, *minimum* where ATC is crossed.

At the end of this chapter, I would like to draw your attention to the fact that *anyone who has something to sell will try to achieve a monopoly situation*. If you don't understand why, perhaps you went a little too fast in this chapter.

You can find more information about me and my other books here: executivewayto.com

Chapter 4. Behavioral Economics

"When executives make big strategic bets, they typically depend on the judgment of their teams to a significant extent".
(Kahneman, Lovallo, and Sibony., 2011).

We become business economists because we want to know something about the future to shape it ourselves. We want *that* glass ball to tells us what will happen around the next corner, after the next turn, behind the next hilltop, tomorrow to be prepared. Even though we know that it is impossible, we still try hard to get actual answers as well as possible using different techniques from different disciplines to find out what the future *is likely* to bring. Therefore, it`s a smart thing to read on the major conditions in the economy: Trade theory, macro theory and micro theory so that we can see what and why things affect the society around us, and thus our lives. No matter how unique we are, each and every one of us is just one of about 8 billion unique people. So at a good number of incidents we are at the mercy of others. It is now time to zoom in even more on the practical conditions of the economy. But before we tackle the different parts of *business economics*, let's start by reminding you that we are human beings in the middle of all the theories. So, we start with the intermediate version between economics and psychology and look at why we do things that we afterwards wonder why we did it. It is what we call *behavioral economics*.

4.1. Four aspects of behavioral economics

Behavioral economics is the study of rationality. Those who reflect a little on human behavior can easily see that economics and psychology are closely linked. Like the front and back of your hand, like heads and tails on a piece of a coin, etc. One side is dependent on-, and exists only together with the other side, or part. If you're at a dinner party, you'll quickly notice who's a lawyer and who's an engineer. The lawyers are, as always, eager to start a discussion that they expect to "win" since they are God in their own kingdom. That's how they talk their way to high fees when they're at work. They can't help themselves in their spare time either, since they already think that everyone is a potential customer. This is what they are experts in. And regardless of the outcome of any discussion, they must at least have the last word, even if the last word is "sorry." While the engineers, on the other hand, laugh themselves off at the fact that we economists explain economic uncertainty with *"the human factor"*. Because then the engineers must put two lines under a fixed answer to rest. Everybody seems to think that economists knows everything about the future, but we just like to know more of it, just like anyone else. This is where behavioral economics comes to our, and everyone else interested, to rescue.

4.2 Thinking fast and slow

If the aforementioned typical social lions had taken a quick look at the book *"Thinking fast and slow"*, which is the very readable book by psychologist Daniel Kahneman (2011), many misunderstandings and hesitant topics of discussion about economics could have been avoided. Amos Tversky and Daniel Kahneman, two scientist investigated and explained a wide range of phenomena that lead to anomalous human decisions. Their research have broadly influenced the social sciences. In economics, they gave rise to the burgeoning field of behavioral economics. This field, skeptical of perfect rationality, Daniel Kahneman and Amos Tversky researched attention, and proved, as we knew already in the 70s, the humans are not at all as rational *as some economic explanatory models must take as a prerequisite* for explaining basic economic relationships. A number of their published experiments attracted a lot of attention. The discovery of how humans *assess probabilities*, as well as the development of the theory of *how we make decisions under uncertainty*, later earned Daniel Kahneman and Vernon L. Smith a joint Nobel Prize in economics in 2002.

From the insight that people are not at all rational all the time, an entire discipline of economic thinking springs. Research in the field is about how we actually act in different situations, and what influences the choices we make, because we are not only motivated by our self-interest and that we are therefore not completely rational. With the help of various research experiments, behavioral economists study what people's decisions are based on. About which moral and economic decisions are based on narrow self-interest and rationality, or whether there are other reasons why we choose the way we do.

Behavioral economics is about how we actually act, and it explains how limited rationality, limited willpower and social preferences affect the choices we make. Kahneman divides this into two *Systems Thinking*:

- *System 1:* Fast, intuitive and emotion-driven decisions
- *System 2:* Slow, rational and logical decisions

Thinking in this way can have practical value. For example, by thinking backwards or seeing analogies, we can make decisions without them being justified by being correct in principle. Thus, you don't actually know if the correct result is due to chance or something else. Decisions in daily life are based on solving problems by choosing the familiar over the unknown. The book *"Thinking fast and slow",* (Kahneman, D., 2012) is about just that; How we think and act in two completely different ways. Kahneman calls it two characters for or *selves*, the experiencing and intuitive self (system 1) and the controlling and monitoring self (system 2) as follows:

System 1	***System 2***
Unconscious and automatic	Deliberate, controlled and precise
Not very mentally demanding	Mentally demanding, consumes a lot of energy
Fast, high capacity – process a lot of information	Slow, with low capacity – happens slowly
Holistic, and experience-based	Analytical and reflective mindset
Contextual context	Abstract thinking
Applied to most decisions made	Not used as often as we think

4.3 The paradox of freedom of choice

We are all unique and so different that we would like to have all kinds of personal choices. Precisely because all possible manufacturers will adapt to you and your wallet, and which we of course expect to have access to, all these options we are faced with actually create problems for us. Products or services can be perceived as relatively similar and being able to distinguish them from each other can be difficult. This thus presents us with a problem of what to choose and where we may not make the best choice. This is called the *paradox of freedom of choice.*

In other words, most people want as much freedom of choice as possible. But already as a young sales manager in the 1980s, I quickly learned that when customers were given too much freedom of choice, it just became a mess, which in turn led to our sales being lackluster. We sold fashion clothes to boutiques for young adults. For example, if we included 10 different trouser models, all of which could be delivered in 10 different colors each, we sold different trouser models in different colors to each and every customer. It was an expensive production for the manufacturer, horrible logistics and it delayed shipments considerably. However, I quickly discovered that customers many times choose 5 different trouser models in maximum 5 - 6 colors. So I cut down the collection to 5 models and 5 of the season's fashion colors and pushed three of each. Thus, almost all customers chose usually only a total of 4 of the models, and strangely enough mostly 3 of the same colors. And to top it all off, I sold 50% more pants to much happier customers. The fact was that by limiting the choice, I made my customers happier, more confident that they made a good choice, and I increased my sales at the same time.

Barry Schwartz, who has written a number of interesting books, is a professor of psychology at Swarthmore College in the United States. He explains this paradox in his book *"The Paradox of Choice: Why Less is More"* (Schwartz, B., 2004). He argues that the freedom of choice we have longed for in the past 50 years is the root of today's dissatisfaction. Whether we're buying a pair of jeans, ordering a cup of coffee, or something else, everyday decisions have become increasingly complex due to the overwhelming abundance of choices that we're presented with. A cup of coffee is no longer a cup of coffee, as we learn when we enter at café. See also a later chapter on innovation management. Schwartz summarizes as follows:

1. The more options you have, the harder it will be to decide and make a good choice.
2. The more options you have, the less satisfied you will be, no matter what choice you make.
3. *Good enough* is the best way to be satisfied.

The fact is that people are generally quite simple, and like what is easy. The thing is that we don't really want any other development than a private economic improvement, and easier ways of doing tasks, because we can then buy products or services that give us a simpler life: More energy in for less energy out, the basic exchange rate for all living organisms. But the problem of today has become all the different options.

4.4 Loss aversion

"People do sometimes lie deliberately, but self-deception and rationalization are more common problems".

(Kahneman et al., 2011).

Although we are constantly reminded of winning cultures from various more or less well-articulated actors in various media, it has been established that it is actually more important for us not to lose than to win. We recognize this in the statement about *"the sorry fourth place"* in sports, when ending up outside the podium in competitions is experienced as a gigantic loss, while when you *"luckily saved the bronze medal"* is experienced as a great triumph even though there may be a difference of 1 point between the two places. We call it *loss aversion.* We can also recognize loss aversion in everyday speech with the proverb: *"I know what I have, but not what I get".*

In other words, it is a fact that losing a $1,000 note does not feel twice as bad as losing a $ 500 note. The same goes for winning a $ 500 note doesn't feel half as good as winning a $ 1,000 note. We get sad or happy anyway, and the difference in feelings cannot be measured twice as much as we can mathematically. Loss aversion has diminishing sensitivity from a reference point that provides a weighting function that is convex in the loss domain and concave in the gain domain. The reference point acts as a psychological point that separates gains from losses. (Tversky & Kahneman., 1992).

Since it is more important for us to avoid losses rather than to win a certain gain, we tend to make decisions that are not related to what *"the rational, economic man"* should presumably have done. In other words, we do not make a choice for what makes the most sense from an economic point of view. We would rather take an uncertain risk for a win, than a certain loss. When a situation looks like a loss, we will act as a risk-taker. Conversely, if the situation looks like a profit opportunity, we become risk-averse.

If we link this to the stock market, small investors in the stock market will often keep stocks that are declining in value even if it seems that they will not rise again. Or that stocks that have risen in value are sold before they reach their potential and may fall again. This is because taking a loss feels far heavier than a possible gain. This is often the problem for the unprofessional private savers, the inexperienced small investors who lack experience, as opposed to the experienced and professional investors who often manage to operate more rationally (Awais, Aziz, Usman, & Bhatti, 2021). The professional investors follow the principle: *"Stop loss: Let profit run",* while the unprofessional investors feel that the loss of their taxed small investments is perceived as much heavier. For they *"know what they have, but not what they'll get",* and it is, after all, *"Better with one bird in the hand, than ten birds on the roof".* This is how we rationalize ourselves away from both gains and losses.

Of course, I could have written a lot about different elements of behavioral economics, but the thing is that I bring to the table what I think you could benefit from. Also it`s not a part of my formal education, but afterwards such, we continue to read out of self-interest. One of my master's thesis was written on *Data Strategy, Data Mining and the Use of Big Data.* See more about this in a later chapter, where you will get a more detailed introduction to why public administration is almost in panic in its search for newly qualified computer engineers, mathematicians and statisticians to engage in nudging and controlling tasks. And anyway, there is quite a limited room for everything in a small paperback book that will encompass 5 years of studies on two Executive Master's degrees plus a couple of other interesting certifications and courses I have conducted. So I'll give you chapters which naturally belongs together for you as a Business Executive in making of which I believe you will need in respect of the major subject of this book. This chapter on Behavioral Economics is so important that I think we should end this chapter with a section on the concept of "Nudging".

4.5 Nudging

"With an eye on these NUDGES, Choice architects can improve the outcomes for their Human Users.". (Thaler & Sunstein, 2008)

The book *"Nudge. Improving decisions about health, wealth and happiness"* by Nobel Prize winner Professor Richard H. Thaler and Professor Cass R. Sunstein (2008) is about this: Steering you by nudging you in the "right" direction. First, let's take an analogous example from any café I've never visited before. When the barista asks what kind of coffee I want, I`ll be guilty of an answer because I've never been there before and don't know the selection. And then again I`m stupid enough to fall straight into the trap, answering *"which ones do you have?".* Thus, I`ll have to go through a wide range of options that I have never heard of before. The barista understands I need help because of to many choices if I`m are not just going to turn around and leave. He therefore asks me a few questions about *"Iced or hot coffee, with or without milk, with or without flavoring, African or Brazilian beans or perhaps Blue Java? Easy, medium or French roasted?"*, and so it goes on almost endlessly confusing me even more.

If you are as novice as I am, and the barista is professionally interested in your satisfaction (they want customer satisfaction because of repurchases), they nudge you via a couple of suggestions of *"we sell a lot of this these days, I think you will like it"* and thus towards a choice that you accept with great relief. You don't really have a clue what you're getting, but you're happy to escape both the *paradox of freedom of choice* with too many choices, and *loss aversion* because you get something that may be better than a worse alternative when you have to choose for yourself completely without any help. Even if you could probably have a much better cup of coffee if you knew something about coffee making. This is nudging in practice, in an analogous way.

Due to the fact that almost everything takes place digitally today, we give away a huge amount of information for free. When you act online, the online stores or domain owners can thus steer you around by nudging you, and in this way they guide you around the online store. The only thing they don't want is for you to leave the site again without having purchased something. That's why they hire behavioral economists, system architects, mathematicians and statisticians to predict what you're looking for and nudge you towards choices that suit *themselves* and thus what products or services you actually purchase, in real time, while navigating inside the online store! In addition, they tempt you with *"others who have bought this, have also chosen this one"*. You may swallow on this bait as well because it gives you a confirmation of yourself as smart and reflective person, although you didn`t intent to purchase what you just ordered. Thaler & Sunstein's point out that system architects must think carefully about 4 questions about which incentives must be answered:

1. Who is the user? 2. Who chooses? 3. Who pays? 4.Who earns?

They further write that *"Free markets often solve all key problems by giving people an incentive to create good products and sell them at the right price."* (Thaler & Sunstein, 2008). They believe that if the market is well-functioning, there will be such fierce competition that the bad products lose out to the good ones that are priced according to people's tastes. Nevertheless, it is the case that many markets are filled with what they call incentive conflicts and uses the American health care system as an example of far too many players riding their own fads and therefore not creating the best solution for the patients.

If you have Kahneman's system 1 and system 2 in mind, you`ll realize that you did not shop reflected and thoughtfully online, but most likely on impulse. And the reason why you don't feel cheated is that, firstly, you are not aware of what is happening, and that you have subsequently ended up in Schwartz's rule no. 3: *Good enough is the best way to be satisfied.* And this makes you accept the purchase as "perfectly fine" for the lack of achieving perfection as the website doesn't have anyway, and you may never find. Also, the impulse to buy what *"others have also bought..."* makes you feel smart and reflective. Even if you haven't decided much more than that you're going to enter the site and look for something on your mind. The rest is cleverly controlled by the site's algorithms built up by system architects, behavioral economists, statisticians, and mathematicians.

For example, Microsoft makes it so that they automatically steer you into their own browser Bing if you are looking for something that is not available on your own HD (Hard Disk). Whether you want to or not. The same happens with Google, or Facebook, and all other digital platforms such as your online banking. This is of course because they want free information about you to both learn what you think, like and prefer to buy. The concept is called *Big Data*, which is the collection of enormous amounts of data, which with the help of algorithms later can predict yours- and everyone else's user behavior for their own benefit. See more detailed on this topic from the practical part of my thesis on *"Data Strategy, Data Mining and the use of Big Data"* in later chapter in this book.

This is how they build up their algorithms, reduce their staffing and costs, and also sell your user data to third parties. So, regardless of industry affiliation, smart business leaders will look at how they can use Big Data for what it is, a management revolution. (McAfee & Brynjolfsson, 2012). By the way, at the time of writing this, Microsoft is in dire straits because they have used tens of thousands of New York Times newspaper articles to train its algorithms without asking permission. In addition, the European Commission has recently denied Microsoft the opportunity to force Windows users onto its Bing browser, so Europeans can now freely choose any one browser and search engine they prefer.

The point of all digital operators is that user data is worth its weight in gold, and it is market power. They want more power, they want to decide what you should think, at least what you think *about*, and thus be able to profit from this information. Thaler and Sunstein writes that in understanding their readers' limited memory, they provide a sketch of the six principles of good architecture:

*i**N**centives*
***U**nderstanding mappings*
***D**efaults*
***G**ive feedback*
***E**xpect error*
***S**tructure complex Choises*

In other words: **NUDGES**.

You can find more information about me and my other books here: executivewayto.com

Chapter 5. Cost- and Management Accounting

"*Economics is 50% psychology and 50% realism*".
(Ole Stavad, former Danish Minister of Finance).

"In planning for the future and in an attempt to influence an organizations development, successful managers are likely to need to draw on a range of skills and knowledge. These include accounting and finance, business strategy and the management of people." (Bowhill, Bruce. 2008).

We have now zoomed from the overall level: international trade theory, national accounts, inflation and what governs unemployment, further through what governs monopoly, oligopoly and industry-specific conditions and different market structures from monopoly to in perfect competition, and also looked a little bit at behavioral economics, it is time to zoom in to the specific company level.

First, ask yourself why I think you should know a little about cost- and management accounting. My answer is that it can be nice to understand how the pricing of goods happens at the specific company level. Of course, the companies' pricing affects you, whether you like it or not. We can of course discuss the order of the chapters and my pedagogy in this, but the idea is that you should get a 360-degree view of your finances: What affects you, what you affect yourself through your choices, and how you can adapt and improve your personal finances. Whether you are a manager or an employee.

So, how do they think, and how do they act? Let`s zoom in on the economy at the specific company level to understand the mysteries of cost and management accounting. There are some clear dividing lines that nevertheless interfere with each other. We can say that we divide this company-specific part of finance into three parts, or disciplines according to when things happen: past, present and future.

The accounts are based on historical and factual information, i.e. the past. We take a closer look at this in the next chapter. But the present is about the business administration's product calculations and the need for cost control. We will go through the most common calculations in this chapter. When it comes to the future, we are concerned with investment and financing the operations. Budgeting is somewhat unique, because it intervenes in all three disciplines.

We can of course discuss the order of the chapters and the pedagogy in this, but the idea is that you as a reader are either thinking about establishing yourself, are already in an establishment phase, are a first-time manager or aspire to become a manager soon. If you manage a business today and feel that you need a "Brush Up" on dormant knowledge, this should be an equally stakeholder approach. Thus, we follow the tradition of strategic thinking (and which is typical of the MBA perspective) first an overview: What is the current situation? We need to get a good grasp of the present before we can plan for the future. In the future, you will know what the result was, so you must have control of the accounts, which are a thing of the past. The past again gives us a basis for understanding the present, so then the circle starts all over again.

5.1. Five important factors in business finance

The first commandment for business managers is to keep the company alive. The second commandment is to create growth. The most important thing to understand is that you are dependent on getting people with you and not against you. Naturally, you want the business you lead to survive, grow, and thrive. In a world where the competition for attention from customers is getting tougher and tougher, and price competition is getting tighter and tighter, you need to have control over both revenue and costs to get a result to live on. In chapter three, we discussed the basic competencies for entrepreneurs.

So, working through the topics of economics it's now natural to continue with the finances. Regardless of whether you have an idea to establish a business to commercialize one or more products or services as we speak, or you are, or will become, a leader with finance and profit responsibility, it is natural to start with the present tense. The most fun and interesting thing is to look at the revenue potential for your products or services. Let's start with calculations.

First, a basic clarification of concepts, which is a simple but important rule of thumb: Expenses relate to a point in time, for example something that has been, or is to be paid. Costs are something that is incurred in connection with the consumption of a good or service. That`s not time-specific.

5.2. Important abbreviations and what they mean

When you are going to have managerial responsibilities, there are a number of things you need to know before you make decisions and initiate processes. First of all, you need to have an overall view, see things "from the heights" or the helicopter, which is a common metaphor. Many people claim to have this *"helicopter gaze"* but often it is just empty boasting because it sounds so cool. But you must have full control over the components and costs included in the goods or services that will be included in your decisions, and that requires both an overview and detailed knowledge. Secondly, it is important to acquire qualified knowledge or help from specialists in exactly what the MBA education is all about: *the core subjects*! That's why we started this article with business finance and the basic types of calculations.

When we make product calculations, there are a number of variables that we must calculate before we can offer our goods and services so that we do not lose money on producing and selling them. We will therefore briefly review what they mean now, because we will need them both in our calculations, but also in the analyses later on. In fact, many of these variables and terms are repeated in, or used in, performance analysis, or Key Performance Index (KPI), although there are many other abbreviations. in addition. In addition, we discuss the background for and benefits of such investment analyses in more detail in chapter 8. But for now, here is an overview of the most important abbreviations:

Shortname:	What it stands for	Measurement unit
FC	Fixed costs	Measured in money or percentage
VC	Variable costs	Measured in money or percentage
TC	Total costs	Measured in money or percentage
Rev	Revenue/Earnings/Yield	Measured in money or percentage
Fin	Financial revenue	Measured in money or percentage
ROV	Total Operating Revenue	Measured in money or percentage
TCu	Total Costs per unit	Measured in money or percentage
FCu	Fixed Costs per Unit	Measured in money or percentage
VCu	Variable Costs per Unit	Measured in money or percentage
NOPAT	Net Operating Profit	Usually measured in money
EBT	Earnings Before Tax	Usually measured in money
EBIT	Earnings Before Interest and Tax	Usually measured in money
EBITDA	Earnings Before Interest Tax and Depreciation	Usually measured in money

Table: Abbreviations used in both calculation models and in accounting analyses. The last four are usually used primarily in accounting analyses and are therefore usually stated in money.

5.3. Five factors that affect manufacturers

As we move on, we must remember to analyze everything, always. With both sudden worldwide pandemics and sudden major wars in Europe, Africa or Asia, most people have realized that they know less about the future than they like to think about. This makes both the calculation work and especially the budget work complicated. But we must build the uncertainty into both calculations and budgets as best we can. Because even though we are supposed to live according to a budget, we do not live better than what the customers actually pay to our bank account. Not only should we take into account what we think might happen in the future, or a few things we can't know anything about, but on top of it all, we should try to abide by it in a good way.

As we now move into Cost and Management Accounting, we are first and foremost moving into the *value configuration* we call the *value chain* - those who produce things. Michael Porter described the structure and functions of these *value chain businesses* in his book *"Competitive advantage: Creating and sustaining superior performance."* (Porter, M., 1985), in this way:

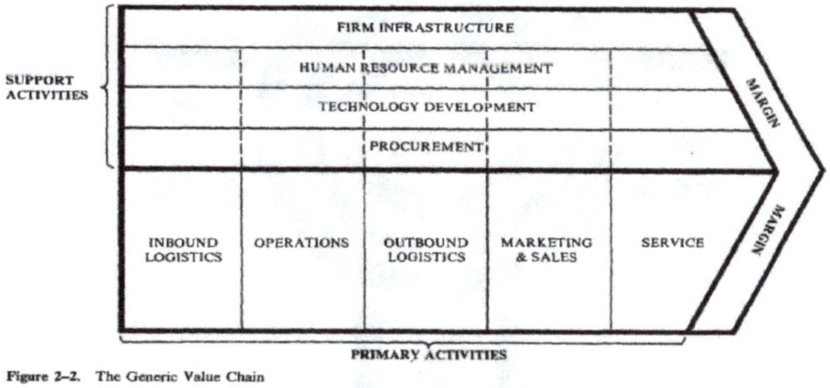

Fig: *Example of the value chain (Porter, M., 1985)*

Therefore, we also include the most well-known and fundamental competitive analysis model and keep Porter's five forces in mind because they affect all businesses in the value chain in this way. We will also take a closer look at different value configurations the book on *"Strategic Management for business Executives"*, but Porter's model shows the forces that affect any producers of the value configuration of the value chain as follows:

1. *Retailer power*: The cost of goods is constantly increasing. The smaller you are, the more expensive it will be.

2. *Customer power*: "Small discounts are received with joy, big ones with greed!". Be careful!

3. *Substitutes*: Think carefully about what an alternative costs; do your calculations still hold?

4. *Competitors*: Check your competitors' market power. Are your products and prices better?

5. *New entrants*: How difficult/expensive is it to establish/produce/copy your products?

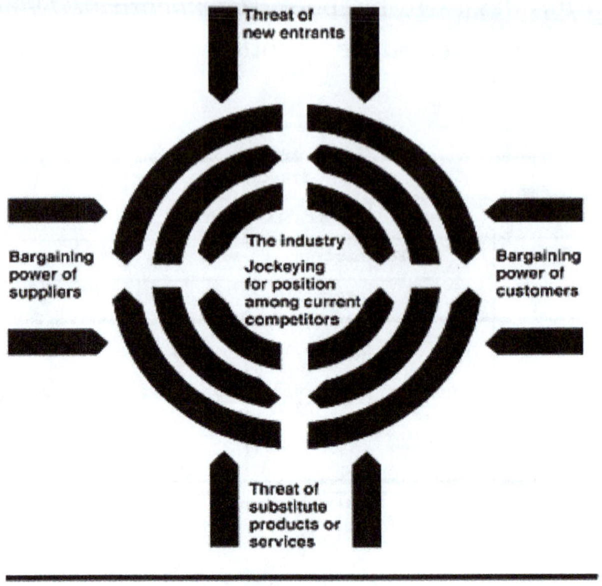

Fig: *Basic competition analysis model Five Forces* (Porter, M. 1980).

In other words, we not only use Porter's five-force model in the strategy discipline, but also in the economics and marketing disciplines because we need to do different analyses, including a competitive or a *competitor analysis*. It is so basic that it should definitely be done before launching your new products, whether you are new to the market, are a middle manager or a manager of an existing business. But for now, we will move on to three basic standard calculation models.

5.4. Three traditional and basic calculation models

Three different traditional calculation models have basically covered most of the calculation needs: the full-cost method, the mark-up model or the contribution model. Other calculation models, such as ABC calculations (which we will go into in the next section and in detail in the online course) are in use, but we will start with these three are the most common, and easiest to understand. The first two are based on all the different cost categories, such as fixed and variable costs incurred in connection with the production and sale of the product.

1. Absorption Cost method

The Absorption Cost method is common in e.g. manufacturing and industrial enterprises. The full-cost method is based on absorbing all different types of costs such as fixed (e.g. rent and fixed wages) and variable costs (e.g. consumption of goods and hourly wages) that are incurred in connection with the production and sale of products or services. Here, care must be taken with the allocation of variable and indirect overhead costs, such as pure administrative costs. The full-cost method is common in e.g. manufacturing and industrial activities.

2. The Mark-up method

The mark-up method is common in wholesale and retail trade and service industries. The markup method is very simple. You simply take all the costs associated with the purchase of the product, semi-finished product or raw material, both fixed and variable, and multiply it by a coefficient (a factor) and divide by the number of units. For example (total purchase price of the item + fixed costs + variable costs + VAT = 100) * coefficient = sales price. Ex. retail price can then be calculated as follows (100 * 3) = 300.

3. The Contribution method

The contribution method is based on or expected market price minus the costs, to see how much the sale will contribute to the result. The contribution calculation is therefore used where the market price is "given" in micro-conditions, in the event of strong competition and equivalent products, and takes into account a demand-based price that the company must accept in order to sell its product. For example, coffee shops, where you have to differentiate yourself in other ways. More on this in Microeconomics. The calculation will then be retail price per unit – variable unit costs = profit per unit.

Traditional calculation models:

Full cost + Absorption Cost calculation:	*Mark-up calculation:*	*Contribution calculation:*
All Direct Materials	Purchase price	+ Selling price
+ Salaries	* Factor (coefficient)	- Variable unit costs (VAC)
+ Other costs (rent, heating, etc.)	= Selling price	= Profit
= sum		
+ Profit		
= Selling price		

Example: Schematic comparison of the most common calculation models.

You can find more information about me and my other books here:
executivewayto.com

Part II: Endogenous Conditions

Chapter 6. The Opportunity Cost

We are now going to start on something very educational and very fun. We will look at the opportunity cost, and I will explain one of the most fundamental tings in finance, applied personal or professional. Because now we have arrived at the very core of *Applied Personal Finance.* We start with basics. We must learn to crawl before we can run.

Finance may sound intimidating to all non-economists. But don't worry, because you don't really need any prior knowledge beyond what you learned at high school. And if you didn`t, I`ll show you here. Also, I think you should have learned this by the end of it, at least at high school! But we stay clear of the heavy parts of finance, the "self-tormenting" parts of options theories and advanced financial instruments. It`s far beyond the goal of this book, and it belongs to the level of professional studies at business schools. Maybe I'll write another book of it together with my son. Because even though he didn't have to, as a reader of my book, he himself have just finished an MEA (in finance!) from one of the best financial top 50 Business Schools in the world!

Anyway, if learning math, or economics was not a success in your previous school careers, I have created Excel apps/models for you to download from our website. You will find directions in the first chapter we are using them, so read on! In these Excel-apps, you only need to enter a few numbers. The only thing you need to do is think through and understand what you want to know and interpret the answers you get. For this, you need insight. Therefore, I have made *"test-yourself-questions with summary answers"* to all finance chapters, except this chapter which is the basic as chapters 11 and 12 are too. Just start looking forward to it already!

I strongly recommend you read all the chapters in due order because it will broaden your understanding. All relevant formulas have been entered into the text and explained. But you do not have to memorize them. You don't have to emphasize understanding financial math either, although I'll show you how they work so you can build the models yourself in Excel. I think it's an important point that you should be able to do it yourself and have therefore written all the formulas right here in the book in the same way as you build them up in Excel. But fear not, all the formulas are described, and it is explained how we use them and for what reason. You can use pen and paper and a simple calculator if you want to test your "little grey" a bit. You don't become an Olympic champion by lying on the couch reading about it, that`s for sure! This is precisely an important point: *What`s not used is quickly forgotten.* So that's why I recommend you do what I did myself: Practice the *test-yourself-questions with summary answers,* of course! And to succeed, I have outlined all the formulas for you to build the same apps in your very own spreadsheet! If you like. Either way, take your time and read the chapters in order. There is of course a good reason why I have chosen to set up the chapters in the order the way I did.

If you don't have the energy to create the models yourself, you can find these Excel apps ready to download at my website. Should you be unlucky and do technical antics, being unsure if something is wrong, you can just enter the numbers again, because the apps/models are locked. So, you have to use them as they are. You can just type the numbers that you need, and then press Enter to get your answer immediately. By the way, I have put the screenshots of the models in the book here, they are incredible easy-to-use and self-explanatory. Thus, the idea is that you only read just one chapter and then tackle the *test-yourself-questions with summary answers,* while you still have the chapter fresh in your mind. In any case, you should quite rarely enter more than two or three different numbers. Therefore, you can spend the time to reflect on what happens when one or more assumptions changes, put it in and immediately get the new answer as soon as you hit the Enter button! That will increase your understanding further.

I should warn you from using the Excel Apps before you have read through the chapter to understand how the models work, and neither the author nor the publisher takes responsibility for how you choose to use them anyway. Because *"Shit in, means shit out".* You won`t get more sensible answers from the models from what you put into them. So, whether you are an experienced economist or not, please read the chapter before you get to grips with the Excel Apps. They follow the chapters in the book, and you have to understand the connections and assumptions to get it right. My models are made in an Excel format that should be suitable for all known versions of Excel. You must have Excel, or another fully equivalent and compatible program to use my models. Otherwise, you have to find a calculator and compute it yourself with pen and paper or build it from scratch in your own preferred spreadsheet.

When my first version of this book was published in 2002, there were simply no books on these topics for non-economics students that focus on how to get answers to personal finance questions, or that had simple models that you could use yourself. Also, there was no FIRE movement in 2000, however these Millennials and Gen-X is the children from that times which now is adults who makes the FIRE movement. But still there is no book like this one. If you want to have this kind of competence as I show you here, you have to enter a business school or to buy yourself a textbook for master's students and grapple with that kind of frustrating studies, and you still have to ponder on how to use it personally. Like I did myself. Those books are focused on companies, and it prepares you for a heavy exam and thereafter a professional life. But not everybody wants to become an economist.

At the time of writing this book, I have still not found anything similar to this. Other authors will tell you what to do, or what they think is smart. But I`ll just show you how economists with an MEA or MBA thinks of financial topics on private matters and that will in turn show you how you can solve your own situations. You`ll figure it out. And that's quite a different approach because that will itself teach you how to learn from practice. Also I will give you tips for books for professionals at The Appendix B. When you undertake a formal study in finance, you must expect to build models in Excel yourself. Or you also have to buy an expensive financial calculator for your exams and of course spend a lot of time to master them. If you don`t, *I've already done all that work for you!* And made it simple and easy to read so you don't need to.

You may be able to find simple calculators, apps and "smart tricks" on the web, especially banks' websites. But they don`t give you the knowledge to fend for yourself. On the contrary, they try to make you dependent on constantly returning to their website as often as possible so they can sell you new products. It's because they have another agenda too. They make money on a concept called *servitization*, which is the business of selling you user data's to third parties i.e. other business companies. If you want to know more about why and how, on Data Strategy, Data Mining and how they make use of Big Data, you can find more material on my website. It`s a good thing in life to remember that nothing is for free. And when it comes to the banks, they are the most successful business organizations of all times.

Other books on personal finance focus on how to pay as little tax as possible. That`s OK because it focuses on keeping you *inside the legal framework* of the laws of the state or country you live in, and it's both legal and perfectly fine. But tax regimes vary both from year to year, and from country to country. In addition, taxes are a "*luxury problem*": If you don't earn anything, you don't pay taxes. So that's why I don't include taxes in a book on personal finance since finance and investments is the main point: How to get the most out of the few dollars you already have by looking at how the MEAs and MBAs solve personal financial challenges themselves.

In this book, we therefore start from the viewpoint of a luxury problem: You have money, or you get money that you can handle yourself. So, I show you both the knowledge of how the economists and the MBAs solve everyday problems themselves by using their professional knowledge on real issues. In this way, serious professional knowledge is transferred to you in a simple way, which you in turn can make you independent and become *FiRE@40* if you want to. In this book we go through everything you normally want to know more about as a private person. Straight to the point, in other words. You will recognize the models when you have read the text, because you will find screenshots of them. And then they'll be self-explanatory. Logical and easy. So, even if you are already an economist, do yourself the favor of reading the chapters in the correct order and through. It increases both understanding and applicability.

6.1 What is financing and investing?

First, a definition of investment and financing: When we think of investing, we first and foremost think of something that will give a return for the better at a later stage. In the future that is. Whether it is in the form of increased well-being or in increased prosperity that we can use tomorrow or save for future use in a rainy day. Or both. When we think about financing, we think first and foremost of finding a solution for how this future return can take place by means of an intervention that will take place today or in the immediate close future.

An example could be a student who takes on a student loan to *finance* an investment in a longer education to obtain a master's degree. In other words: the financing of the investment that in the future hopefully will provide a better job position and better salary. Which in turn gives a hopefully increased well-being both personally of working with something you like and getting a better salary that gives more or better benefits. Another example could be that you invest your savings in an apartment that your daughter will use as a student dormitory for a few years and that you hope it also will increase a little in value over time, both a benefit for her and for you. In economic terms, we think first and foremost of monetary values. But it`s applicable in everyday situations: If you invest in behaving nicely to other people today, they will always remember to behave nicely to you in return.

In finance, we distinguish between two types of tangible investments, financial investments and real investments. The financial investments can be, for example, loans, deposits or mutual funds. Real investments can be properties like for example land, a building or a house or a car that you can mend yourself. You can also make intangible investments, such as in your own education. Or in your children or your family, neighborhood and society in general. But since the return is not necessarily measurable (you may not get that job) or that your family don't think you are as cool and hip as you think yourself, we will stay away from the intangible investments in this book. First and foremost, because you cannot quantify the intangible, and this book is all about understanding quantifying. But regardless of when we talk about investing and financing, we are talking about a subject which you drop into on a daily basis, whether you want to or not. It is probably the most practical of all sciences in our everyday life because there is economy in everything.

40 years ago, there wasn`t much talk about finance other than when someone was buying a house or a car. At that time, it was usually only done once in a lifetime. As the standard of living increased, it became more common to have a car, washing machine, new refrigerator, TV, a boat or a cabin and so on. When I wrote my version of this book 22 years ago on investment and financing, it just about began to become a more common expression that larger parts of the population used more than once or twice in their lives. In the last 10 years, it has become common. Nevertheless, a long period of artificially low interest rates in the aftermath of the Covid pandemic has led to the fact that almost everyone under the age of 40 who is not an economist does not understand even elementary economic conditions. In other words are illiterate in finance. But you who read this book will soon master it!

Regardless of how we talk about investing and financing, we move along a time axis! If we are to define what *finance* is really about, we can say that it *is the allocation of resources over time.* By allocation, we mean moving or distributing. From this, we instinctively understand that increased consumption today means reduced consumption tomorrow. And not least the other way around, reduced consumptions today means savings to increase consumptions tomorrow. Let's dig into that!

6.2 One dollar, two dollars, three dollars...

I have actually been interested in economics, - and economic contexts since I was quite young. I hadn`t finish primary school before I was nicknamed "The Bottle King". You know why, I picked them up and took them with me. Not that I was looking specifically for empty bottles other than during holidays then, but I couldn't just leave them there and maybe hurt some animals. Most of the kids I knew had fun throwing stones at them until they shattered. I didn't like that at the time, and I don't do it now. But in my country, as in more and more these days, you could exchange one bottle for a quarter. So, I did get something back for the effort of carrying the bottles to the nearest grocery store, because of a deposit system: You pay a deposit of a quarter of a dollar on each bottle you buy in the store and then get the quarter back in return when you bring the empty bottle back to any grocery store. If you don`t, the cashback is there for someone else who can be bothered to bring it to the grocery store. Like I did. So, it was a no brainer. I picked bottles from wherever I found them and returned them to the store to buy candy in exchange. Or to save for another day. Such efforts can finance chocolate and candy for both one and two kids of that age, weekly. It wasn't fun being called "The Bottle King" but I soon realized that those who did were only envious because I constantly had a big bag of candy and a soda while the others had nothing but sour faces and bitter comments because they didn't understand a very simple, but important economic principle. Namely, that for a little extra effort (carrying an empty bottle or two to the store) I got some interesting in return.

In this chapter, we will review three very important and fundamental economic principles:

1. *Many small streams becomes a river*
2. *The concept of opportunity cost*
3. *Value for Money Principle*

In my early years I could of course wonder how Peterson could buy a car for several thousand dollars when he worked as a newspaper boy. Questions such as *"Should I take the mortgage as an annuity loan or serial loan, and which will be cheaper?"* was one of the things I tried to figure out. Without getting anything but a headache! It was never quite right and the uncertainty about where the errors in the formulas had almost made me crazy because I didn't have the right formulas. Until I hated my own incompetence in the field so much that I simply had to undertake a serious study of economics. But then I became happy, because I then knew how to compute the numbers. Later in life as a senior business advisor to around a hundred other business managers, my customers have many times met me with problems like *"What does that loan cost me?"*, or *"Is it worth saving or borrowing money for that boat?"*, *"Is it worth it to lease a car, or borrow money and then buy it?"*. So, in this book you will be able to receive some of the knowledge I have in these matters as well as some of the models I created during my studies to understand the finance subject better. You simply don't have to take a formal economics degree; *I've already done the work for you!* Nice, right?

Well, truthfully speaking, I haven't always been as good at saving money. I have always have something to share with others. Unfortunately, some have been surprisingly good at exploiting this. But my own lesson from my childhood is still clear: *"Many small streams makes a big river!"*. The case is that small and simple discoveries of your own can have quite big consequences, and that is what you remember best. Another important point is that I now at least have the knowledge to both discover and be able to control all *"small streams"* in a way that suits me and my family much better. In addition, I can quickly calculate what such a lack of control, possibly or alternatively, will affect. And this brings us to another very important and fundamental economic concept, namely the concept of opportunity cost.

6.3 What options do you have?

Basically, you must firstly and lastly learn to think about what options you have. We are talking in an economic sense, however applicable in many ways. You may dream of an amazing sports car, or a gorgeous house, a wonderful cabin, or that incredible speedboat. Or *the* holiday trip of a lifetime. Or simply about retiring at the age of 40-45? Yes, all of this is actually possible. But usually not at the same time or at once. First, we need to think about the consequences of the choices we make and then we need to ask ourselves if it's worth it. Both in dollars and cents and in renunciations. One of the most useful concepts in economics is called *the opportunity cost*.

The opportunity cost is about the fact that in order to choose one thing or a solution, you have to sacrifice another thing, - or another alternative because there is never enough money for everything. Actually, this is the essence of all strategies. You probably remember from the introduction that economics basically deals with the fact that there are not enough resources to satisfy all needs that exist. The opportunity cost is often explained briefly and concisely as follows: *"The cost of the best opportunity forsaken"*. In a somewhat more elaborate language, we can say that the opportunity cost is the cost of the difference between what we ultimately chose, and the alternative that we *did not choose*, including any income. In other words, we can say that the opportunity cost shows the value of the best alternative use of a resource. Interest is a typical example of an opportunity cost. Reflect on it.

When it comes to the finance textbooks, there is a sad tendency to add all the examples to a hypothetical company with all possible and impossible combinations of alternative use of resources, cost structures and financing options. But of course we will not do that in this book. We will look at the issues based on the day to day need as private individuals. If you are looking for textbooks for business world situations, there are a lot of great books on the market, in almost all possible languages. I`ll give you a few tips in appendix B at the end of this book. Enough about that. Now let's take a simple example right away and *note that the amounts and percentages I use in my examples do NOT affect the academic reasoning*. These are just examples:

You are considering buying a car, which you do not already have. You don't need to have a car to commute, but you and your wife have a penchant for traveling to a shopping mall in the neighbor town where you can both cut your hair, buy toys for the kids and fishing equipment for yourself. After the trip to a well-stocked grocery store, you will be both hungry and thirsty and want to enjoy a meal at the mall. You know that after all bills have been paid, you can save about $ 400 per month if you go for it. You have already saved $ 5,000 in your payroll account, and the car you are drooling over is an AudiA6 that you believe takes care of both your family's overall transport needs and your personal status. It is also beautiful silver-gray. It is in mint condition and asking price is $ 15,000,- only run 60,000 km. The car dealer "Car Shark Ltd" offers you a loan of $ 10,000 to 15% interest (arrears annuity), *paid over five years. You quickly calculate in your head that this would be 10,000 /5=-2,000 per year /12mnths = $ 166.67 per month. Then we should probably add 15% on top. This is where you start to break into a cold sweat because your brain goes into a "loop" over doing percentage calculations in your head.*

Mr. Smiley at *The Car Shark Ltd* explains that this loan will only cost you $ 248,59 per month including interest. Thats a total payment of $ 14,915.78 of which the interest must therefore be the amount of $ 4,915.78. In chapter 8, you will learn to do all such calculations yourself before you visit Mr. Smiley at *The Car Shark Ltd* or similar places. In a snap! However, this was more expensive than you had expected, but since you know that you can save

400 per month, you think that this will be fine anyway. *"Pretty manageable"* you say, grinning broadly. So you ask him to pick up the contract. While he is away, you remember that you have read something about opportunity costs, and that such things can be directly smart to keep in mind. Where does the opportunity cost come in here, and not least, - why on earth should you think about such a thing?

The answer to the opportunity cost lies in the reasoning *"What would the situation be like if we don't do it"*? Well, I mean buying the car. An alternative is the current solution where you either have to limit yourself to the sparse range of shopping options where you live, or that you hitchhike with your neighbor ($ 5 for gasoline and takes 1 hour) to the mall. You can alternatively take a combination of bus and ferry ($ 10 and which takes 2 hours) or take a taxi which is unreasonably expensive ($ 25 and takes 1 hour and 10 minutes each way), including waiting time for the taxi. Although this probably is better for the neighborly relationship.

If you do not buy that car at all, these money can be alternatively spent. We can, for example, choose to put the $ 5,000 on a savings account which gives a slightly better interest rate than the payroll account, let's say 7% p.a. (per annum). The interest of such amount will actually finance the trip to the mall every fortnight (bus and ferry), as well as a lunch for $ 9.67 once a month. Or a taxi once a month and a few cups of coffee once you're there. Alternatively, you can hitchhike with your neighbor every week and spend the remaining $ 9 on lunch or coffee cups on various visits throughout the month. And then you still have the original amount of $ 5,000 to possibly (or alternatively) spend when the washing machine, TV or refrigerator breaks next month, next year, or the year after. Another option may be that you want to undertake a full vacation for the whole family abroad next summer.

In these choices, the $ 5,000 is still resting in your account. Now let's look at what, for example, a *negative cash flow* (borrowing the $ 10,000 with a downpayment period over five years at 15% interest) of the amount of $ 248,59 per month could alternatively have been used for something else! Because they are part of this story. *If you can afford to borrow, you can afford to save: Never forget that!* In this case you have still not signed the loan papers, so you can save these $ 248,6 every single month. This is

248,6 * 12 = 2,983.2 per year. Let's say you save this $ 248.6 every month for five years and you are such a cynical capitalist that you would like to get the best possible interest rate on your savings. The bank in which you have a payroll account currently gives you 7% annual interest (also arrears annuity). After a year it will be $ 2,983.2, after two years it will be $ 6,175.2 and after three years it has grown to $ 9,590.7 and after five years you will have a total of $ 17,155.6 on your account, and still you have your original $ 5,000 to spend to begin with or put in the same account, adding another $ 6,097.27 to that savings account. Assuming the bank actually gives you an annual interest rate of 7% for the *entire period, your wealth would have grown to a whopping $ 23,252.87*. What's more, you don't have to spend money on maintaining jobs in both the car industry, the oil industry and the insurance industry. How did this growth happen? Did I catch your attention now? If not, you did probably not read thoroughly, reflect on it or perhaps the content of this book is not for you.

But this is what the economists know and act upon. Don`t they buy cars? Yes of course they do, however, they know exactly what they do and chose consciously. Because in addition to increase your wealth, you did not have to spend money on maintenance, gas, oil-, and insurances accordingly But we cannot include these costs until you actually have bought the car and drive it from the car shop. They come exclusively with the car, just like repaying the loan and the interests. These other costs are difficult to calculate in advance because they vary depending on how much you will be using the car. That is why it is called variable costs. But if you don't buy the car, you will of course also completely miss the indisputable pleasure of sitting behind the wheel of a silver-grey Audi A6 and enjoying your neighbor's envious look as you cruise past his living room window.

For us who are wage earners with relatively small budgets and modest means, it is important to stop for a moment to reflect on what we could alternatively use the money for. Because if we buy the car, we have to sacrifice something. Therefore, the opportunity cost is also often called the sacrificial cost. Maybe you'll sacrifice your family's vacation trip to your mother-in-law next summer (maybe not a sacrifice for you?) or the salmon fishing in Alaska you've dreamed of since you were a little boy, the amazing wedding dress of an otherworldly dream or maybe your children's future college education. Maybe you sacrifice a small extension to the overly narrow living room, or a new bathroom that in both cases would increase the family's wealth. Maybe you're sacrificing supporting a charity project on the other side of the world because you "can't afford it" right now? Well, you can alternatively use a rental car once a month, and probably still be able to save 250 per month after gasoline and insurance have been paid for the rental.

You may have noticed that I switched from the accuracy of two decimals to no decimals in the middle of the example? So, please remember that economic understandings with all its assumptions does not become more correct with an accuracy of five decimals. That belongs in foreign exchange rate transactions and two decimal places in cash registers and in the financial statements like I as professional CPA must do at work. The decimals in our context only interfere with the understanding of the numbers we are working on. We are simply looking to understand the principles, not to impress the economics professors. The exact numbers with two decimals can be found in the applications you will use from the next chapter, but my *points* does not get any more correct.

There is always something to spend your money on, and the economists' task is not to decide for you what to do, but rather to *point out the financial consequences* of the choices you make. That said, I will admit that economists are not equally sensible at all times. We suffer as much as everyone else from the pain and agony of choice as explained. We are no less human than others, but we choose willingly and knowingly of the consequences. And now you understand better what we have in mind all the time. But now you're looking forward to the next 9 chapters, right? However we will first go through a little more stuff in this chapter, because there is more to think about.

6.4 Be smart, think twice!

Some people are more impulsive than others. While others, on the contrary, are completely vacillating over the most banal things. Regardless of the type of person, it can be worthwhile to think more than once. We continue with the Audi, which you can't easily forget about anytime soon. *"Yes, but after taxes?"* you say, *"I get less tax when I take the loan? It will only be 211,1 (248,5 minus 37,5) after tax because I pay a 30% tax rate?".*

Maybe so. But now it's definitely time to think twice! What amount do you have to pay each month? $ 248.6, or $ 211.1? Didn`t we just outline that the loan of $10,000 at the rate of interest at 15% should have a cost of 248.6 per month over 5 years? In chapter 9, I will show you how to calculate the tax effect of debt, or tax reduction on investment, but let`s take one thing at the time. Anyway relax, because the car salesman Mr. Smiley is not trying steal your money to fill his own pocket straight off. He`ll get it there anyway. But now it's time for a warning right away. Mr. Smiley makes you focus on net borrowing costs (after tax), which is a cheap sales trick even if it is never so true! This makes you focus on a lower cost than what you should, which makes it looks cheaper. The amount to pay, contracted with the lender, including interest of 248.59 must be paid *every month* until the debt is paid off! This is the negative cash flow you have to deal with.

If a salesperson is pounding on the net borrowing costs (after tax), you should ask *"Is that the amount I have to pay each month? Where does the $248.6 come from then?"* I myself usually ask if this means that salesperson have decided to pay the difference (of my taxes) for me. Then they usually quickly explains that I can go to the tax authority office and have my tax reduced. But that's not the point here. If you can afford only the tax reduced amount, you can of course *not* buy the car. It will probably stay in the garage, because you wouldn`t be able to drive the car because of the running costs like gas, insurance and maintenance as well. People tend to forget that when they fall in love with items. That`s my point; If you cannot finance the cash flow and then some over your disposable income every single month until the debt is paid off, there is no point in signing the mortgage. If you don't have a penny to save, how are you going to pay a penny? Not to mention insurance, the gasoline and everything else that comes with the use of your car. Once you have started serious economic thoughts, you can think about the fact that you are not really dependent on a car anyway.

Another important principle we will include in this chapter is called *the "value for money principle".* Economists call it "*the cost/benefit concept"* or, to put it a little more explanatory, *"the utility value per dollar".* Not a dumb thing to have in mind, so let's take an example. We continue where we left off with the Audi:

We have already realized that you and your family will travel to the boring mall both steadily and constantly to let your money run. Your need is transport, and you find the previously reviewed alternatives unacceptable. The neighbor is definitely tired of you (but not the rest of the family), you are just as tired of the bus and ferry because you want to spend your time at the mall and not on transport. And you think that it will be too expensive with a taxi.

An alternative to buying this silver-gray Audi A6 right now is to buy another far cheaper car *in cash* for a maximum of $ 5,000. It will probably cover the same transport needs, although it may not cover the need for status in your neighborhood. But you can save the $ 400 from your salary minus running costs on the car. Let's say that the running costs of a car for $ 5,000 amount to an average of $ 151.4 for petrol, insurance and a minimum of service per month on average. You can save 400 – 151.4 = 248,6. You now know this will be 248,6 * 12 = 2,983.2 per year. Plus, interest income if you add them to your savings account. If the car lasts for a while, you can buy a newer one for $ 17,155.6 in five years! Provided that the bank will give you 7% interest on your savings account *for the entire period.*

You remember that *"if you can afford to borrow, you can afford to save!"*. In this example both the core of the *"value for money principle"* (you get a car anyway even if it is not that expensive), the essence of the entire chapter *on the concept of opportunity cost* and that you see that by *saving a small amount each month*, you can relatively quickly increase your wealth.

I've learned a couple of tricks when the itches for buying stuff becomes unbearable:

1. Firstly, I ask myself what I can *alternatively* get for the money, and if I want to sacrifice this other alternative?
2. Secondly, If the answer is *yes* to the previous question, the next question is whether the chosen solution provides the *best value for money*, i.e. is there a similar product that is cheaper?!

You won't be too surprised when I tell you that I never buy the latest version of any products, do you? It's just nonsense because the penultimate version is usually very little different, just some ditty dab that I probably don't need. If for once it should be exactly *the ditty dab*, I just need to have, I'll wait until the last ultimate product turns into the penultimate. It usually happens tomorrow, at least within a year. The manufacturer constantly has to deliver new models with new and improved *ditty dab* simply to keep the turnover, and hence the share price in the stock market happy. Advantage for me, but cruel for the one who burn their money at the latest *ditty dab* all the time. Well then, this was the text of the day. We have discussed and reflected on three very important and fundamental economic principles:

1. Many small streams becomes a river
2. The concept of opportunity cost
3. Value for Money Principle

What do we get the most benefit from per dollar? What you can do, what you should do and what you ultimately choose to do are not necessarily the same.

You can find more information about me and my books here:
executivewayto.com or at fireat40.com

Chapter 7. The Value of Money over Time

We are now going to start on something very educational. We will look at the allocation of resources over the time, and it will explain another of the most fundamental tings in finance. Pay attention! This is precisely what finance is all about. One of the most fundamental points in financial theory is that a dollar today is worth more than a dollar tomorrow. Why is this so? Well, if you were given the choice between getting a hundred dollars today or a hundred dollars in a year, you would of course choose to get the money today. Firstly, because you`ll get interest on the hundred dollars by lending it to the bank. In other words, a dollar today is worth more than a dollar tomorrow. Secondly, you can alternatively spend the hundred dollars today.

7.1 Value over time?

But not everyone is quite aware of how to calculate on it. To get into finance, we have to go through how to compute the interest. There is no way around this. We will concentrate on two dimensions in this chapter. One is called the future value, or the final value (FV), and the other is called the present value or net value (NV). I prefer to use future value rather than final value when we talk about a fixed amount both in the book and in the applications. The future value (FV) is the value of an amount in the given future. The net value (NV), on the other hand, is the value of a given amount in the future converted back to today's value. In other words, we compute in the opposite direction.

7.2 Perspective

To help us get some perspective on these things and to keep our tongue straight in the mouth in our upcoming insights, we start by drawing the time axis. We must *keep this time axis in mind at all times* while we operate and search for the value of an amount. Either in the future, in the present or in the past. Let's jump right in. Here is a picture that hopefully explains the connection: The time axis points both forward and backwards.

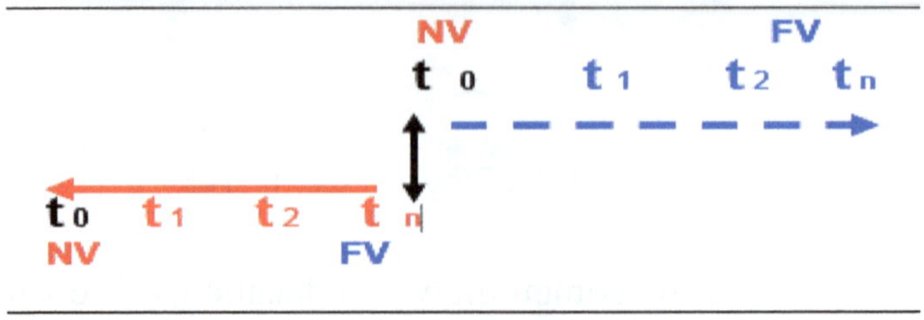

Fig:
We look at the time axis to understand in which direction we are moving in the calculation of the value: From the FV in year zero, we can calculate our way back to the NV for any year in the past, and the opposite way from NV in year zero, we can calculate our way to the FV for any year in the future.

The dotted arrow points *forwards* from the letters t_0 to t_n. Above this, you can probably see that it says NV and FV in the mentioned order. Below this, you can see that the solid arrow points *backwards* from t_n (FV) to t_0 (NV). So, now the t_0 is on the far left. This *t* with a zero behind it reads as t_{null} and it represents *now-in-this-moment* on our time axis. T_n represents a very different year in the future. T_1 will be next year (year 1), and the connection will then immediately become clearer to see. NV means net value, and FV means future value. I will come back to what the little black arrow pointing up and down between t_0 and t_n stands for, a little later in the chapter.

7.3 Future value

We must keep this time axis in mind when we allocate money over time. Let's start by agreeing that a given amount today is worth more than the same amount at some point in the future as explained in the introduction of the chapter. There are several reasons why the value of money "grows or decreases" over time. But we call this the time value of money.

Let's take an example:
We can perhaps imagine that you have a hundred dollars. Imagine considering lending this to me, but you are not quite sure if I will be able to pay it back in, - let's say a year. Also, if you lend it to me, you can't use the hundred bucks for caramels or ice cream in the meantime. Therefore, you want some kind of compensation. We call this compensation interest. Let's

say that in your local bank you`ll get 5% interest on your account. Therefor you demand the same from me so that you will not lose any money by lending it to me rather than the bank. We refer to the interest rate as ***i****. What are you going to have from me in one year?*

The formula is very simple; we learned to calculate an equation with one unknown X already in secondary school:

FV = Future Value, and i = interest

We write the formula like this:

$ 100 * (1+ i) = FV

It's as simple as that! In our example, the amount is: 100 * (1+ 0.05) = FV

That`s: FV = 105

If you didn't quite understand why we wrote the interest rate ***i*** as decimals, lets refresh the interest calculation from secondary school where we learn that *percent* means *in hundreds*, i.e. (i = 5%).

In plain language, this means that

$$5\% = \frac{5}{100} = 0.05$$

It was actually not difficult at all. Now, let's imagine that I get to borrow a hundred dollars for another year. How much should I pay you back when these two years have passed? Of course, you should have the interest rate for the first year plus the interest rate for the second year. In addition, you must have your hundred dollars back. So, then it would be 5 dollars in interest * 2 years plus 100 = 110 dollar? No, that's not correct. In that case, you are cheating yourself out of 25 cents. It may not be so important on small amounts and few years between good friends, but if we are dealing with big numbers and a long timeline, you will see that the growth series gets quite large.

We fill in the interest rate 100 * (1 + 0.05) * (1 + 0.05) = FV
and calculate that it will be 100 * (1.05) * (1.05) = 110.25

We write the formula like this:

$\$ 100 * (1 + i) * (1 + i) = FV$

You are now bitten by the lender shark bug and suggest that I can borrow the money for yet a third year at the same interest rate. You have seen that you get interest on both the amount lent and the interest itself, namely the effect on interest on interest rate as we call the *compound interest effect*. It's fun, and not at least it`s better than you was thinking. The amount you will have back from me in three years can be calculated as follows:

*100 * (1.05)*(1.05)*(1.05) = FV*

As we recall from school one hot summer day just before the holidays was the teacher chanting something about how a number that is multiplied by itself can be written as the elevated power of n, like this $\mathbf{x^n}$. The elevated power of $^{\mathbf{n}}$ of times the number must be multiplied by itself. In this case, we are talking about three years. That is, in this example, 3 times:

We calculate:

$100 * (1.05)^3 = FV = 115.76$

*We can now see the universal formula for a fixed rate of growth, where the amount we are going to calculate is called **NV**, the interest rate is called **i** and the number of years is called **n**:*

We write the universal formula this way:

FV = NV* (1 + i)^ n

If you are wondering where this "hat" sign like this ^ comes into the picture, it is a common mathematical expression for *"elevated in power"*. Even fairly inexpensive calculators tend to have this ^{x} function. So, if you have such a simple calculator with a parenthesis function too, you can very easily calculate FV in a snap. On other calculators, you may have an y^x button. If you don't have a calculator, you'll have plenty of opportunities to play around with the applications on Excel. You can now e-mail the publisher to get the workbook: https://fireat40.com. The workbook is named FiRE@40!

But first, let's go a little further. The formula has an elevated power function, which means that the amounts grow faster and faster. We call this the compound interest effect. The higher the interest rate we get, the faster our initial amount grows. Let us therefore pause for a moment and look at what happens to a dollar on a time axis over 30 years, and at different interest rates.

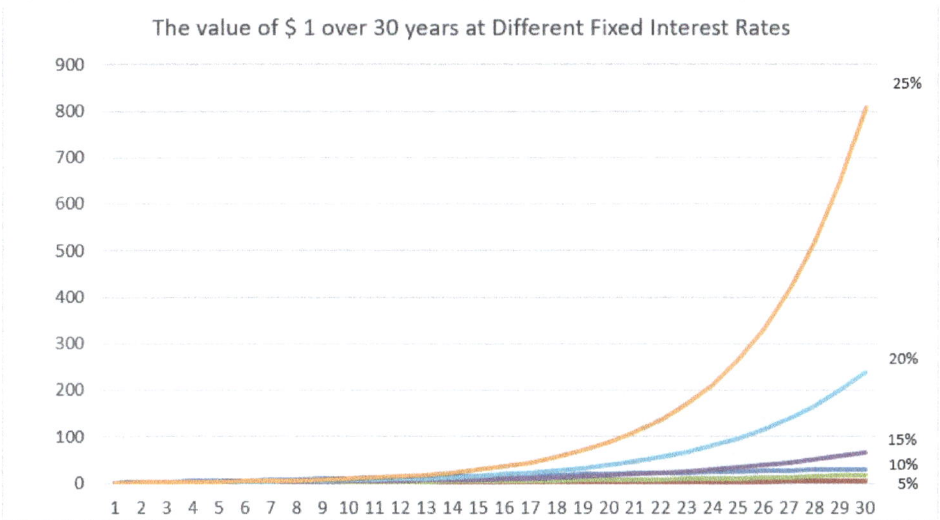

Fig: By leaving $ 1 in a bank account at 5% *fixed interest rate*, it will grow to $ 4,32 in 30 years. At 10% fixed interest rate, the dollar will grow into $ 17,45,and at 15% fixed interest into $ 66,21. At 20% fixed interest, the dollar will grow into 237,38 and with 25% fixed interest into a whopping $ 807,79! This is why it is so important to understand *the compound interest effect.*

As you can see from the graph: The longer timespan and the higher the interest, the steeper the curve rises. The graph shows the development for different fixed interest rates over 30 years. If you recollect, this is also the model from the illustrations on the front cover of this book just because it is so incredibly important, and of course I wanted to catch you attention! The secret is already in the open, explained just now; it`s because of the fact we also collect *interest on the interest itself* i.e. what mathematicians call a *geometric series* and we economists call *the compound effect*. In my front cover image, I show you what happens if you put one single deposit into the bank and let it rest for 30 years, calculated at 5 different interests. Just like the example of 1 dollar in this example!

This knowledge should wake the dead and the ignorant! The same thing happens with your debt collectors if you don`t pay your bills. It certainly grows over your head! From the front cover design I could have put 25 dollars, but for the fun of it I put 25,000 dollars. Here showing you the development every fifth year:

Interest	1	5	10	15	20	25	30
5 %	25 000,00	31 907,04	40 722,37	51 973,20	66 332,44	84 658,87	108 048,56
10 %	25 000,00	40 262,75	64 843,56	104 431,20	168 187,50	270 867,65	436 235,06
15 %	25 000,00	50 283,93	101 138,94	203 426,54	409 163,43	822 973,82	1 655 294,30
20 %	25 000,00	62 208,00	154 793,41	385 175,54	958 440,00	2 384 905,42	5 934 407,84
25 %	25 000,00	76 293,95	232 830,64	710 542,74	2 168 404,34	6 617 444,90	20 194 839,17

***Table**: The debt of 25,000 developing at 5 different interests over 30 years, or a deposit.*

7.4 Present value

We will now turn around and look the other way. This means that we are going back in time. In the previous chapter, we saw that if we got 5% interest on a hundred dollar for a year, it grow to 105 dollars. We can say that the 105 dollars in one year at 5% interest is 100 dollars today. Neither more nor less. It is exactly the same amount, so there are two equal amounts measured completely different places on the time axis. Or to put it another way, they are directly comparable.

We also found the future value of an amount by multiplying the one hundred note (x) by 1+i. We usually say that the present value is the discounted value. We divide the final amount of 1 + the interest rate *i*. In this example, it will be:

$$NV = \frac{105}{(1+0.05)^{\wedge 1}} \quad \textit{which becomes} \quad NV = \frac{105}{1.05} = 100$$

Plain and simple. It's not more difficult than this, when it comes to a year. What if we calculate the three years? Let`s try:

The future value of: x =$ 100

The time is: n = 3 years

At the interest rate: i – 5%

We calculate the future value as follows *(FV_3 means the future value at the end of year 3):*

$FV_3 = 100*(1.05)*(1.05)*(1.05)$

or we fill in the mathematical formula, and get the answer like this:

$$FV_3 = 100*(1,05)^{3} = 115.76$$

In general, we can simply say that if we are computing *the present value* of an amount over ***n*** number of years, we must turn the entire future value formula upside down. In other words, we divide. Thus, *the present value* of 115.76 in 3 years at 5% interest *can be discounted* as follows:

$$NV = \frac{115,76}{(1+0,05)^{3}}$$

Which can be written like this: $NV = \frac{115,76}{1,1576} = 100$

In other words, I have proven to you that the hundred-dollar bill we calculated forward in time is the same hundred-dollar dollar we came back to in this calculation. Thus, we can write the general formula for the present value in this way:

$$NV = \frac{FVn}{(1+i)^{n}}$$

The correct mathematical expression of *the discount factor* is:

$$NV = \frac{1}{FV * (1+i)^{n}}$$

That`s it, and nothing short of absolutely correct. *It applies to all amounts, all (fixed) interest rates and all (full) years you want to compute!*

7.5 Is back and forth the same distance?

It is by now a natural thing to ask ourselves a couple of questions. Are future value and present value really two sides of the same coin? Is it simply not more difficult? And if so, what on earth are we going to use this knowledge for? Where does it come in handy? As we saw in the previous chapter, we can calculate the future value of any amount over any given time perspective and required (fixed) rate of return according to the formula:

$$FV = NV * (1 + i)^{\wedge n}$$

Then it turned out that the present value of any amount, claim or time perspective can be calculated by turning the whole formula on its head:

$$NV = FV * \frac{1}{(1 + i)^{\wedge n}}$$

The one formula is thus the other formula turned upside down. This will also be the case if we now think about the time axis again. We can clearly see that we are moving back and forth along the same axis. FV moves from present and forward, while NV moves back from the future to the present. We can also draw the time axis in this way:

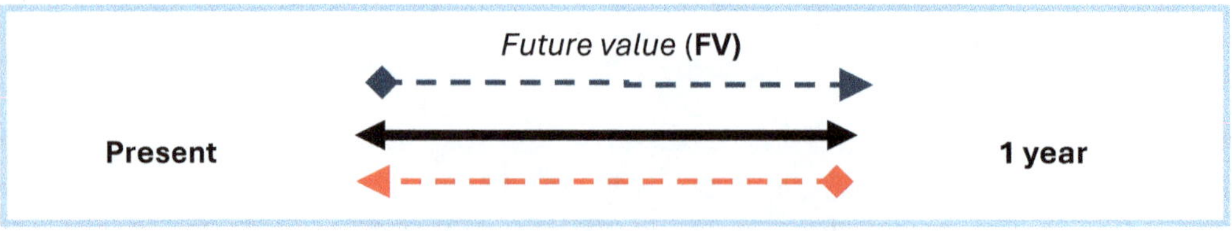

As we know, repetition is the mother of all learning. We can now see why we have the little black arrow between the two time axes. It represents point zero, the very starting point for our calculations! If we are to calculate forward in time (FV), we calculate from t_0 to t_n. If we are to calculate to the present (NV), we start from the future value t_n and calculate back to the present in t_0.

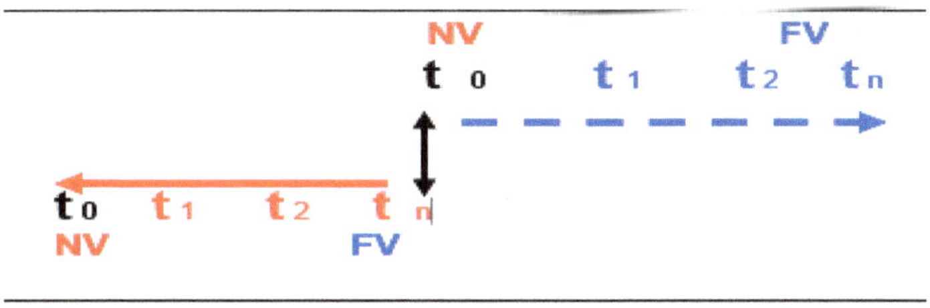

***Fig**: If we are to calculate in the future, we calculate from t_0 to t_n. If we are to calculate backwards to the present, we start from the future value and calculate the opposite way. Hence the little black arrow between t_0 and t_n.*

The model in which we started the chapter and which I personally prefer:

But let's make a summary on present value, future value and the time axis one last time. Let's combine the mathematical theory with the practical life.

We want to know how the amount of USD 250,000 "grows", as well as how it "shrinks" over time. Let`s use a *discount factor* of fixed 5%. How much would we have to start with *in the future* 30 years from now if the amount were to be 250,000 *today*? And alternatively, what will USD 250,000 *today be in the future* with the same discount factor?

We can see that an amount of just over one million dollars *30 years in the future* is the same as $ 250,000 in today's monetary value at 5% fixed discount rate. Alternatively, 250,000 today will become just over a million in the (1,080,000) future if the return is the same:

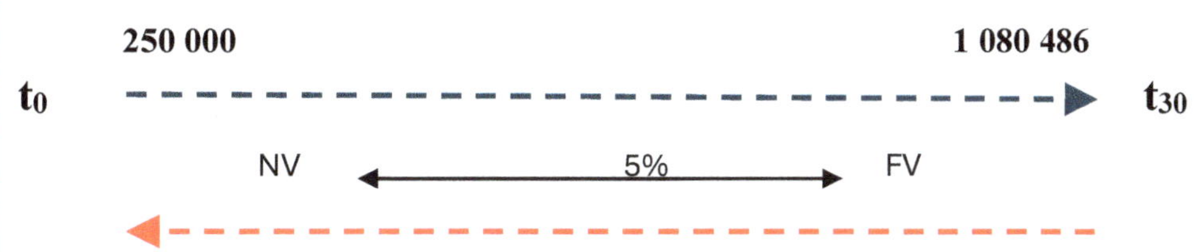

That`s how we can calculate until we turn blue on what the car you bought last year should have cost in today's money, or what you could possibly have had in your account instead. Or how much you have to sell the house you bought 15 years ago if you are to get the same return as the bank would have given you in the same period at the same interest. Or how much you earned in your previous job would have been in today's money. Yes, if you knew what the real interest rate was then. But you don't know, because we haven't gotten that far yet. But it's not harder, I can promise you that!

For the time being, we will stick to fixed nominal interest rates, as we have done all the way throughout this chapter. By nominal interest rates, we mean the bank's offer rate. But by now you should be almost ready to try the apps yourself. We will do that in the next paragraph!

7.6 A little about the applications and their use...

You have now reached the point where you should be let off the edge of the pier alone. But you will get a small life jacket along the way. These are the applications I have created for you in Excel, which you can download, and which come free with the book you have in front of you. You can now copy the entire workbook *«Fireat40.xls»* to an appropriate area on your hard drive. I'm not going to tell you how to. Nor where you should store it. Because it's your machine, and it's not necessarily like mine. But it might be natural to call the workbook *"Fireat40.xls"* since I refer to that name further in the book.

When you open the workbook for the first time in Excel, you will automatically come to the top of the worksheet of this chapter, which is chapter 7. The previous chapters was about important theories, something other than calculations, really. Even if it was with a couple of calculations for the sake of examples. The first model you encounter is called *FV of an amount* *. Here you do your calculations, and it looks like this:

Future value of an amount: *		
Nom Interest rate	5,00 %	
NV	250 000	
Terms in years	30	Years
FV	1 080 485,59	

And just to the right of the calculation model you will find the graph:

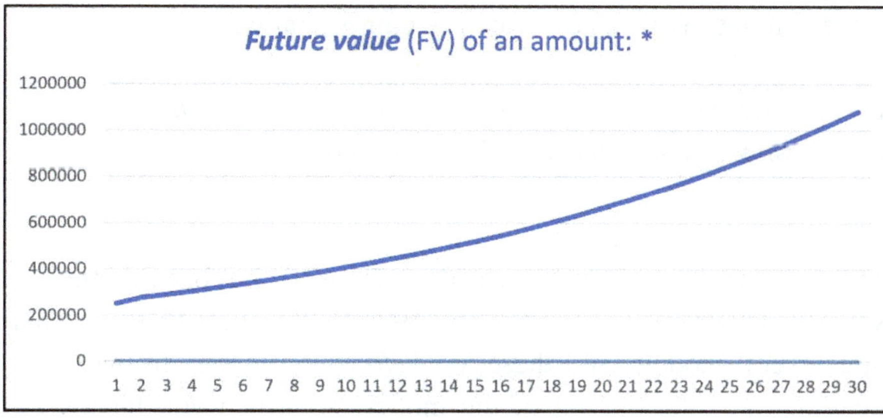

On the same screen, just underneath, you will find *the NV of an amount:*

Present value of an amount: *		
Nom Interest rate	5,00 %	
FV	1 080 486	
Terms in years	30	Years
NV	250 000,00	

The following graph looks like this:

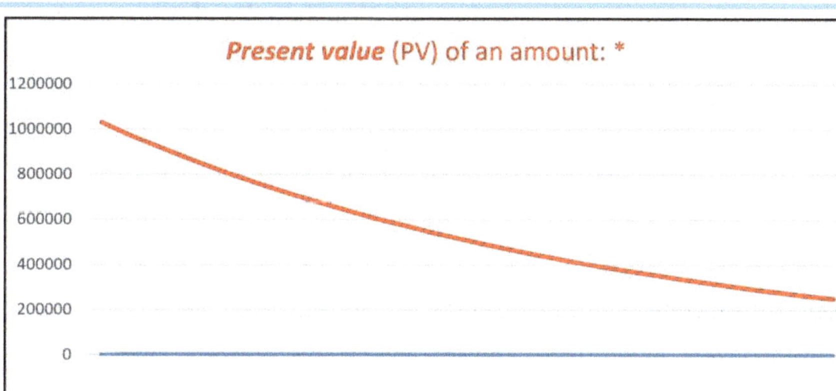

If you really want to see the compound interest effect in practice, you can try some "wild values". For example, try to fill in 25% instead of 5% in the apps. In this first chapter, I have put a formula collecting the numbers from the FV model, down to the NV model, just for the fun of it. Just to show you we are computing the same numbers therefor getting the same results as you can see from my examples. You can override my numbers at will.

Please note that when it comes to these Excel apps and the accompanying graphs, you should remember the following points:

1.

You can customize your own screen the way you like, but my applications follow a standard screen resolution of 1920*1080 pxls. In some chapters, there are several models, and these are *below each other*. In that case, you can see *PgDwn* at the bottom of the model. So, when you hit the *PgDwn button* on your keyboard, Excel jumps to the next model.

2.

Note that you should fill in only the yellow cells in any of the applications. No matter what model or chapter you're in! If you should be unlucky and type outside those cells, it doesn`t matter. The models are locked outside the yellow cells so it`s not possible. If you do, Excel will show you an error message stating that *"this spreadsheet is protected"*.

3.

Note that you can point the mouse at the graphs at any time to see the underlying numbers you are pointing at. You just let the cursor rest on the line for a few seconds, and Excel will show you the value. This way, you don't have to calculate new numbers all the time, you can just read the graph for the other years than the number you have entered.

4.

Note that the models calculate whole calendar years, starting from January 1.st. With very few exceptions, the graphs shows periods over 30 years. This is no coincidence. It can be interesting to calculate things over short periods, like we'll do in chapter 9, whilst it is really exciting to see investments over a longer time perspective. That`s why the 30 years are standard.

5.

The color schemes are pretty consistent. You'll see this as we progress through the chapters. This becomes especially important if you repeat from the book later. Especially important when we are looking at comparisons of several formulas in the same graph.

Oh well. I think that was the most important thing to remember, so we're going to playing as we learn. In order to really understand this matter, I have made some *test yourself tasks with accompanying summary answers.*

On next page you will find these exercises. You can try for yourself. I strongly advise you not to cheat!

7 a. Test yourself

(We assume fixed interest rate, and we disregard taxes and inflation)

If you like to exercise your brain, you can try with a pen, paper and a calculator first. If not, it's okay to tackle the Excel model in the workbook that we have now named *"Fireat40.xls". Please remember that the numbers in these examples doesn`t change the point of the knowledge itself.*

1.

I thought that you would initially help me with the following little nut:

I am the happy owner of a small house in the country. The home is currently worth USD 500,000 and with today's price increase on homes, I expect it to be worth USD 1,000,000 in 15 years. If I put 500,000 USD in the bank today, the bank guarantees me that I will get 8% interest over the entire period. If I sell the home, I can stay with Aunt Edna completely free of charge since she is so gregarious. We have always liked Aunt Edna so it could go smoothly. She's also not so old that I have to expect to be put on the street pretty soon again. What can be in the account in 15 years if I sell my home and put the money in the bank while I live with my aunt for free?

Tip:

Nom. Interest (*i*) 8,00 %
Amount : 500 000,00
Term (in years) : 15 år

t_0 t_1 t_2..... ....t_{15}

2.

I want a brand new silver-gray Audi A6 wagon, no later than when I turn 40 in 5 years. We estimate that it will cost 250.000,- by then. How much do I have to put in the bank today to be able to buy it if the bank gives me 8% interest for the next 5 years?

3.

My son Ole will start university in the fall of this year. As well-meaning parents, we have decided that if he passes high school with at least an average grade, we will treat him to two years of higher education at a private college afterwards. We estimate that this education will cost $ 100,000 when he starts of. My wife and I have a high-interest account that currently offers 6% interest. The rate of interest is expected to remain at this same level in the whole period ahead. What do we need to put in the account today?

4.

Since you have now become a devil at present value calculations, you promise your hopeful 10-year-old daughter that she will get half a million dollars for her own home when she turns 30 years old. How much is the promise worth in today's money if you invest the correct amount at a guaranteed return of 5% interest over the entire period?

5.

In yesterday's newspaper it was stated that by entering into an agreement on pension savings with a lump sum of 50,000, you will be paid 250,000 when you retire in 35 years. Do you think it is interesting if one can assume that the interest rate in the same years will be e.g. 5%? Would you do that if you could buy a government bond today that yields a guaranteed 7% over the period?

6.

You have made a New Year's bet with a friend to quit smoking. He burst already on New Year's Day, so now your friend has to make amends and pay up. Since he is a student, he can only give you 3.000 today. At the end of the year, you'll get 5.328.

***a**. How much money did you bet when the interest rate is 11%?*

***b**. What can you consume at the maximum at the end of the year?*

***c**. Suppose you get 5,000 right away to consume at will. What do you get at the end of the year?*

***d**. If you want to spend 7,548 on a ski trip in January next year, what can you spend now?*

It can be worthwhile to structure your thoughts on a sheet of paper before you start typing in on the models. Draw the time axis and put the values on them. If you're completely stuck, you'd rather get a sneak peek, because you'll learn from it too!

7 b. Summary answers

1.

We draw the time axis:

NV = 500,000 ⟶ *FV = ?*

We know the current value and want to know the future value. Seen along the time axis, we can say that we are in NV and want to know the value of FV in 15 years. We fill in the model for future value: i= 8%, NV = 500,000 and n = 15. The answer is that the FV will be USD 1,586,084.56 in your account, which is far preferable to a possible sales value in 15 years of 1,000,000.

2.

We draw the time axis:

NV = ? ⟵ FV = 250,000

It is the other way around here. We will know the value in 5 years and want to know the NV (or t_0*). We enter in the model (Present value of an amount): i = B% , FV = 250 000 and maturity n = 5. The result is that I have to deposit only 170 145.80 in the account today. Check the time axis if you have received an answer that is greater than 250,000!*

3.

We draw the time axis:

NV = ? ⟵ FV = 100,000

Same problem here! Ole will start in the fall, while we count the whole calendar year. He spends 3 years in high school, so the maturity n = 3 years, i = 6% and FV = 100,000. So, we must deposit 83,961.93 now!

4.

We draw the time axis yet again:

NV=? ⟵ FV=500,000

The pledge is worth USD 188,444.74 in today's money!
(We will calculate NV of i = 5, FV = 500,000 and maturity n = 20.)

5.

Here we have to wrap our brains around the problem: We know that the agreement costs 50,000 today and that it will yield 250,000 in 35 years. We must therefore compare two amounts, namely 50,000 today compared to 250,000 in 35 years.

Again, we draw the time axis:

NV = ? ⟵ FV = 250,000

We get that NV = 45 322.57 at 5%. You are not interested in exchanging 50,000 today for something that is actually worth 45,322.57, are you?

In the second question, we try to bring some "alternative" thinking into it well. What would you do if you could buy government bonds at 7% instead?

Let`s look at the time axis:

NV = 50,000 ⟶ *FV = ?*

It is easy to understand that 7% is better than 5%, however, we want to calculate all three options. We find that this agreement on pension savings worth of the 50,000 today becomes FV = 533,829.07 if we`re buying government bonds at 7%. In other words, we will have a loss of 283,829.07 if we enter into the pension savings agreement. In both cases its bad business for you, but good business for those who sell pension savings.

6.

You can draw the time axis for yourself now:

***a**. NV of 5,328 = 4,800 plus the 3,000 you have already got. The total amount of the bet is 7,800.*

***b**. **FV** of 3,000 to 11% = 3,330 plus the 5,328 you are going to get will be 8,658 at the end of the year.*

***c. FV** of 7,800 – 5,000 = 2,800 at 11% becomes 3,108 at the end of the year*

***d. NV** = 1,000 that you can spend right away. 7,800 at 11% becomes 8,658 in the end of the year. You can spend FV 8,658 – 7,548 =1,110. NV from this is 1,000.*

You can find more information about me and my books here:
executivewayto.com or at fireat40.com

Chapter 8. Investments and Long-term Liabilities

A while ago, I read in a newspaper an article about *"How to afford a little luxury in everyday life?"* The subtitle was *"Tips for better personal finance"*. Whilst a little chuckling, I read the article about a married couple who really had control over their cash flow, or their wallets if you will. All the tips were well-known material from my economics studies. The couple had just bought a new car for almost forty thousand dollars. Cash. They did not live in a dilapidated shed deep in the deep woods. They lived in a nice, terraced house in a central and expensive area of the country. The husband himself earned a salary of about fifty thousand dollars per year, while the wife's income was slightly better. Hm!

8.1 Major investments, long-term debt.

A townhouse in this area is not cheap, and cash payment for a car of almost forty thousand dollars. In addition, the couple had two adult children who had recently received a couple of hundred thousand to establish their own homes. It is natural to imagine that the couple had debts far above the pipes, but that is not true either. They still hadn't emptied their savings account. It was still just above fifty thousand on the accounts. And they paid barely two thousand dollars a month on a loan, so the loan can't have been that large. The husband stated that the loan was planned so that they will bc dcbt-free approximately when he retires. You`d think it smells scorched! A little drug dealing perhaps? Maybe the old man is a moonshining in the cellar? Wasn't there a big liquor smuggling gang in that area? But no, the couple hadn`t done anything criminal, and all economists who read the article would immediately see that.

But the married couple were certainly not stingy, neither with themselves nor with others. For example, according to the article, they donated hundreds of dollars every single month to charities. They had almost four thousand for savings or allowance every month. The key to the couple's success was, of course, full control of their cash flow. There were no surprises there. The husband says that planning is important. When they go to the grocery store, they only buy what is written on the Post-it note. Neither more nor less. There was no room for impulse shopping, so we understand that the luxury in everyday life was planned! The key to that success is a budget! The basis for the budget was held by her husband in a binder where he collected all bills as they were paid. Neatly separated according to what type of bill it was and in chronological order by due date. At least no one can claim this couple for the same bill twice, with impunity!

8.2 Budget, budget, budget!

If you want to become a real FIRE, you need to be in control of your personal finances, and that means your cash flow. To get control of the cash flow, there is no way around a thoroughly prepared budget. You can laugh or cry, swear or yell. But the way to become a FIRE on your own salary can be summarized in four words, as I wrote in the introduction on page 1: *Knowledge, Will, Savings and Investment.* Thus, you cannot avoid the budget that is part of the most basic of everything economics. The knowledge you gained about opportunity costs in Chapter 6, and about the allocation of resources in Chapter 7 is really important knowledge, but it does not help if you don`t have control over your cash flow. Here in ***Applied Personal Finance,*** I will try to convey more of this important knowledge in the chapters to come. But you have to stand for the will to do something about it yourself. If you don't have it or obtain it, it's because you choose the differently. You already know what it is. Party on today, don't think about tomorrow with cold sweats and peasant regrets when your accounts are empty, and the bills just pour over you. That's why we're starting with a budget *now!* You can do it any way you want but make sure to add up your and your family's income for each month throughout the year. And write down all expenses. Now it is a good thing if you have copies of your old bills. At least from 12 months back whether it`s digitally in your internet bank, paper bills or both. Preferably also the whole of the previous year. So, feel free to scroll your internet bank while you`re at it. Make sure that you find everything you spend money on. Perhaps the bank has such a budget model you can download? The most important thing for you to get absolute total control.

If you think that creating a budget yourself is difficult, I have made a layout for you on the spreadsheet called Chapter 8 in *FIRE@40.xls for* you to use as a starting point. The model looks like this:

Budget for :		Hannah	&	John		Year:	
INCOME:		JANUARY	FEBRUARY	MARCH	APRIL	MAY	JUNE
Salary	Hannah	200,00	200,00	200,00	200,00	200,00	200,00
Salary	John	200,00	200,00	200,00	200,00	200,00	200,00
Other income	(Example)	40,00	40,00	40,00	40,00	40,00	40,00
Additonal income	(Example)	10,00	10,00	10,00	10,00	10,00	10,00
Variable income	(Example)					99,00	
Sum Income		450,00	450,00	450,00	450,00	549,00	450,00
COST							
YEARLY		JANUARY	FEBRUARY	MARCH	APRIL	MAY	JUNE
						125,00	
			65,00				
HALF YEARLY		JANUARY	FEBRUARY	MARCH	APRIL	MAY	JUNE
TV / Netflix(o.a)				10,00			
					50,00		
			25,00			90,00	
QUARTELY		JANUARY	FEBRUARY	MARCH	APRIL	MAY	JUNE
Electricity			15,00			15,00	
Phones			25,00			25,00	
Gas bill			65,00			65,00	
MONTHLY		JANUARY	FEBRUARY	MARCH	APRIL	MAY	JUNE
House rent		100,00	100,00	100,00	100,00	100,00	100,00
Food/Groceries		75,00	75,00	75,00	75,00	75,00	75,00
Clothing		35,00	35,00	35,00	35,00	35,00	35,00

Fig: Screenshot from the budget module. The numbers may look a bit small, but that doesn't change the point of the model. You can only type in all yellow cells.

When you press the PgDwn button, you get to the rest of the budget (monthly, variable expenses), and a graphical analysis of the budget year. At the bottom you will find a "wave" that shows your net cash flow throughout the year in a graphical analysis. As you know, a picture is worth a thousand words. As you can see, things go up and down! From the presentation, you can easily see that I'm in deficit in February, May, August and November, while the rest of the year is in profit. The question now is whether you are making a profit for the whole year as a whole. Note that this budget shows few, large and cyclical costs and that's okay. The best thing we economists know is large, fixed incomes, and few and small fixed costs. Many fixed costs tie up liquidity and kill your freedom to make changes or strike good, essential items on offer. Therefore, fixed costs are the worst thing economists know.

When you need to fill this in yourself, you start by filling in who the budget is for and what year it applies to. Yes, because you're probably going to want one for next year too. Now, let's fill in the income. Then you continue down to the expenses. Make sure you fill in the expenses in the correct month!

As you can see, there is room for some variable expenses. After all, it's not every month you spend USD 350 on shoes or clothes or at the hairdresser. But now you have a basis for seeing what the net cash flow looks like. You can of course sum up in the cells, so you can put in more costs than I have set up in my example. The more careful you are in filling out this budget, the better overview you get and the more accurate the annual result will be.

When you press PgDwn again, you get another graph, which is a common way for economists to show a simplification of the movements in the economy of a company, an organization or a project. As you know, a picture is worth a thousand words. The annual profit or final sum (in numbers) can be found by scrolling to the right along the cash flow with the arrow keys.

Commuting		25,00	25,00	25,00	25,00	25,00	25,00	
Loans(s)		65,00	65,00	65,00	65,00	65,00	65,00	
Other costs	Shoes	15,00					28,00	
Gasoline								
Sum costs		315,00	495,00	310,00	350,00	620,00	328,00	3
2024		JANUARY	FEBRUARY	MARCH	APRIL	MAY	JUNE	
NET CASH FLOW		135,00	-45,00	140,00	100,00	-71,00	122,00	2

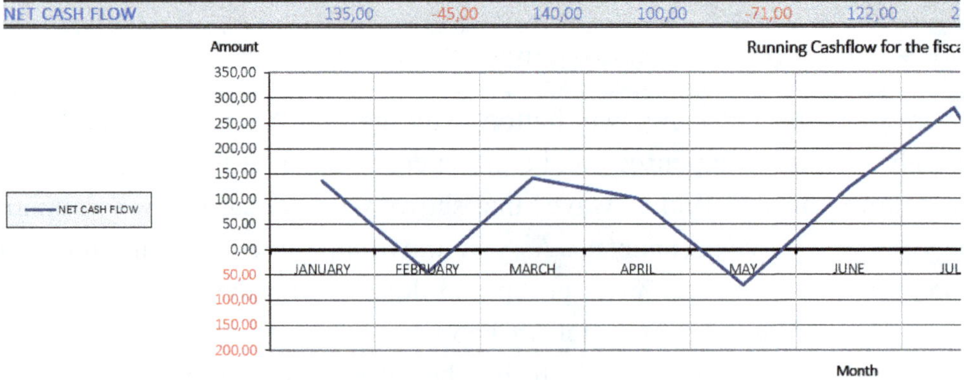

Fig: *Excerpt from the second screenshot in the budget module. The numbers may look a bit small, but that doesn't change the point of the model. You are supposed to use your own numbers. Here is also a graphical analysis of the net cash flow in your budget year.*

You had to do this to fill in the income and expense items, so you will probably find it again. It is located along row 36, specifically in cell O36. In this example, there is a small profit. If you don't get a profit in your own accounts, something is completely wrong! Either you really have too many expenses, far too little income, or you have typed something wrong. Take a break and then go through the expense items at a slower pace.

Now, instead of looking at a cash flow that moves like the waves of an autumn storm, we can use PgDwn button again.

There you see a graphical analysis of our budget example as a business leader would like to see it, (although without the explaining arrows):

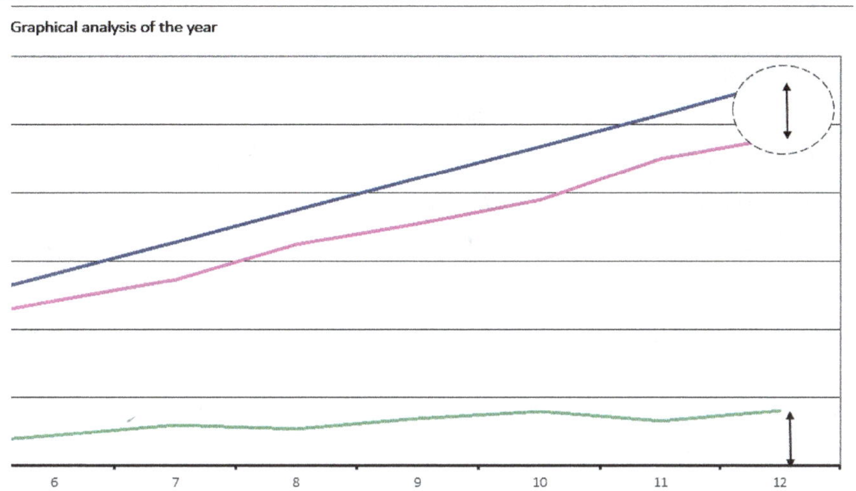

Fig: *When we zoom in on the graphs' endpoints on the right side, we can see there`s a gap. This gap shows the surplus, (or deficit) in the budget. I've put on an arrow ⟷ between the accumulated income and the accumulated expenses with a circle around it to highlight this gap.*

A small digression here:
Did I mention to you that I know of a guy who collected the bills in a plastic bag? Yes, the unpaid bills, that is. It was at the beginning of the hard 90s. The guy, like so many others during that period, did not have a job. He quarreled with his parents and wanted to get out of the family nest. So, he rented an apartment with a friend who also didn't have a job. So, he bought a mobile phone so potential employers could get hold of him. He couldn't cook meals for himself and didn't like sandwiches, so he stopped by the hot dog stand both morning and evening. When he was broke, he borrowed money from friends, and if he got some money, he naturally paid his friends first.

Well, to make the story short, he went on like this for three or four years. But since he didn't have much income, he just collected the unpaid bills in a plastic bag so that he could pay them when he just got a job. Today he has both a job and a girlfriend. They live at home with his parents and are expecting their first child. He will turn 33 pretty soon, and just the interests on everything he owes from the early 90s takes all of his entire salary. They live off her salary and wonder how they will manage when the baby arrives. Unfortunately, that is a true story. So now you are warned not to make the same mistake!

Now, back to the text as we were. The work you have done in creating a proper budget is at least as important as understanding the concept of opportunity cost and the time value of the money! *These three things are the very foundation of your financial success*! Without a proper budget and budget control you will not succeed! That`s why I put these chapters after one another in the beginning of this book! From now on, the rest will mostly be a matter of techniques and understanding how to use them in everyday life to become *FIRE i*f you are in the first half of your 20s. Or get *significantly much better off than before* at any other age. If you are not trained in finance, it will be very interesting for you to broaden your horizons!

8.3 Serial loan

Now that we have finished the budget, we have come as far as we know that you have a surplus every year. You`re not very often on bars and restaurants with your friends either. Maybe you should have a surplus most months even if you feel that you almost go bankrupt with only a few pennies in your account a week before the next payday. Either you are hard on your savings with a tight budget control, or the opposite where you`ll have to dig into your memory to see if there are “holes in your pockets” somewhere. Now let's imagine that you don't have any holes in your pockets but a surplus to save most months of the year. So, we have now established that you can afford to go to the bank to borrow money for a new house, or boat or car or whatever it may be. Or you can continue to save more for a rainy day. Anyhow, you can prove to the bank's little loan shark that you are in control and are credit worthy, fully capable of repaying a credit or mortgage loan.

So, by now we should look at the easiest loan to understand, namely the *Serial Loan.*

It's really easy to understand. We tackle the example of the same Audi that you can't get out of your head. Upon showing your budget to the bankier, he offers you a serial loan of 100,000 to 15% interest over 5 years since you can prove that you make a profit every single year. To make the example simple, let`s say that it is a serial loan with annual installments that are paid in arrears. If you now take on a serial loan, it works in the way that you calculate the interest on the remaining loan for each period. The payment series is calculated as follows:

Installments	= Total amount of the loan / number of years
Interest payment	= Interest rate * residual loan
Residual loan	= The total amount of the loan – paid instalments
Annual benefit	= Interest + Instalments

When we put the calculations from this case in a table, it looks like this:

Year	1	2	3	4	5
Installments	20 000,00	20 000,00	20 000,00	20 000,00	20 000,00
Residual loan	80 000,00	60 000,00	40 000,00	20 000,00	0,00
Interest	15 000,00	12 000,00	9 000,00	6 000,00	3 000,00
Interest pr m.	1 250,00	1 000,00	750,00	500,00	250,00
Totalt pr m.	2 916,67	2 666,67	2 416,67	2 166,67	1 916,67

Fig: *A Tabular layout for a serial loan of 100,000 at 15% interest over 5 years.*

It's as simple as that! You can easily manage this with a pen and paper.
But you can just go into ***"FIRE@40.xls"***, set the cursor in cell A1 and type PgDwn 3 times until you come to this model, just below "*Graphical analysis of the operating year*" as we used in the section on budgets. Here you`ll find the model for serial loans. It looks like this:

SERIAL LOAN * :		Amount of benefit		
Interest	15,00 %	Year 1	35 000,00	* Point the marker on the pink graphic line to read the residual loan
Loan amount	100 000,00	Year 2	32 000,00	* The graph show you the residual loan for a total of 30 years.
Duration	5	Year 3	29 000,00	(Never mind what`s below zero, the loan is paid in full anyway)

The following graph for these calculations looks like the one shown below. If you are wondering why the line falls *below zero*, it is not because the bank pays you back half a million after you have paid off the loan. It`s because the graph shows for 30 years. Don't bother with what's below zero after 5 years. The loan was paid off at 5 years anyway. Our example looks like this graphically:

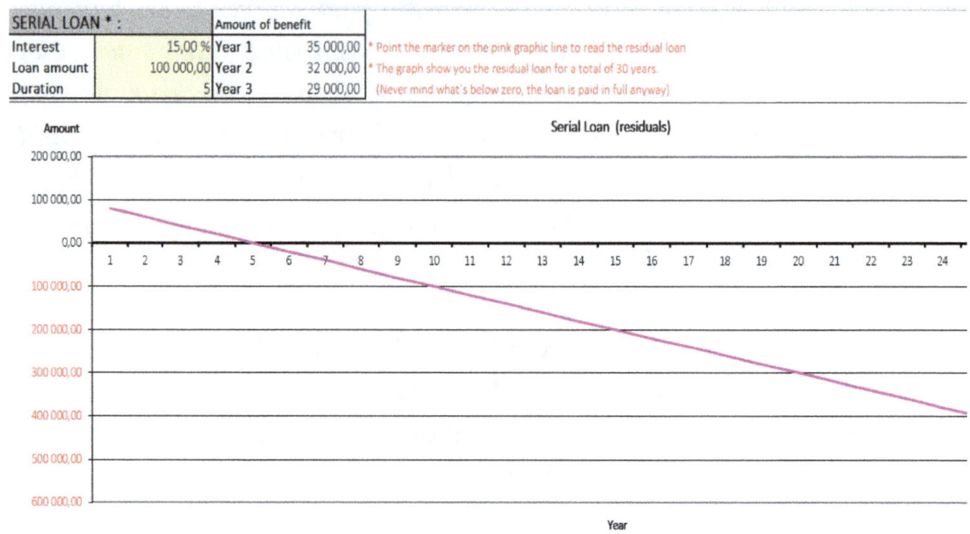

Fig: *The model for a serial loan is shown graphically. Never mind that summer below the y line (zero). The loan is paid off anyway by then.*

8.4 Annuity loan

Now, let's do the same example, however, calculate it as an *annuity loan*. We`ll still assume that you pay once a year and that we are talking about *payment in arrears,* i.e. that the interest is paid at *the end of the period*. The whole point of an annuity loan is that we pay a fixed amount each term, unlike the serial loan where we pay less and less interest for each term. In this case it will be December 31st since it is an *annual annuity*. This fixed amount is thus intended to cover *both* interest and instalments. What will the annual payment be then?

We are going to calculate the periodic payments, which in total correspond to NV of the 100,000 we borrow. However, at a fixed amount every month, all the time through the down payment. The formula we're going to use is the inverse (the opposite) of an amount of savings with equal payments. We haven't been through that formula yet, because it will come in the next chapter. But to answer the question, let's think a little about what happened

$$NV = FV * \frac{1}{(1+i)^{n}}$$

when we calculated the present value of an amount in chapter 7. The mathematic formula looked like this:

However, the formula we are going to calculate by now looks like this:

$$NV = PMT * i * \frac{(1+i)^{n-1}}{(1+i)^{n}}$$

It looks a bit difficult, *but it's not*. If we look at the formula for the present value of an amount, we recognize at least parts of the formula. **PMT** stands for *Payment*. In this equation, PMT is the unknown *X-factor* in the equation that we are going to calculate, so we have to make it stand alone on one side of the equal sign. The mathematical expression now looks like this:

$$PMT = \frac{NV}{\frac{(1+i)^{n-1}}{i * (1+i)^{n}}}$$

It looks a bit messy, but we can rewrite it like this:

$$PMT = NV * \frac{i * (1+i)^{n}}{(1+i)^{n-1}}$$

If you find this expression difficult to read, you are probably not alone. But when we fill in the numbers from our example as we took on the serial loan *(100,000 at 15% interest over 5 years),* we see that everything becomes more understandable, reading:

$$PMT = 100{,}000 * \frac{0{,}15 * (1+0{,}15)^{5}}{(1+0.15)^{5-1}} = 29{,}831.56$$

In other words, by multiplying the present value by the *inverse annuity factor,* we get the annual performance of the loan. But enough about that.

Right now, we are only interested in finding the *difference* between serial loans and annuity loans. In other words, what we actually have to pay in total. The loan is for 100,000 and it will not be paid until the end of the year. So, the debt we are going to calculate interests on is easy to see will be 15,000 the first time. But what about the installments? Let me remind you that the annual payment on this annuity loan, without fees and commissions of any kind, amounts to USD 29,832 per month, fixed.

You can go straight to the model in the workbook *FIRE@40.xls* when you want to check for yourself. The model can be found on the screen under the model serial loan. Below you can see the tabular of the loan as I showed you with serial loans in the section above:

Year	1,00	2,00	3,00	4,00	5,00
Yearly paymer	29 831,56	29 831,56	29 831,56	29 831,56	29 831,56
Installments	14 831,56	17 056,29	19 614,73	22 556,94	25 940,48
Interest	15 000,00	12 775,27	10 216,82	7 274,61	3 891,07
Residual loan	85 168,44	68 112,16	48 497,42	25 940,48	0,00

Fig: *The same loan of 100,000 at fixed 15% interest over 5 years, but as an annuity loan.*

We can say that if you know the annuity, it is easy to find the different parts. The annual annuity is 29,831.56. The interest rate for the first year is 15% of 100,000 = 15,000. Thus, the installment must be 29,831.56 - 15,000 = 14,831.56.

For year two, interest and instalments are calculated on the remaining debt of 85,168.44. This will be 12,775.27, and the instalment will be the annuity minus the interest we have calculated = 17,056.29. This is how we continue until the loan is paid off. A little easier to understand how the loans behave, right? Let's drill down to *the Annuity model* in *FIRE@40.xls* using PgDwn once more. Your screenshot should look like this:

Annuity loan *					
Interest (nom)	15,00 %		Per mont:	-2 485,96	* The graph shows 30 years
Loan amount	100 000,00		Per Year :	-29 831,56	* Annuity in arrears
Duration	5	år	In total	-149 157,78	

Fig: *The model for calculating an annuity loan*

Following with a graph looking like this:

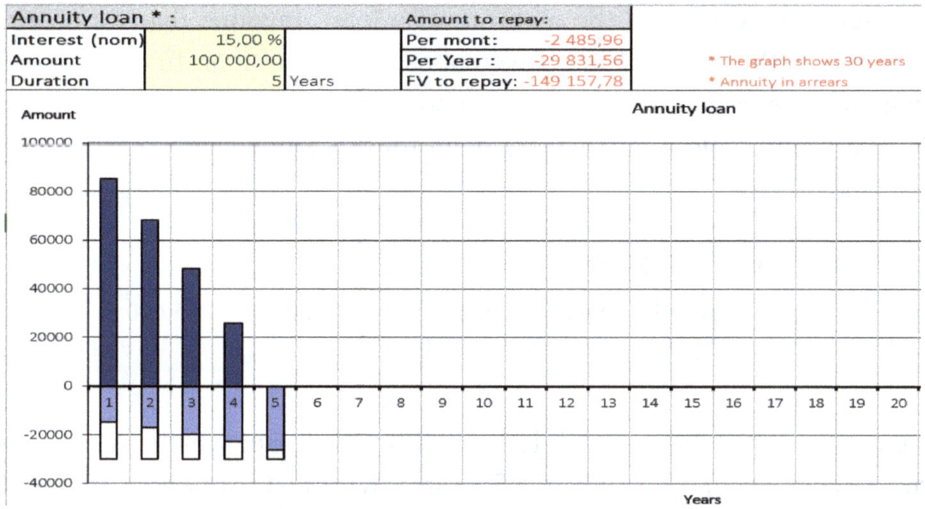

Fig: *Screenshot of the Annuity Loan model*

If you are wondering why parts of the columns are on top of the zero line and some parts are below, this is because of the structure of the formulas and Excel's way of showing this. You can say that the residual value is positive for you until you have paid it, while interest and instalments that have to be paid now is emptying your pocket today. So that's why! If we want to compare the payment structure of a serial loan and an annuity loan, it will graphically look like you can see from here:

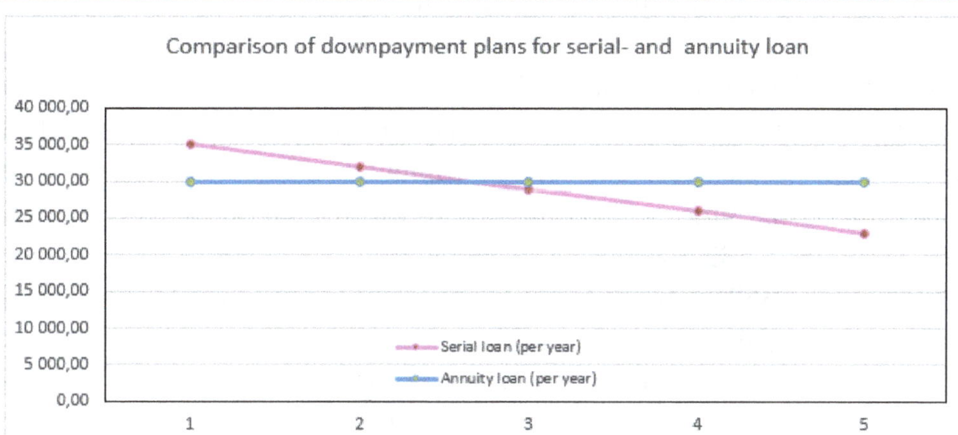

Fig: *Comparison of downpayment structures for the two long term loans.*

The annuity loan has a fixed payment over the entire period-, while the serial loan's payments decrease as we follow the downpayment plan.

8.5 Choice of maturity for the loan

Let's discuss the choice of the maturity of a loan. Imagine that we continue the example with the car. What if we choose the serial loan first? To be able to compare, we need to think closer about the total payment that will be made. We'll first look at the total payment for those selected 5 years. We find that we should pay:

Annual repayment in 5 years:

Year 1:	Year 2:	Year 3:	Year 4:	Year 5:	Total cost = 145,000
35,000	32,000	29,000	26,000	23,000	

As we can see, the total payback is 145,000 in total. But what if we choose a shorter repayment plan of only for 3 years? We must, of course, expect the annual benefit to increase. The following payment series calculates like this:

Annual repayment in 3 years:

Year 1:	Year 2:	Year 3:	Total cost = 130,000
48,333.33	38 333.33	43,333.33	

We can clearly see that the total downpayment reduces to 130,000 dollars. Is it this not less than the 145,000 then? It definitely is. Money saved for other things, if you can handle the larger yearly downpayment.

Now that you have become such a devil at present value calculations, you can ponder on this a bit. Why do we pay interest? It is because of the depreciation, or the wear and tear of capital as economists call it, of the money during the time we borrow it. It turns out that at 10 years, the loan costs a total of $ 182,500, which is almost twice as much as we borrows in today's value. Will it be different with an annuity loan? You can try it yourself. I put up three options:

At 3 years, the total costs is 43,797.70 * 3 = 131,393.09
At 5 years, the total costs is 29,831.56 * 5 = 149,157.78
At 10 years, it total costs is 19,925.21 * 10 = 199,252.06

In other words, we can say that the loan costs less with a shorter repayment period, and more with a longer repayment period. After all, we pay interest on the remaining debt, so the longer the repayment period, the more expensive it is. It is really expensive to be short of cash and low on liquidity! What if you could reinvest the difference at 15%? We`ll dive into that interesting part in chapter 10 and 11 for sure.

8.6 What the bank does not say, but which you must ask about.

Stop for a moment! All the total amounts of the annuity loan are higher than the serial loan! Why is that? Well, it comes from the fact that the structure of the loans is different. On the serial loan, we pay the interest on the remaining loan each year plus an instalment that is the same over the entire period of the loan. If we take a closer look at the annuity loan, the total payment or annuity is fixed each year throughout the period, while the interest rate is also calculated on the residual loan at any given time. Therefore, the instalments are increasing. In the end, we almost only pay installments.

We can see from the figures that an annuity loan is slightly more expensive than a serial loan. This is related to the fact that an annuity loan takes a little longer time to pay back than a serial loan. It will not be surprising to see that the annuity loan therefor will be a little more expensive. We can show it graphically in this way:

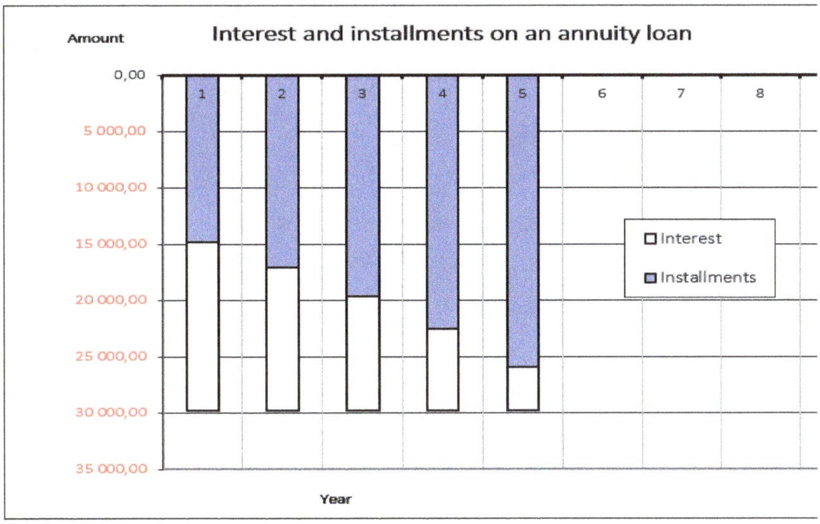

***Fig**: The payment of an annuity loan is fixed, split in increasing installments and decreasing*

So why should we choose an annuity loan if it is more expensive? It has primarily to do with your liquidity. In other words, what does your cash flow look like after budgeting. An annuity loan has fixed payments, while the serial loan decreases. The choice of whether to take the one or the other depends on both your financial liquidity, as well as how big the investment is. If you are in the start-up phase in life, or in business, it may be good to choose a long repayment period annuity loans with fixed payments initially rather than risking breaking your neck financially on large payments to begin with. You will probably get better economy over time since you may make a career and get paid better and then can refinance it. If you make a smaller investment, it may be good to choose a serial loan to finish it as soon as possible anyway.

Another thing to consider is if the loan is "flexible", meaning you may be able to pay off a little extra on the loan when you have a little to spare, also without being extra charged in fees and other punishments. If you can, such an extra repayment will reduce your remaining debt. So, in that case the loan will suddenly behave just like a serial loan during that period. But still an annuity loan in the remaining periods. Great, isn`t it? You choose; you win!

Let's exemplify with the extremely expensive Audi, yet again:
You have obtained an annuity loan on the car and must pay $ 29,831.56 for five years. But at the end of the year, you have a whopping $ 5,168.44 in your savings account not used for Christmas presents, and that will not be spent on the pile of bills in January. You put the money into your loan in the bank since the bank thinks it's okay for you to show a little extra willingness to pay, and you don't have to pay a fee to do so. By now you have paid the expected $ 14,831.56 that you were supposed to according to the payment plan, plus you have paid an extra $ 5,168.44 = $15,000 in total this year. If you remember well, the instalments in the first year of serial loan were 15,000. Your remaining debt for the next year will be USD 85,168.44 - 5,168.44 = 80,000. Isn`t this the same as the remaining serial loan? Yes, it is! And the interest should be calculated on the remaining debt regardless of the type of loan, right? Abra-Cadabra! The annuity loan became a serial loan this year. But if you don't have extra money for next year, it doesn't matter. Because you know that you have an annuity loan that you can afford.

Maybe the bank clerk provided you with such details, or on the other hand maybe thought you weren`t smart enough to understand, or maybe just didn`t think of it. Or maybe too busy because of all their other tasks, and too much else on their mind? In any case, it is important to ask at the bank before signing the papers to finance some private investment:

"Is the loan flexible, meaning I can pay in extra if I have a little to spare?"

"Do such additional payments cost extra money in the form of fees and commissions"?

If the bankier answers yes to the first question and no to the second, you can smile at your knowledge. And then you can manage your loan according to your personal wallet and well-being.

However, before you sign the papers, there is another thing you should consider. It is whether you should choose a *fixed rate* or a *floating rate*. This can have a major impact on your personal finances. Just try to simulate yourself in the models and see what the difference will be if the interest rate on the loan you are going to calculate is 1.5% or 3%. Economists as well as bankers is calling this a *"stress test"* and this is first and foremost a question of what we think about the risk in the future. We will look at risk in more detail in Chapter 10, so we will now deal with the question of the future first. What do you know about interest rates next year? What do you know about inflation next year? I don't know much more than you do, I`m afraid. Although, if you bought my book *"**Fire@40!**(Applied Personal Finance)"* or *"Applied Economics and Management for Business Executives"* you'd bc much better off understanding why it happens and how it will affect you.

So, let's simplify the problem a bit: if you have tight finances, for example in a start-up phase of adult life itself, or a start-up business, you can choose a fixed rate. At least for a period. This means that you tie the interest rate on your loan for a period of, for example, 5 years. In that case you know exactly what to pay in these agreed years because the interest rate is fixed during that period. And then after 4 or 4 1/2 years, you can consider whether you should perhaps still choose a fixed rate for a new 5-year period or renegotiate for a floating rate. If you can afford it (as the loan doesn`t tie up a too large part of your income), you can choose a floating interest rate. You can both gain and lose from your choice. Historically, it has paid off in the long run, but in recent years developments in the aftermath of the pandemic, it has turned out to be not such a good idea. It depends on how society develops, and how central banks both domestically and internationally regulate interest rates to stimulate or cool the economy this year, next year or the forthcoming years. Please read more about this in my books *"Fire@40!(Applied Personal Finance)"* or in *"Applied Economic Management for Business Executives"* which you'll find at www.fireat40.com or www.executivewayto.com. It may however be a smart thing to keep in mind that the fixed interest rate is usually more expensive than the floating rate in the long run. But whether your finances can withstand fluctuations, you must answer yourself.

Although the point of the book is not that you have to understand the formulas to get the context, but the other way around this knowledge. You may wonder what economists have to go through during their 5 years of education. So, if you think that there has been a lot of derivation of formulas in the chapters, the consolation is that I have kept it to a minimum as far as I can. But I think we need to go through the most basic formulas so that you appreciate how they work. In that way you can also use a pen, paper and calculator. The comforting fact is that this was the penultimate time. Only in chapter 10 (on savings) will we do it again. In the rest of the book we shall concentrate on what the formulas look like and how they are used, okay?

Shouldn't we take on some tasks and practice a little on this knowledge with test-yourself-questions with summary answers?

8 a. Test yourself

(We assume fixed interest rate, and we disregard taxes and inflation)

Well, we don't need a lot of questions to clarify the points of this chapter. The models are easy to use and to understand. You can pretty soon think of many examples for yourself. There is always something you would like to finance and therefor calculate. *Please remember that the numbers in these examples doesn`t change the point of the knowledge itself.*

1.

Your son Ole has turned 17 and thinks it's time to start learning to drive. You're horrified at the thought of having the young dude behind the wheel of your new Audi A6 and start wondering if you should buy him a small car to practice on instead. A bit later you find a nice little car for \$ 45,000 (or \$ 4,500), and since you have no money in your account, you take on a serial loan in the bank at 11% interest over 5 years.

a) What does the loan cost in the first year?

b) What is the remaining debt after 3 years?

2.

You dream of a boat of the "*Smuggler*" type but doubt whether you will ever be able to afford it. You are absolutely sure that by the time you have saved the half million dollars that the boat costs today, they will have stopped producing it a long time ago. But maybe you can afford to borrow money from the bank to buy it? A quick call to a few banks make you sure that the interest rate will be 12% per year, with monthly instalments. You and your wife (she really wants a cabin in the mountains instead) have by using *«Fireat40.xls»* budget model concluded, with prudent consumption, you have a *surplus liquidity of an average of 5,510 per month. How long will it take to repay the loan, and what type of loan should you choose?*

3.

Your daughter is hooked on sailboats. Since she is competing in races, you see a need to switch to a different model as the little hopeful both grows and wins. The boat she has put her eyes on, costs a handsome \$ 50,000. But you do not have money ready and must therefore borrow. Since you have just bought a car for Ole, and a *"Smuggler"* for yourself, you feel the need for a little more control on your cash flow so that your liquidity will not be too strained. The bank is accommodating this time as well since you are such good customers. They understand the problem and offers an annuity loan over 10 years at 11% per anno (per year) in monthly installments.

a) What will be the annual annuity and what will be the monthly payment?
b) You ask the bank if the loan is flexible, and the bank answers yes to the question. What will the remaining debt in year 3 be if you pay in so much extra that the loan behaves like a serial loan?

4.

Both you and your wife earn good incomes. In total, you earn $ 500,000. Your wife has long been begging to move into a house where the kids can have their own living room in the basement. Also, she thinks she can build a beautiful garden where you can have your own little carpenter's shed also. The house she has found is of course absolutely perfect. It costs $ 1,500,000. The apartment you have can be sold for $ 950,000, of which the bank should have covered the rest of your loan of $ 450,000. Your budget template from chapter 8 still shows a monthly average profit of $ 5,100 per month. The bank does not grant loans in excess of 2.0 times your joint income. The bank always requires a mortgage on the house and an interest rate of 8% p.a. (per anno/year) *within* 80% of the loan appraisal. Beyond this, the bank does not provide loans. The maximum repayment period is 30 years.

a) What will the bank answer when you submit the application for a loan?
b) How long will it take to repay the loan if the bank approves the loan?

5.

Your house is beautiful, and you moved in last week, which was a freezing cold day of January. Like all other wage earners, you have a loan on your house. It is an annuity loan of $ 1,000,000. You pay 8% interest p.a., and the term of the loan is 30 years.

a) On the way home from work, you hear on the news that the central bank has raised its signal interest rate by 1/2 %- point during the day, and that your bank followed up by 1 %- point. What will this cost you extra per year if the interest rate stays a whole 30 years?

b) How much will your personal wealth be reduced in total if the interest rate remains for the entire term of the loan?

c) The next day, your colleagues laugh that you have misheard. The interest rate is reversed, so your bank has (amazingly) lowered the lending rate by as much as 1% -points. How much do you save on this action if the interest rate stays the whole year?

d) How much does your personal wealth increase if the loan interest rate remains the same throughout the term of the loan?

8 b. Summary answers

1.

Let's go to the model for serial loans and finds that a serial loan of $ 45,000 in the bank at 11% interest p.a. over 5 years.

a) Performance in the first year can be read to the right of where we enter the interest rate: $ 13,950.00

b) *We point to the graph* and see that the remaining debt after three years is $ 18,000. We can also calculate the instalments to be $ 45,000/5 = $ 9000 per year. Since you have been paying for three years, the remaining debt is (5 - 3) * 9000 = 18 000 (The graph shows the text Series "Residual loan" Point 3 Value : 18,000 when you point to graph just above year 3).

2.

We stop by the serial loan model first and try on different values for maturity. The loan amount and interest rate are given. Even at 30 years maturity, the payment in the first year is just over $ 10,000 more than you can manage. Therefore, we move on to the annuity model. Same procedure here until you find a match that turns into $ 5,510 * 12 = $ 66,120 per year. The answer is that it takes 21 years to repay an annuity loan on these terms.

3.

a) *The annual annuity will be $ 8,490.07, and the monthly payment will be $ 707.51.*

b) We`ll find this by entering the information in the model for serial loans. We then point with the mouse cursor at the graph over 3 years and can read the remaining debt of 35,000. Or we can take out a simple calculator and calculate $ 50,000/10* (10 -3) = $ 35,000.

4.

a) The bank lend you a maximum of 2.0 times the household's total income: $ 500,000 * 2.0 = $ 1,000,000. and probably says that they will look into the application if you submit it.

b) If the bank would approved the loan, the calculations will be as follows:

The bank lends a maximum of 80% of the valuation: $ 1,500,000 * 0.80 = $ 1,200,000. But their requirement is $ 1,500 000 - (950 000 - 450 000) = $ 1,000 000. If we try the annuity model again, we discover that the bank's maximum maturity of 30 years, the annual annuity is $88,827.43. This is a whopping $ 22,707.43 more than your ($ 5,100 *12) = $ 61,200 can afford anyway . . .

5.

a) The loan basically costs you $ 88,827.43 at 8% p.a.
At 9% p.a. it costs $ 97,366.35, i.e. an annual increase in expenses of $ 8,508.92

b) Total borrowing cost was $ 2,664,823 (8%) and is now $ 2,920,090.54, i.e. a wealth reduction of $ 255,267.54 under these conditions.

c) The loan now costs you only $ 80,586.40 in which means an increased wealth this year of $ 8,241.03.

d) The total cost of the loan is now $ 2,417 592.11 which means a total increase in wealth of as much as $ 247,230.89 if the terms remain in place throughout the term of the loan

You can find more information about me and my books here:

executivewayto.com or at fireat40.com

Chapter 9. Current Debt and Effective Interest Rate

In the previous chapter, I showed you how to calculate the costs of loans of the long-term type. And so far in this book, we have looked at nominal values. Now we will take a closer look at debt of the short-term type, and then we might also start using effective interest rates at the same time. It is in fact that the effective interest rate is always higher than the nominal rate, i.e. in the case of loans. The opposite is true for deposits in the bank. The larger the fees, the higher the effective interest rate on your loan. The reason for this can be found in the structure of the formulas, which we will discuss later in this chapter. But I can reveal already now that there will be neither much mathematics nor much to read. In short words.

9.1 Short thoughted?

Just to put it in short, but brutal right away, current debt like credit cards or consumer loans are not the ways to go for an ordinary wage earner if you want to become a millionaire, or *"FIRE@40!"* with an average salary. Unfortunately. You will immediately see that current debt is the expression of short-term loans and it does not only apply to how short a time to repay the loan, but that it can also be directly short-sighted. At least if you are planning a better financial future. Does 20 -30% annual debt interest make the hairs on your head suddenly rise and stand on end? Be aware, especially if you have this type of debt. Because this is the normality, unfortunately not the exception. What if we ourselves got such a return on our savings?

9.2 Effective

As we know for sure, we must include *all costs incurred* that comes with a loan when calculating the effective interest rate. Among these costs, we can mention both fees, commissions, registration fees, term fees, invoicing fees and all sorts of other specified fees and costs incurred on a loan. There is also a fee for a possible appraiser if you may need a mortgage collateral as a reasonable assurance for the loan. Just to name the most common costs. The formula for *Effective interest rate per year* (arrears probability) we write as follows:

$$p = ((1+q)^{\wedge m})^{-1}$$

Note the double parenthesis. From math's lessons, we have learned that we dissolve (and calculate) the innermost parenthesis before we calculate the next one outside. *The "small p"* here stands for the effective interest rate as opposed to the previous *"i"* which stands for the nominal interest rate, or i_{nom} as it is also often written as. "*Small q*" stands for the interest of the period and *m* stands for the number of periods per year. In this way, we can calculate the effective annual interest rate from this one formula, even if there are semi-annual, quarterly or monthly maturities. We just have to be consistent with what we put into the formula so that the answer we get back is what we actually ask for. This formula shows you the *effective interest rate* if all the interest is paid at the end of the period as in *arrears probability.*

If we have to pay interest and instalments *in advance* instead, the effective interest rate is calculated according to this formula instead:

$$p = \frac{i}{((1 + m - i)^{\wedge m})^{-1}}$$

If you by now think that this will be a "math chapter" you are completely wrong. But I have written the formulas for those who like this type of brain teaser, and for the sake for you to be certain that I do not write mumbo-jumbos. For example, what will be the effective interest rate on a loan that is paid every month when the nominal interest rate is 10%? Well, you can now choose to play with your Mickey Mouse calculator. But keep in mind that you must use decimal numbers for the expression of nominal interest rate (which is the letter *i*) in the expression above. The answer is 10.56% effective interest rate per year. Where does the last 0.56% come from? Well, they come from the fact that you pay 12 times a year *in advance*. If You don`t like to calculate with pen and paper, my included app looks like this:

Effective interest: *	
Nominal interest rate:	10,00 %
Times of Payment/Year:	12
Effective interest/Year:	10,56 %

* Arrears annuity

Fig: *Calculating the effective interest of arrears annuity in a snap*

Let's no longer dwell on this fact, but dive further into the world of examples:

Let's assume that you have to go out to buy a new bed for little Ole since the old one said goodbye last Friday. Since you don't have cash and also think you've been excessively eager on the loan market lately, you consider different financing options and wonder what will be cheapest for you.

We're now going to take a look at a few different short-term financing methods to see the different costs of these options.

9.3 Credit cards

It's quite amazing to see how many people use credit cards in modern society. I have it myself, it`s convenient and can hardly be avoided anyway. But as long as I don't use them, it doesn't cost more than maybe the annual membership fee of $15. You could say that I pay a kind of insurance of $15 per year to have reserve liquidity in case something unforeseen should happen.

Throughout the world, credit cards are widespread and accepted almost everywhere. There are mainly three types of these plastic cards that we most often somewhat misleadingly call credit cards. Because some are pure debit cards where users are charged to their bank account directly. So, you cannot use it when your account is empty. One type is called a payment card where you get the bill once or twice a month for what has been consumed in a certain period. Another type are the pure credit cards where you have credit at a predetermined limit that is repaid over a longer period of time, as with a loan. The development in recent years is that there is a greater degree of combination cards. Here, the account is debited immediately until it is empty, and then you get to *pay off the overdrawn amount*, on the *predetermined credit limit* with a variable interest rate and variable repayment time dependent of your use.

These plastic cards are so nice to have since you don't have to run around with cash in your pocket. It feels safer since it is not so easy to get robbed in a dark street after a late and perhaps damp night out in a bar. Those who are robbed have all been robbed of large amounts of cash, right? Yes, amounts of cash are robbed by criminals who sneak around in more or less dark alleys. But that may only be half the truth. Credit cards are stolen and misused as well. But we will not go into the world of criminology here. We're going to take a closer look at what cash disappears from your account, whether you're aware of its size or not. Unfortunately, many people tend to forget to keep track of the account's balance when the cards are swiped or tapped through the payment terminals. Losing track is anything but cheap!

It`s expensive to have a credit card, the average consumer is aware of that. We have gradually become surprisingly good at just accepting the banks' "taxation" in the form of various fees without hesitation. It is not surprising that this particular interest rate is high, because the risk of unsecured loans is very high for the lender. We will take a closer look at the connection of price and risk in Chapter 13. But these fees are added on top of your debt regardless of risk. You may not be quite as aware of how much the plastic cards actually costs. There are many different brands of cards, with just as many different types of conditions. In any case, common to most people is that you have to repay a debt with a small monthly interest rate that is calculated on the remaining debt as we saw earlier on. We have been through both main types of long term loans in chapter 8. We also went through the effective interest rate was just two paragraphs earlier in chapter 9.2.

Now, let's say you're considering using your credit card to buy Ole's bed. You suspect that there is something strange about this account, because you are always broke. You also never quite manage to calculate the correct balance from month to month since the card issuer charges installments at the beginning of the month. On your bank statement it says that the card has a (nominal) monthly interest rate of only 1.25% and you have never bothered to calculate the interest p.a. (per year) since it is such a low interest rate

anyway. Well, "Try again" as we say. It is a whopping 16.08% per year without different fees, commissions, and other charges.
Just calculate it for yourself! Or you can test the model to be found in *FIRE@40.xls*. The model for interest in advance looks like this:

Interest in advance: *	
Interes rate per period:	1,25 %
Times of Payment/Year:	12
Effective interest/Year:	16,08 %

* Payment in advance

Fig: *This model shows you how to calculate the effective annual interest rate for advance payments of an annuity loan of fixed interest.*

For obvious reasons, I have not made a graph here. We are not going to look at the development over 30 years' time, we are going to have *a specific amount on a specific day* at the end of one year. This model is a pure calculator, pre-programmed and ready for you to play with.

On most credit cards, you usually get both a fee of some kind, and usually you often get an annual fee or commission or whatever we call it, in addition. The bottom line is that all these costs that come in addition, the installments affect your effective interest rate. Later in the chapter, we will go through a model called Consumer Loans, where we can use this model. Without dwelling any more on this now, I will just make you aware that such "loans" or credits as it is called are expensive. It is not uncommon to have an effective interest rate of 20 - 30%. Even in our days! Imagine if you could get over 20% on your savings? Well, we did that in chapter 7. Good business for you as a lender, but terribly bad for those who are not smart enough to avoid such an "offer". The most expensive thing in the world is to be poor and low on cash. No wonder I write about savings already in the next chapter, right? You can start looking forward to it already.

9.4 Installments credit

For now, we continue with our efforts to get Ole a new bed at a, under the circumstances, a reasonable financing cost:

In one of the stores you visit, the seller offers installments on the bed for 10,465. You must pay the first instalment of $1,010 in cash, and the rest in equal instalments over a whole year. You nod cheerfully and happily, because then Ole can sleep in a new bed tonight since you have $ 1,010 but not much more in your account. But what does this cost? Well, you know that. It is easy to multiply $ 1,010 by 12 which becomes $ 12,120. But we want to know the effective annual interest rate as well, since we will be comparing the price of different financing choices. We no longer put up with being broke from month to month. We will also see specifically on our account that we are taking part in the general increase of welfare we hear so much about in the news.

Choosing an installment credit in the store means that you choose to take on a loan of $10,465. You must pay the first instalment in cash, and the rest must be paid in equal instalments until the debt is paid off. Now it is easy to say that the effective interest rate can be calculated roughly as 1010 * 12 = 12.120 and that it therefore must be (12,120 – 10,465/10,465)*100 = 15.81%. Is that cheaper than the 16.08% we got in the previous example? But of course this is wrong. In this way, we do not get the time value of the money, or that the loan balance decreases as we repay. The correct answer is twice as much. The effective interest rate in this example is 31.84%. If you didn't get hiccups in the example with credit cards, you`ll get that now, right? Without going the way through the interest table (we don`t really use them anymore) or mathematical interpretations, I will explain it as briefly as I can:

We borrow 10,465 with a monthly payment of 1,010. Or to put it in a word you now are familiar with, we say that it is an annuity loan. The installments are fixed over the entire period. We can use our annuity model from the previous chapter and try our way until we get an interest rate that gives us 1,010 in installments. Just try it for yourself, it`s called to interpolate! You find that at 2.334% interest rate and 12 periods (it says years in that model) we'll get installments of 1009.98 per month. But we have to find an annual interest rate. So, by now you have filled in 12 periods (months) on the cell for years, then it is of course the period interest you have received an answer for. And as you know, it`s 12 months a year. We now fill in the 2.33% in the model for Advance Interest in this chapter since we advance the amounts *each month, and we find the answer of 31.84%. Just try the elaborate steps yourself.*

You don't have to rummage and search between the different *FIRE@40.xls* spreadsheets to do this operation. The description above is included for the sake of explanation only, so I hope that you appreciated it. I have made a model even though the hope is that you will never use it on real life example calculations, only for the test of it. I hope that you learn as you read.

As for the model *Installment Credit*, you can find it on the same screenshot in the spreadsheet (Chapter 14) in *FIRE@40.xls*, it is made for your comfort. All in one place as usual. This app is based on the recognition that an instalment is a series of payments, or cash flow, on which we can therefore calculate the internal rate of return. If you are not already an economist, forget the term internal rate of return right away, because I will not go into the explanation of this term in the book. The interest rate we arrive at is the monthly interest rate, while we want to find the annual interest rate. Therefore, the model includes the formula for the advance effective interest rate since you have to pay the first installment before taking the bed out of the store. In this case, you pay in advance.

In your eagerness to learn as much as possible, you will now naturally notice that the app has calculated an effective interest rate of 31.90% and not 31.84% as with the second method! But relax, it's nothing wrong with the apps. It's just that *this one* includes all the decimals, while we only write the first two.

Installment credit: *	
Loan	10 465,00
Cash payment	1 010,00
Installmets	12
Monthly fees	0
Effective monthly interest:	2,3344 %
Effective yearly interest:	31,90 %
Total cost:	12 120,00

* This model calculates for 1 year only

* Cash payment equals monthly downpayments

Also note that the model takes into account invoicing fees etc., which here are called monthly fees. In other words, it takes into account monthly fees, but not one-time fees. Now try on your hand at, for example, an invoicing fee of $50 per month. Then suddenly the effective interest rate now jumps to almost 45% effective interest rate! It's the way to make good money in a hurry for a lender! Yes, if the customers pay it that is!

9.5 Bank overdraft, perhaps?

Well, you'll find that paying an effective interest rate of a whopping 32% or even worse 45% is both immoral and completely out of the question. You have a lot of other things to spend your money on, so you continue to look for financing for Ole's bed. Shocked by the information, you stop by the bank anyway. You will check the costs of overdraft on your account in the short period before the next payday. But here the bank is not very benevolent.
A rather strict bank clerk will tell you that you will be charged in the following way, at best:
Amounts between $ 20,000-50,000, the effective interest rate is 11.95% per year Between $ 50,001-100,000, the effective interest rate is 11.35% per year In addition, the bank calculates a commission of 0.25% of the remaining balance per 30 days, a minimum of $ 250. The minimum open maturity of an overdraft facility is 1 year, and the minimum loan amount is $ 20,000.

As you sweat trying to calculate it all in your head, you exclaim: *"But is this really common then, and what will be the effective interest rate?"* The strict bank clerk replies that *"No, but fortunately it is not common to use a credit you do not have, so the bank treats this as an overdraft facility at best"*. Since the bank's lowest limit is $ 20,000, this is the amount the bank clerk calculates and comes to the conclusion that this will cost you $ 149.58 per month. This would then be an annual effective interest rate of 19.50%.

But we have to remember that the minimum amount of the bank's commission is 250 $, so must it be even more expensive than this? So, you start to lose interest since you find that the installment had an effective annual interest rate of 31.90% excluding invoicing fees cost you net of $ 1,010 - (10.465/12 = 872.08) 872.08 = $ 137.92 per month in financing costs. That's more than ten dollars cheaper than what the bank charges if you overdraw the account! You can try for yourself on the model (PgDwn) :

Bank overdraft*:	
Total Bank Overdraft:	20 000,00
Average draft:	50 %
Nominal interest:	11,95 %
Commission on the limit:	0,25 %
Cost pr. number of days:	30
Cost this period	149,58
Eff. Interest per period:	1,50 %
Eff. Interest per Year:	19,50 %

* Cost of the credit in this period

Note that we have entered $ 20,000 as an overdraft facility here since the bank has stated this limit amount *as the minimum for this type of loans*. We will calculate the average consumption whether you pay off after a month, or in a year. Because the minimum time the overdraft facility is open is one year, otherwise there will be no "shop" for the bank. Regardless of whether you only need $10,500 for a month. We enter 50% as the Average use of "Total Overdraft" since this is what you need to use.

If you enter the *average in use cell* at 100% since this is the lower limit the bank operates with, you get a period cost of $249.17. Imagine that it matched so surprisingly well with the bank's "minimum 0.25% of remaining balance per 30 days, minimum $ 250! This costs at least $ 3,000 per year.

Now you begin to despair, and you understand much better the phrase *"It is extremely expensive to be poor"*. But it's even worse to be stupid. In fact, there is nothing more expensive than that! You might ask yourself if there isn't a certain connection here somewhere.

9.6 Consumer loans, anyone?

According to statistics, many of us have so-called short-term debt. These are small consumer loans with more or less flexible repayment periods. In the previous chapter, you could read about the couple who could put $ 40,000 in cash on the table for a new car and far from being broke afterwards. And this despite a beautiful home in a better part of the country's more expensive residential areas. There where nothing in the article indicating short-term debt, neither of the consumer loan type nor of the credit card type. No wonder they both had a good economy, and a little luxury in everyday life.

Well, back to the example:

The bank clerk thinks that you may be able to come to an agreement after all. The bank has a product for situations like this, and you arrange for a meeting later in the day since the bank needs to go through your finances more closely, which "has taken off a bit" lately. For this, they need some overview of the family's finances. The bank has been quite nice so far, so you hope to get out of the situation pleasantly without Ole having to sleep on the floor for a whole month. He has already spent a couple of nights on the couch that should also have been replaced several years ago. Now he complains of back pain already.

The bank's terms and conditions are as follows for a loan up to $ 50,000:

Establishing fee : 500
Nominal interest rate : 15.60% (advance interest)
Term fee: 25 per term.
You can choose whether you want monthly, quarterly, semi-annual or annual instalments.

Let's say you choose monthly installments since you can pay back in smaller installments. You can now go into the model *Consumer loans* in FiRE@40.xls's spreadsheet:

Consumer loan*:				
Nominal interest	15,60 %			
Start up fees:	500	dollars		
Interest per term:	1,2153 %		Cost per term:	-967,50
Loan amount	10 465	dollars	Total cost	-11 609,98
Terms:	12		Eff terminrente:	2,43 %
Fees per term:	25	per term	Eff. Yearly interest:	33,43 %

Here you will see that you cannot fill in the first field. It is just presented so you can try your way under *"Interest per term"* since some banks only state this rate, while others states both the nominal and effective annual interest rate. If you are given the annual interest rate as in this example, you can try and fail interest rate per term until you get the given nominal annual interest rate. Another thing is that the model is designed for a repayment period of 12 months since most people with poor liquidity will choose low repayment amounts. You know the rest of the numbers, so you can just fill them in.

Note that *the different fees* makes the effective interest rate doubled in this example!

9.7 A little sigh, then!

It is with astonishment that we can hear topics of conversation around the lunch table in different workplaces in the news. Adults and apparently sensible people get almost cranky during lunch discussions about nominal and effective interest rates. They don`t agree on which interest rate matters or not when talking about loans. Even some bank employees do not seem to understand the difference. Shudder and horror!

Most of us have mortgages on houses or other large investments such as a cabin, a boat or cars. If you don't, you're probably so young that you're at least well prepared for what's coming to you in the future. But then again, that`s why you read my book. Keep it close to heart! The nominal interest rate is the bank's *"bait rate",* so to speak, just to get you hooked on the offer. However, as you now know, the end result is affected by both set-up fees, commissions and other costs that are incurred in connection with undertaking on the loan. Of course, there are also expenses for the appraiser in connection with the pledge on your fixed assets like maybe a house. All kinds of monthly commissions and fees also affect the final result. As we know, the flow of money must be distributed exactly on the time axis if we are to get an accurate answer! But all of us who have read all the way up til here know this. And that the whole point of this chapter is to see that the effective interest rate is always higher than the nominal interest rate on loans. So it is the effective interest rate that we want to know something about since it is the one we pay. It affects our cash flow and that`s what is important.

If you thought that the "next step" would be to look at leasing, or renting, you have to think twice. Not because I don't have a model for this. Because I do.

But you don't need such a model to understand that "renting a thing for a few years" for a few hundred bucks every month for several years is financially completely out of bounds for you as a private individual. And if you still don't get it, think about this: Someone makes a good living from you renting instead of buying. They live well.

Now I'll leave you to play with the models until the next chapter. Have fun!

9 a. Test yourself:

(We assume a fixed interest rate, and we disregard taxes and inflation!)

1.

On the way to work, you pass «Household Bank Ltd» daily. You have a habit of looking in through the bank's windows and over the past year you have seen constant interest rate changes. On loans that have a duration of one year, the bank has operated both 10%, 12.4%, 9.75% and 7.85%. The loans are in arrears and are granted without set-up costs or term fees.

a) *What is the effective interest rate per year for these monthly instalments?*
b) *What is the effective interest rate per year for quarterly installments?*
c) *What is the effective interest rate for semi-annual installments?*

2.

You currently don't have cash, but you're considering an offer for a photography equipment package. The package costs $ 45,000 and as the keen photography enthusiast you are, you believe that this is exactly the equipment you need. The equipment, which consists of both camera bodies and an assorted selection of pro-class lenses, can be financed in different ways. What will be the total cost and effective interest rate if:

(a) *You take installments from the dealer over 12 months at $ 4500 per term. The invoicing fee is $ 50 per term.*

(b) *You use a credit card that is paid off in advance over 12 equal instalments with a period interest rate of 2.56%, establishment fee of $ 150 and monthly term fees of $ 35?*

(c) *Take a consumer loan in the bank with a start-up cost of $ 500, nominal interest rate of 19.56% per year with monthly advance instalments and term fees of $ 75?*

9 b. Summary answers

1.

We`re going to the Effective Interest app:

a) With 12 monthly instalments and arrears annuity,
10% nominal interest = 10.56% effective interest rate
12,4% nominal = 13.27% effective
9,75% nominal = 10.29% effective
7,85% nominal = 8.19% effective

b) In the case of quarterly instalments and arrears annuity,
10% nominal = 10.66% effective interest rate
12,4% nominal = 13.42% effective
9,75% nominal = 10.37% effective
7,85% nominal = 8.25% effective

c) In the case of half-yearly instalments and arrears annuity,
10% nominal = 10.80% effective interest rate
12,4% nominal = 13.66% effective
9, 75% nominal = 10.51% effective
7,85% nominal = 8.34% effective

2.

The total cost and effective interest rate of the photo package will be:

a) *The instalment of these terms gives an effective interest rate of 44.38% and a total cost of $ 54,600.*

b) *The credit card behaves like a consumer loan. The term interest rate is 2.56%, the start-up fee is 500, the loan amount is 45,000, the number of instalments is 12 and the term fee is 35 per term. We see that the total cost will be 53,254.48 and that the effective interest rate will be 38.43%*

c) *Same model here, but new conditions. We try on different values on the cell for the forward rate and see that 1.50% gives a nominal interest rate of 19.56%. But we are surprised when we discover that the total cost is 50,407.20, and that the effective annual interest rate is 26.40%.*

You can find more information about me and my books here:
executivewayto.com or at fireat40.com

Chapter 10. Savings and Final Values

Now you're probably scratching your head a bit and wondering where all the millions go. Wasn't it so that you could become a millionaire as an ordinary wage earner? You don't become a millionaire by depositing one amount into an account and leaving it there, do you? Because if you get that high interest your country has such serios economic problems that the currency is constantly devaluated, and your money won`t not be worth anything in a couple of years. Or opposite, surely the deposit must be so incredibly large, or it must take a few generations before there are millions of it. Both yes, maybe and no. To read more about this, please visit my website Fireat40.com

10.1 Savings, - how wise is it really?

In chapter 6, I explained to you about the opportunity costs and what you would have to sacrifice if you let go of your finances. In chapter 7 I showed you what the time value of money is and means to you, and even though the chapter may have been a bit technical in some places, you quickly understood the points just by reading the text and solving the problems in *FIRE@40.xls*. That kind of thing can lead you to decide to start your journey as a millionaire, and several people who read my first book 22 years ago have done the same before you. Or maybe you're a real FIRE and want to take an early planned retirement when you turn 40? We moved on in chapter 8 where we became practical again and something that is just as fundamental, namely budget, control and liquidity management. Thus, we had the basis for looking at what it costs to finance your dream home, boat or car, and your budget showed whether you would manage the investment. And in Chapter 9, I showed why the opposite led straight into misfortune and desperation, how incredibly expensive poor liquidity management and thus expensive consumer debt is.

I have shown you that economic relationships have to do with both the amount of effort, time perspective and return. But also that the two fundamentals: *Knowledge and will* are the basis. Thus we have arrived at the third point in the four basic *knowledge, willingness, saving and investment* that I wrote in the introduction on page 1. We must have knowledge, which leads to a *willingness* to set up *a budget* before we get to the point of *saving* in order to be able to finance some *investment*, which is the fourth point

Now, not everyone who has half a million or so in a salary account that doesn't yield a return. Or who can run into the bank to buy shares, bonds or otherwise lend such amounts at high interest rates. But it's amazing how many people have a whole gross annual salary sleeping in such an account! My wife worked in a bank where she saw shocking examples of ignorance, lethargy and some cases of pure idiocy from customers. We should not include pensioners in this context, who have everything they own in a bank account that pays so little interest that the bank should blush. And banks should do so when interest rates are barely keeping up with inflation and perhaps not even that. But the pensioners would prefer to have this opportunity to collect one 100 dollar- bill at a time. When you are 80 or 90 years old, you have minimal interest in what the economy will look like in 10-15 years. They need to make a short walk to the bank or store to pick up the 100 dollar bill because they need to meet other people. Both the familiar and unfamiliar faces. Without being foisted on investment objects with a glittering past and claimed an even better future.

But it is not at all these pensioners I am talking about. I'm talking about people in their prime, and many younger than that. Surprisingly many of these have a net or a gross annual salary on - hold your breath, their salary account! At an interest rate that is *below* inflation! When my wife wanted to talk about investments with them (yes, she is also an economist) one can wonder why she gets answers like: *"No, I will live today, not when I turn 50!"*. Sigh! Yes, like that! Others may look up from their chores in horror and say *"Savings?! Is it really that wise?"* Maybe you did just that too, before you had second thoughts and bought this book. While we've played our way through four finance chapters in "*Applied Personal Finance"* we have learned that we can calculate in seconds what half a net annual salary will be if we invest it for a 15-year period at a 1% better return than before. Not to mention what it will become when we have let it ferment for 30 years. It will not be so small. We know what an acid reflux we get when we calculate what we have *lost* on the difference between 4% and 8% of such an amount in the 20 years they have slept on our salary account. Or maybe you don't dare to?

Maybe you're young and smart? Only 20 years old and don't really know what you're going to become, so you're working a bit in the meantime? Or maybe you got the book as a gift for your confirmation or bar mitzvah? Maybe you had a smart teacher who understood how to bring algebra into life? That's how I thought about my one-year-old son when I wrote my first book on personal finance for him. So he would be free to choose his life for himself but still get this knowledge as easy to read as possible, as early as possible in life to understand the knowledge and start as early as possible in life. Preferably as a student. For your information, he took the point of it long before he read it. In fact, already at the age of 13, he exclaimed that he wondered how on earth he would be able to afford to buy a home when he grew up? He did not know about the book I had written to him a decade earlier but spoke on the basis of the TV-news and the development in house pricing. But the younger you are when you find and understand this knowledge and these connections I share with you here, the luckier you are! Simply because the time perspective works *for you*, maybe twice as long as the person you got the book from. We will immediately look at what you can do with your pocket money, and how much will be gained from it. Or how much it will be with fairly small monthly profits even if you are 40 years old now and have always been broke from payday to payday. It's never too late, just stay tuned!

10.2 Final values

In chapter 8, we emphasized the practicalities, namely using the loan models and taking on some tasks so that you can get answers to your own calculations. We simply took a break from the mathematical deductions so that you wouldn't think that this was still a fancy way to trick you into reading a master's thesis in financial economics. It is not. Far more is required of both the author and the reader. But I also thought it was important to show already in chapter 7 how a geometric series, i.e. the compound interest effect, arises and works, so that not everything comes at once now. In practice, you already saw that relatively modest amounts can grow quite powerful! It all depends on the time, the interest rate and, of course, the amount of the bet. We will now continue that line of thinking here. You will also benefit from this chapter even if you just read the text and ponder a little about the graphic representations. Don't struggle through the mathematical deductions if you don't want to. But that's the smartest thing.

You probably noticed the heading "Final values". This is the same as future value, as we learned already in chapter 7 about the time value of money. The reason why I use a different word now is that we will calculate deposits of equal amounts over a longer period, while in the case of future value (FV) we only relate to a single amount with a fixed return over a fixed period. So we will not do that now. To get off to a good start, we start as usual with a small example:

You like to go out on the town with the guys. It doesn't happen very often, only 4 times a year. On the other hand, you hit the big drum when you are at it. You usually spend $ 2,000 each time. Since you are of the social type, you join your colleagues every Friday after work to have the "Friday beer". It will only be a couple of pints and a "small sharp one" a total of 150 dollars. Since you are generous with your wife and the trust is mutual after 20 years of marriage, she does the same as you. Yes, she goes with the girls then, the boys are left alone. You don't notice much about these amounts because you are so well off and lack nothing in this world. With the exception of a cabin in the mountains. Well, yesterday's party was nothing short of amazing, but today you have a hangover, and the peasant remorse has taken you. While you sit there and feel sorry for yourself, you ask yourself what you could have had in the account today, if you instead had put this money in a high-interest account at, for example, 8% for the entire period?

You get a sheet of paper and set it up: (40 working weeks * 150 * 2) + (2000 * 4 * 2) = (12,000) + (16,000) = 28,000 per year! Now you suddenly wake up. What can you *alternatively* get that does not cause a hangover for 28,000 per year? You run over and start the computer and bring up the model for *annuity loans*. After some trial and error, you will find that you can pay off a loan of 112,000 at 8% interest in just 5 years! Or a cabin in the mountains for 300,000 in 25 years at the same interest rate. Isn't that what you want then? Party and monkey pranks in the bars, versus a cabin in the mountains. Hm! Maybe not a luxury palace a la Onasis, but still perfectly acceptable size and standard for you and yours. And isn't little Ole crazy about snowboarding, and you and your wife for salmon fishing?

You wake up your wife, whose daily condition, if possible, is not far behind your own. Truth be told, both you and your wife feel a little too old to dance at the bar with a lampshade on your head. It was fun the first time, but now it's become routine. The guys kind of expect it. Eager about your newly acquired knowledge, you post about the cabin that can be financed by cutting out today's overconsumption. But then your wife wants you to do some calculations on what it would be like if you bought mutual funds instead. Maybe you can get the castle of your dreams anyway, she nags. Anna boasted about how fantastic a return they had had on a mutual fund. Yes, it was so good that they could soon buy "half the city". In any case, they were going to travel to the mountains to look at a dream cabin with a swimming pool and all sorts of cool solutions. Therefore, you stumble back to your computer and find your FV model in FIRE@40.xls. *You stare a little at the model and realize that the formula for the future value of an amount looks like this:*

$$FV = NV * (1 + i)^{\wedge n}$$

So, you start thinking. If you put 28,000 in the account at the end of the year this year, it will have grown to as much as 30,240 after a year when the account you get the highest interest on gives 8% interest. Then you deposit another USD 28,000, so you have USD 58,240 at your disposal there. You do the math:

After 1 year, it will be 28,000 since we deposit at the end of the year every year.

After 2 years, it becomes 28,000 $*(1 + i)^{\wedge 2}$ = 30,240 +28,000 = 58,240.

After 3 years, it becomes 28,000 $*(1 + i)^{\wedge 3}$ +28,000$*(1 + i)^{\wedge 2}$ +28,000 = 90,899.20

After 4 years, it becomes: 28,000 $*(1 + i)^{\wedge 4}$ +28,000$*(1+i)^{\wedge 3}$ +28000$*(1+i)^{\wedge 2}$ + 28000$*(1+i)^{\wedge 1}$ = 126,171.14

At the beginning of year 5, there would have been 126,000. But this is almost halfway to the 300,000 you calculate at the beginning. And now you are also starting to get a little tired of keeping track of which amount should be raised to what power for which year. Naturally, you find it regrettable that all amounts have to be calculated manually. You therefore take a "quick one" and calculate 300,000 / 126,171.14 = 2.38. Since you have a fixed rate of return and savings amount, you multiply the 4 years by 2.38 and get 9% yearly. You sigh and stumble back to bed as the headache starts to get really nasty. But it didn't have to be so difficult to find the right answer if you had the energy a little longer. The rest of us, on the other hand, continue on, because we see that your last reasoning must be wrong. That's because you've suddenly forgotten the whole argument for *geometric* series and switched to an *arithmetic* series in the middle of the job. So it must go wrong. The correct answer is 8.05 years, but since we do economics, not mathematics, and also only calculate whole years, it is only called 8 years. This is precisely because of the geometric series. We'll see why soon.

10.3 Bank deposits

Banks don't run charity, no matter what anyone might try to make you believe. They certainly don't exchange money for fun. Because then they could put their own money in another bank and earn their money there. The banks make money on both the interest margin and on all kinds of fees, commissions and other activities. The interest margin is thus the difference or margin between the borrowing and lending rates. Not only have you bought the home by borrowing from the bank, but your car, your insurance and soon you will probably be able to buy all your clothes there too. At least the workout clothes, we are to believe the thousands of Sunday hikers who wander around in the nice weather. As a goal for this section, we will therefore show what the formula for bank deposits looks like and look closer at what you get back from the bank after a while if you save a fixed amount annually.

We remember that the formula for future value of an amount was:

$$FV = NV * (1 + i)^{\wedge n}$$

$$FV = PMT^* \left[(1+i)^{1} + (1+i)^{2} + (1+i)^{3} + \ldots + (1+i)^{n}\right]$$

$$FV = NV * (1+i)^{1} + NV * (1+i)^{2} + NV * (1+i)^{3} + \ldots$$

Then the formula for a number of equal payments must be written as follows: Or more formally like this:

PMT is, as previously mentioned, an abbreviation for *Payment.* The expression inside **[ ]** The parentheses are called a *geometric series*. In the previous chapter, we had an example of a loan for $100,000. We were going to find the annual annuity which we explained as follows: *"We can say that what we are going to arrive at are the periodic payments that together correspond to the present value of the 100,000 we borrow".* You may recall that the formula for present value is the inverse of future value and looks like this:

$$NV = FV * \frac{1}{(1+i)^{n}}$$

This expression can also be written as a geometric series, just like in the case of FV above. But it becomes the inverse

$$NV = PMT^* \left[\frac{1}{(I+i)^{1}} + \frac{1}{(I+i)^{2}} + \frac{1}{(I+i)^{3}} + \ldots + \frac{1}{(I+i)^{n}} \right]$$

Since I don't want to torture the readers with mathematical deductions, let's take it a little fast forward. Those who are good at math will certainly be able to keep up. The clauses inside the parentheses can be written as:

$$\frac{1}{I+i} * \frac{(1+i)^{-n})^{-1}}{((1+i)^{-1})^{-1}}$$

Which can be simplified to:

$$\frac{(1+i)^{\wedge n} -1}{i*(1+i)^{\wedge n}}$$

after we multiply the previous expression first by $((1+i)^{\wedge n}$ and then by -1.

But never mind because now we are almost at the finish line. You may also remember the formula for an annuity loan? It looked like this:

$$NV = PMT * \frac{(1+i)^{\wedge n-1}}{i * (1+i)^{\wedge n}}$$

PMT still stands for *payment*. So it's the same formula! Let's take one more example:

Let's assume that you have won a lottery and that the prize is an amount of 50,000 per year for five years. The amounts are paid out in arrears, so we can say that there is a probability in arrears. We therefore wonder how much this is discounted to today's money when the interest rate is 5%: We fill in the formula and get that:

$$NV = 50\ 000 * \frac{((1{,}05)^{\wedge 5})^{-1}}{0{,}5 * ((1{,}05)^{\wedge 5}} = 50\ 000 * \frac{0{,}2763}{0{,}0638}$$

Which, in a completed state, thus becomes:
NV = 50 000 * 4,3295 = 216 475

Or to use a terminology we are familiar with from the previous chapter: An annuity loan (arrears probability) of USD 216,475 that is repaid over 5 years at 5% interest, has an annual annuity of USD 50,000. Just try it for yourself in FIRE@40.xls. You get 50,000.27 and that's a small rounding error because we only used 4 decimal places in the calculation above. Convinced? You understand the implications. You have models for calculating back and forth, both FV and NV of a single deposit, at a fixed interest rate over many years from chapter 7. Now I have proven that the loan model from chapter 8 must be correct, and you have seen that you can calculate the present value of an annual payment (arrears probability) on the model for annuity loans from chapter 8. Two things at once are really smart, right? You can therefore calculate how large a loan you can finance by a fixed repayment over a longer period of time, which you`ll find out after setting up a budget! Let's turn the whole thing on its head and see what the final value will be of an annual deposit that is the goal of this section.

Let's say you sell the lucky ticket to a friend for 216,475 because he would rather have the 250,000 spread over five years. You put these 216,475 in the bank where you get 5% interest. You may not remember the formula for one-time deposits, but then you can retrieve the model in your spreadsheet and try there.

The formula is like this:

$$FV = FV = NV * (1 + i)^{\wedge n}$$

So, let's try our luck with our lottery win:
$FV = 216\,475 * (1\,,05)^{\wedge 5} = 276\,283{,}05$

That is, in the case of one-time deposits. These conversions are exhausting! Surely it must be possible to do this in a somewhat more modern way. What about your friend who gets the five amounts? He doesn't get that much money compared to you, you fool, did he?

Let's say your friend puts the money in the bank as soon as he gets paid this 50,000 so that he is neither tempted to spend it, nor miss out on interest. The interest rate in the bank is 5%. The general formula for the present value of an arrears probability is:

$$NV = PMT * \frac{(1+i)^{\wedge n-1}}{i * (1+i)^{\wedge n}}$$

While what we did to find the final value was to carry forward the present value in *n* years. Then we get the formula:
We'll fill in the formula to make sure it's correct:

$$FV = 50{,}000 * \frac{(1{,}05)^{\wedge 5-1}}{0.05}$$

Which, in a completed state, thus becomes:

$$FV = PMT * \frac{(1+i)^{\wedge n-1}}{i}$$

FV = 50,000 * 5.5256 = 276,281, 56
Voila, that's the same amount! We have reached our goal!

It was more labor-saving, but hardly more modern. We attribute the two dollars difference to *rounding errors*. It's true, just trust me. If you want to check it (you really should), you can go to FIRE@40.xls on the tab called "chapter 10". A

Final Value from yearly savings:					
Nom.interest (fixed)	5,00 %				* Fixed yearly savings
Yearly savings *	50 000,00				* Arrears annuity
Duration	5	years			* Deposit by 31.12
Final Value:	276 281,56		Savings per month:	4 166,67	* Graph showing the ful

Fig: *Model for calculating final values form yearly savings*

And just below you will find the graph as you probably recognize from the cover:

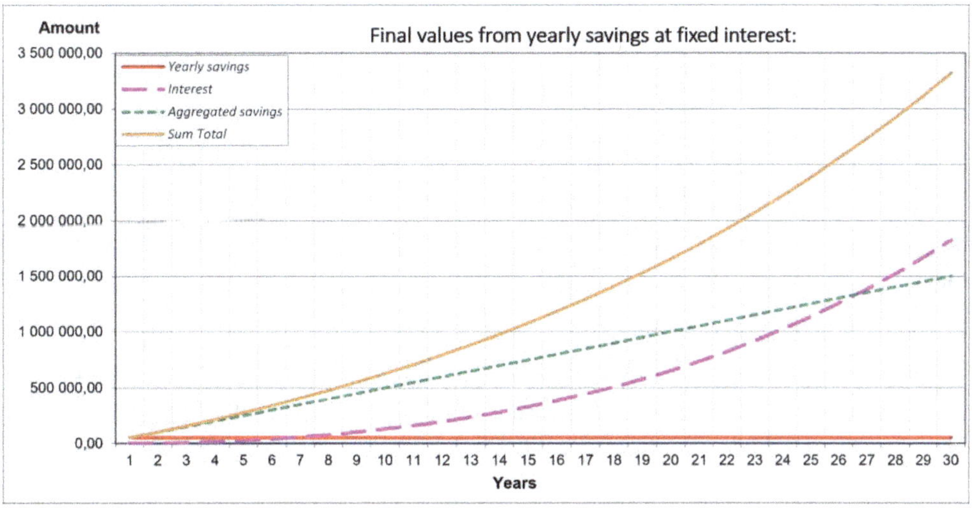

Fig: *The graph shows the development if you save 50,000 (green dotted straight line) for 30 years and get a fixed 5% interest rate for the entire period in arrears probability. The final value, or total amount, is a blue concave line, and the pink dotted line shows how much interest and compound interest you receive each year.*

Now you have yet another new app. This time to calculate a series of equal annual payments. Neat and tidy, right? The prerequisite for the model to be correct is that you receive the same interest rate all the time, such as a fixed interest rate and a fixed payment at a fixed date. The point of these models is *not* that you should get definitive answers for everything, but that you should get *the knowledge to understand* how to adapt to the situations that arise in life and inspire you to think a little more sensibly about the scarce resources that you have at your disposal.

Now you should be itching to try the model yourself. I haven't made that many questions here either, I want you to test your own examples and become a racer at this! I make them first and foremost for you to understand how the algebra can work for you and make you as familiar as possible with the knowledge and how it can be used in your life. And the summary answers are important for you to check whether you have understood the point of the theory i.e. attacked the problem of the questions in the right way.

10 a. Test yourself:

(We assume a fixed interest rate, and we disregard taxes and inflation!)

1.

You are a 20-year-old student and rent a dormitory. You want your own little nest and have no desire to move home to your parents after completing your studies in 5 years. A fellow student has started saving money on something called BSU (housing savings for young people) because he also wants his own apartment. You check the bank's BSU scheme and are told that the interest rate is 7.30%, the maximum deposit per year is 15,000 and that you get a tax deduction for part of the savings amount. Max deposit is 100,000.

(a) *How much equity will you have for an apartment in this account if you follow the savings plan when you stop studying after five years?*

(b) *When you finish your studies after five years, your grandfather decides to pay the remaining amount, which means that the account, including interest, will be as much as 100,000 at the end of the year. How much does he have to deposit today?*

2.

Your fellow student has gotten a job at the local hot dog stand and tells you that you can also start there since they need more employees. The pay conditions are decent, and you can earn 5,000 a month and the employer guarantees that you will be able to work there until you finish your studies. You decide to save the entire amount in a high-interest account that currently offers 6.5% interest. How much will be in this account after completing the study if the interest rate remains fixed throughout the period?

3.

You've been on a trip to Western Norway and completely fallen in love with nature. On the journey, you came across a local farmer who would like to rent away an acre of his property for 99 years for a completely negligible amount. Now you are wondering if you should build a cabin on the plot. After reviewing various cabin brochures, you fell for "Western cottage" to only 250,000. You can actually save 7,500 a month. How long will it take to save up money for the cabin if the bank gives you 6.8% for the entire period?

4.

Your wife tells you that you need to quit smoking, which you have been doing for the past 20 years. You don't want to do this because you've tried to quit before without success, and besides, no other arguments have bitten you. You smoke your 30 a day. A 20 pack costs 58 dollars where you usually shop. If the cigarette price remains stable and but you put the money in the bank instead: How much could you have in your account in 20 years if the bank gives you a 7% fixed interest rate for the entire period?

5.

You want a boat but can't afford it. You never have money at the end of the month, but a review of the budget module in chapter 7 revealed that you should actually have had 35,000 in profit every year. You have debts on the house and cannot refinance it to buy the boat. You wonder if you can finance the boat by stopping spending money on nonsense such as hot dogs on the way home from work, daily canteen visits, drives at random, coffee lattes constantly and constantly and other things you think are really unnecessary. The bank currently offers 7% interest rates, and all experts expect the interest rate to remain at least this level for thc next 10-15 years. How long does it take to buy the dream boat that costs 450,000 today when you need to save up the entire amount at current conditions?

6.

Your oldest daughter wants a pony that costs 15,000. Since you have become a raw capitalist, you want to make her the same. You don't want to give her the pony but tell her that she needs to save her pocket money.

She starts crying and says that you are naughty because the pocket money, which is 300 per week, will never be enough to buy the pony. Is she right when the bank gives 6% interest for the entire period?

10 b. Summary answers

1.

a) After 5 years, you will have 86,778.95 in equity
(b) In the 6th year, he must deposit the present value of the remainder (of 100,000 - 86,778.95) *which is 12,321.58*

(You first drew the time axis, right? Go to chapter 2 *"Present value of an amount"* and enter Nom. Interest - 7.30, FV = 13,221.05, Maturity = 1 and get that NV = 12,321.58...)

2.

There will be a whopping 341,618.46 in the account under these conditions.

3.

You try it out and find out that it takes you just under 3 years to the current conditions.

4.

You spend 30 a day at price (58/20) = 2.90 per piece * 30 * 365 = 31,755 per year. You could instead be a millionaire with a whopping 1,301,811.86 in your account in 20 years at current conditions.

5.

It takes you 9.5 years to save up the amount under current conditions.

6.

This was a trick question, because with 300 in pocket money per week, it takes less than a year (only 50 weeks) to save the amount for the pony... In addition, you will receive interest on your savings for the 50 weeks.

Chapter 11. Combinations

Although we have now played our way through model after model, we have already been through quite a lot of central economic theory during these few chapters. Hopefully, you have struggled a bit with some test-yourself-questions and realized that so-called "trick questions" are not at all tricky, you have just thought a little wrong in relation to the question. Remember that the most essential thing in economics is to think logically before the technically. It is about using common sense. With common sense, we can come a long way. With good tools for the techniques too, half the job is done.

11.1 Combinations

We are neither more nor less human than before, so year after year we wonder if we should not buy a boat to go a little fishing. Or a cabin in the mountains to hunt or go alpine skiing so we can rest between battles at work. Or if we shouldn't simply just move to a bigger house now that the kids have grown so big and require more space. Well, if you have children. But in any case, both the investment and financing issue will come into the picture sooner or later. Therefore, we learned the basic understanding of the opportunity cost, and the basic work of budget control as early as possible in our journey in the world of applied personal economics and finance.

Of course, we don't necessarily have to calculate what the effective loan rate is to become happier as people, and if we go around thinking about such things all the time, we are certainly both single-minded and more or less crazy. On the contrary, some may argue that you can get stomach ulcers from such thoughts. No wonder, because most people will probably get stomach ulcers thinking about the half or the whole million, they have lost in interest income because they did not understand or bother to save a little but spent their money on parties and fun every weekend. Or because they didn't understand the point of moving their savings from a simple salary account to a high-interest account a long time ago. Of course, now you have done the math. At least you have started to move your surplus liquidity from your salary account to your high-interest account in the end of the month, every month that you can. Or maybe you have started to do that every two months or quarterly, depending on how much it is? After reading through the previous chapter on savings, we saw that this would at least make us a little wealthier in the long run. Yes, perhaps quite wealthy after a while, depending on the size of the amounts, the time perspective and the return.

We should not forget that investment and financing in many ways need some maturation in the cerebral cortex before we fully see the connections. We must take the time to let the knowledge sink in better before we throw ourselves into more advanced material. But then again it becomes all the more fun at a later stage. Therefore, in this chapter, we will take a look at what we have learned so far. We will see how we can combine the knowledge from the previous five chapters to get answers to more everyday questions of a more or less complex nature.

11.2 Borrow or save for private investment?

If we see a beautiful sailing yacht in the sunset on a beautiful midsummer evening, our knees may get a little shaky as we wonder how anyone can afford such a beautiful thing. Isn't it true that only *"fat-fifty-year-olds"* can afford that kind of thing? And if so, why is it? Wasn't it the case that the state paid most of the debt of the dessert generation? That *the state*, albeit not Uncle Sam in person with his top hat, traveled around with a large bag of money, and distributed generously to a certain age group at the expense of others? It is of course not quite that simple, which we will return to in a later chapter. The dessert generation is also not fifty years old anymore, they are in their late eighties.

But then we remember that there is quite a lot we can finance with some targeted savings. It is perhaps not too strange that someone can buy a large sailing yacht if they have saved for 20 or 30 years? In that case, I don't think so, and neither does anyone who has read the previous chapter 10 on savings. That's how it works, no matter what anyone tries to tell you. This is the book for you and me who are wage earners, and here this is what we will focus on. So, what do we do then, if this sailing yacht is what we *need* to have to feel like a whole and complete person? Regardless of whether it is sailing with this yacht that makes us happier, or is it owning the beautiful yacht itself? And what if we are so impatient that we cannot wait 20 or 30 years in the meantime?

Even if we have debts on the house, maybe we can finance the yacht by refinancing (we will discuss this in chapter 13) and remortgaging our lovely little house to buying the sailing yacht as well? Then we might enjoy sailing while we are still interested in sailing. We may not think sailing will be the most amazing thing on earth in 20 years' time. But if we save for 20 years, the price of the yacht will probably go up in the meantime and then it is not certain that we can afford it after all, is it? We will take a closer look at that question.

When it comes to private investment, we are faced with a number of such questions. Some questions are more heavily weighted for us than others. Maybe it's the opposite with our neighbor. That is why financial matters become so personal and complicated, because we complicate it with our feelings. We would like to take into account all possible eventualities right away. It may not be such a good idea, but we are like that as humans. And perhaps that is why we are vacillating in many contexts. We all want developments. Or do we? First and foremost, we want *a positive development in our private economy*. When it comes to everything else, it is not so certain we want too many changes and developments at once. Because then uncertainty comes into the equation (uncertainty and risk in chapter 12) and we don't like that. We don't like uncertainty; that's why we want to know as much as possible about the future. Then, we sleep better at night. Like Saul Kaplan stated in the book "Business Model Generation": *"Everyone loves innovation until it affects them"*. (Saul Kaplan in Osterwalder & Pigneur, 2010). So, let's limit the questions we want answers for now just make some assumptions that we can do with a little algebra. Shall we take an example right away?

On the Sunday trips that you usually take to a neighbor marina, you have completely fallen in love with a sailboat of the good old-fashioned kind. Slender lines and pointed bow. The boat is around 35 feet, so you can expect to be able to travel far and a lot with it. The boat, which is immensely *popular, costs $800,000 as brand new from the importer. The importer states that the price of new boats increases by about 5% each year, while last year's prices on last year model have only fallen by 1% per year in the past 10 years they have been on the market. Your bank can refinance the mortgage on your house so you can borrow the $ 800,000 to 8.5% fixed interest over 30 years. You do not have significant savings capital, but the bank's savings rate is currently 6% and it is expected that it will remain stable for many years. The questions you ask yourself is whether you should finance a brand new boat by borrowing from the bank now, or by saving money to get the boat sometime in the future. When can you possibly buy the boat if you save the full amount? Should you perhaps rather finance the purchase of a used model, and if so, in what way?*

Yes, now you're probably wondering if you have to jump from spreadsheet to spreadsheet to get an answer. That is absolutely the right way of thinking, but I reveal right away that I have created an overall model to look at such a combination. That way, we don't have to jump from model to model and maybe lose track of the question in hand completely. As usual, tax effects have been omitted since we have not come that far yet:

TAKE ON A LOAN OR SAVE UP FOR PERSONAL INVESTMENTS?							
Buy new now *		Buy used now *		Final value of savings *		Annuity loan *	
Price increase	5,00 %	Depreciation %	1,00 %	Nom.Interest	6,00 %	Nom.Interest	8,50 %
Price of good	800 000,00	Residual value	593 538,33	Annual savings	74 440,46	Loan	800 000,00
Duration in years	30	*Duration in years*	30	*Duration in years*	30	*Duration in years*	30
FV	3 457 553,90			Final value	5 885 127,77	Annual repayment	-74 440,46
* Evenly price increas (yearly), Deposits pr 1.1, Arrears Annuity, Excluded tax effe				Pr. month	6 203,37	Pr. month	-6 203,37

Fig: *This model is showing us the combinations of buying new or used, financed with savings or loan.*

First, we look at "Buying new*" and want to know how the price of new boats will develop in the future. We get the answer by entering the numbers in the example that applies to this. So, a 5% price increase per year, the new price this year is 800,000, and we will see what it will cost in 30 years since we want to see the development in the long run.

We then enter the depreciation in the "Buy used *" section and get an answer to what today's new boat will cost used in 1 or 30 years in the future, which also will give us an idea what, for example a 5 year old boat would be expected to cost today. Since we believe that we can finance a brand new boat by bank loans, we only enter the loan interest rate on "*Annuity* loans". The other information is already there.

In the first chapter of finance (chapter 10), we learned that if you can afford to borrow, you can afford to save. Therefore, we enter the interest terms in *"Final value of savings* "* which is currently 6%. And therefore, we save the same amount as we borrow to find equal conditions to compare. We can now read from the graph on the same screen:

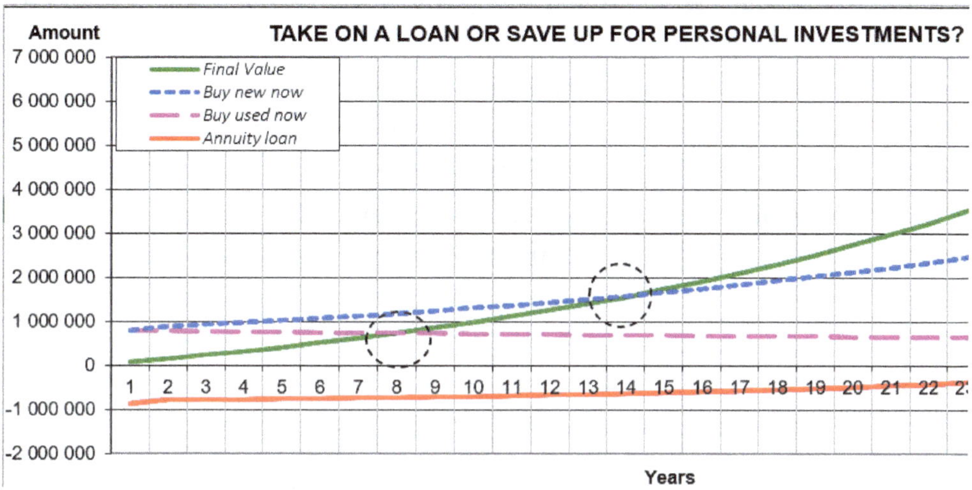

Fig: *Please notice the two circles focusing on the two intersections in the graph, showing the intersection of "Buy used now" and "Final value of savings" at 8 years, and the other intersection between "Buy new now" and "Annuity Loan" at 14 years*

Now, what is the point of the graph, what does it show you? Well, we use graphical analysis of the simple and straightforward kind. It gives us a picture of the situation that helps us to interpret the numbers we want to know about more quickly and more accurately. If you follow the dotted blue color line *"Buy new"*, and the green solid line *"Final value of savings"*, we see that these two criss cross at 14 years. I have drawn a circle around that intersection here, so it will be easier to read for you to understand the point of the graphical analysis. This means that if you start saving as calculated, you can afford to buy a brand new boat under these conditions, in 14 years.

If we follow the green *"Savings line"* you will see that it crosses the pink long-dotted *"Buy used"* line at 8 years of savings, which of course is a far better economic choice. I have drawn another circle around this intersection here in the book. Both of these intersections that I have drawn with *dotted circles*, are of course not so in the apps because you will put in other numbers. But I have done this for you to understand how to read your own examples faster. The choice between *saving* for a new or used boat is of course yours. In both cases, you will not expose yourself to debt, and the savings can always continue. It increases your wealth.

But if you borrow the full amount from the bank, you will be able to buy the boat today. And then you will be able to enjoy long, lazy summer evenings from tomorrow. But then you won't break even for 30 years, and that reduces your wealth. In addition, you may only get 3/4 back for the boat when you sell it. And we know that at the value of tomorrow's money is very little compared to today's money. We have calculated this in chapter 7. It may seem somewhat banal to point out this here, but this is an important economic point! We constantly do things we know don't pay off. We may be impatient without thinking about the consequences of the choices we make, or that we simply cannot bear to wait to satisfy our needs. That`s very expensive.

Now, we could discuss partial financing where we envisage a combination of saving and borrowing. We could perhaps imagine that we were the stock exchange's coolest investor and got a higher return there than with bank savings. Even though we know that this entails risks of the unpleasant kind. Or that you had saved a significant amount already and lacked so little that you wondered when you could buy the boat new with continued savings. Or the car, or the cabin, or whatever makes your knees shivering. But I can't make models for all possible eventualities, and I can't give you definitive answers for your life. I can't think for you either, so I'll show you how to think much smarter about your personal finances, without reducing your quality of life. I feel that you should be able to understand what you can use my models for and make such calculations by now, already. You've got so many smart models and tasks that you can switch between them? You should be fine if you have bothered to take all the *test-yourself-questions*. That's the point of them. Because what one wants to calculate is as different as there are wishes in this world. The only thing I've done here is to show you how to solve a problem with different elements. That's why I've combined the four different models that we've been through so far in the book. To sum up, there is the FV, NV, Loan and the Savings model. And then I show you how to interpret the data using a graphical analysis. As you know, a picture is worth a thousand words.

11.3 The tares and the wheat.

Some people in this country are a quite much better off economically than others, so to speak. Of course, this does not only apply to those who have been saving for 20 or 30 years already, inherited a rich uncle or won the lottery. The banks know this, so they pop up new products like popcorn to increase their own turnover like all other companies do. It's not hard to understand. They don't earn anything from products no one wants. The aim of the chapter is that we will simply learn to distinguish between the tares and the wheat.

Banks, insurance companies and other financial institutions attack us with one brochure or internet banners gaudier and more screaming than the other. Everyone offers their "*amazing products*" in ads with screaming letters and bold print about what you can "win" with this particular product, " *just click here*". If you ask your bank clerk (if you have one) about which product is the best of all, you will usually get an incredible number of strange noises from them. And not at least long politician-like answers. Unfortunately, none of them seems to become particularly wise. The vast majority answers you with counterquestions in return. It's old sales tricks, "*let the customer find the solution to their own problems. But let him do it with or with your help. Then you get the sale and both you and the customer are satisfied*".

Most people have noticed that things go up and down in this world. But since it is not so fun to see that our hard-earned savings are declining, we may stop subscribing to equity funds (we will go into more detail about stocks in the next chapter) when signs indicate a decline, as we have loss aversions. We sort of might just leave the money there "to see what happens", hopefully it'll bounce back up tomorrow. The financial institutions does not gain anything from that. After all, they make their money from buying and selling shares. One such product on the market is funds with guaranteed repayment of the deposit amount. The point is to buy a fixed share of $50,000 or $100,000 or maybe even more that is locked in the fund for maybe 5 or 10 years. Which means that you cannot sell your share when the prices skyrockets or plunges into the deepest abyss. Or whenever else you want. In return, you get your stake back plus any promised return when the locked period is over. Should things go too badly, you will at least get your bet amount back. Surely there must be something. Or have you learned otherwise by now?

Well, the alternative question is what you could have gotten if you put the money in a risk-free high-interest account instead, as you remember. If you think that the price increase will go up more than the interest rate during this period, you buy. And if you don't think so, then you put the money in a high-interest account, right? That is not certain, because we are not always as rational. The banks are so good at focusing on the probability that the future will be like the past. Which should mean that the world lives in its own bubble, without impulses and progress. Then the bank's interest rate terms shouldn't change either, perhaps? But about the future, we only know that most people are creatures of habits who only *occasionally* break their habits, nothing else. It is not for sure that the sun will rise tomorrow! The banks' borrowing and savings rates vary, so we don't live inside a bubble. However, the advantage of the bank interest rate is that it is risk-free, even if it varies. As long as the bank lives and thrives, avoiding a bank run..

You can check what your bank offers to you (read the fine print too) and take an alternative consideration of it all. How much is the share that you get back in 10 years really worth if you only get the guaranteed amount back? And what could they have become if they were placed and yeasted on the high-interest account instead? It's also really fun to calculate for those of you who have played with the models in chapter 7. If you buy a share for an estimated 100,000 and it it`s locked for 10 years while the market stay put i.e. stand still and your high-interest account in the meantime gave 5%, you will *not get* your money back. Because they are not worth more than just over 61,000 in the value you subscribed for. You don't exchange a tenner for a fiver, do you? Already as children, we quickly understood that it would be cheating ourselves after checking in the local candy store a couple of times. In other words, it's downright stupid, and we aren't stupid, are we?

If you had put this money in the high-interest account instead, you would have got both the initial amount it and a little extra back, but not if you let it stand and crumble in your salary account at 0.5%. Although that's slightly better than 0%. It is only with such considerations that we can distinguish the sausage from the delicious bacon that is wrapped around. But we must also never forget that when we talk about the future, we are talking about a hypothetical return. It is neither effective nor real until we have realized it. That is, when the money is in our account.

11.4 Refinance loans to enter into a long-term savings agreement?

As both a kind of warm-up and a foretaste of the next two chapters on risk and equity, we will take a look at another combination model. A smart way to sell mutual funds is to get people to refinance their house to invest the released cash in mutual funds. Smart by the bank, but it is not quite certain that it is smart for you. The bank(s) are great at focusing on the fact that historical returns have been this way or that way. And even though they say in a subordinate sentence that this is not a guarantee, they also say that there is a high probability that it will be high in the next 10 years because of the last year. That is what the historical return tells us! And then they hope that you are both stupid and greedy. Because they need to eat tomorrow like everybody else, and someone must pay that meal.

The point here is whether *you think* the stock market will give you a return that is at least as good as the interest rate in the bank. Otherwise, there is no point, right? What do you know about the bank interest rate in let's say 10 -15 years? What does the bank employees themselves really know about the savings rate in 15 years' time, for example? It may be a good idea to ask them more about this. Because these are questions you need to ask yourself if you don't one day suddenly get an unpleasant surprise! Since this is the book for ordinary students and wage earners who want to get a little smarter, it might be good to keep an eye on the next chapter as well.

I haven't shown you the points about the risk yet. Other than what we already knew before we started on ***Applied Personal Finance*** For the bank, that's fine, they make money every time you buy or sell a share in the mutual funds, plus they charge a management fee if it's their own fund. Of course, they also make money on the interest margin. And of course, they earn from fees and all kinds of commissions. It is quite smart to think twice, read the fine print, and not least to compare the amounts on the time axis. Right?

Let's take an example right out of the hat:

Let's say you only owe $550,000 left in loans on your house that cost you $ 6,500 per month. You will finish your loan (duration) in 10 years. The bank now suggests that you should refinance your house over a longer period of time, for example 30 years at the same interest rates as the past is 7.5%. The borrowing costs (on the new loan) will now be reduced to $ 3,900 per month, and the point is that the difference should be invested in equity funds. A whopping 2,800 per month for 30 years to an expected high return must make you a millionaire. We have already calculated that in the previous chapters, right?

Just try it out for yourself with the model for annuity loans from chapter 8. First the old expensive and then the new refinanced. Put the difference between old and new borrowing costs into the model for fixed savings and fixed returns from chapter 10. If you don't want to, you can go to the tab for this chapter 11, under the previous model we tested in *Fireat40.xIs* and try out the model *"Refinance loans to enter into a savings agreement"* which looks like this:

Refinance your mortgage to save the difference in mutual funds?					
Today`s excisting annuity loan:		Refinanced new annuity loan:		Savings agreement:	
Nom.interest (fixed)	7,50 %	Nom.interest (fixed)	7,50 %	Nom.interest (fixed)	7,50 %
Residual amount	550 000,00	New loan	550 000,00	Invested monthly	2 796,51
Duration	10	Duration	30	Duration	30
Monthly repaymer	-6 677,27	Monthly cost	-3 880,76	Final Value	3 469 885,46

But remember that none of my models are saying anything about risk! And that any savings rate in the real world is *floating*, while this model shows *a fixed* interest rate. As I said, we do not get better answers out of the models than the information and assumptions we put in it. The point is that you should understand how finance works so that you can use it yourself.

So, what do we read from the graph? Well, the first thing we notice is the intersection between the increasing solid (green in the spreadsheet) "savings agreement" that intersects the (pink) solid and falling graph *"Today's loan"* at 6 years. The shortened repayment period, compared to the 10 years you actually had left, is due whether you can afford to save an amount of 2,800 in addition to today's borrowing costs per month, which you then naturally get this savings interest rate on. The graph that accompanies the model looks like this:

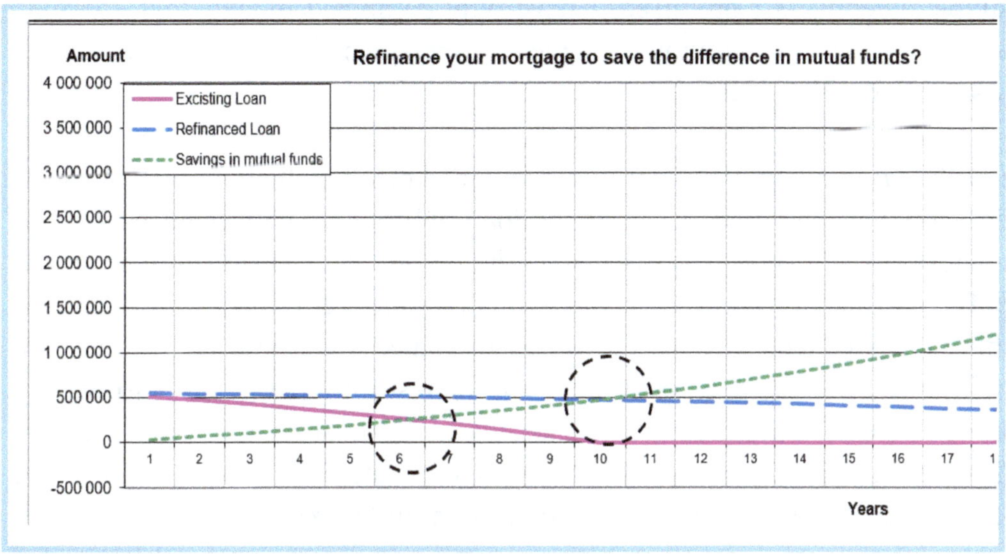

If you cannot save 2800 per month in addition to the current loan and therefore choose to refinance the mortgage to save this difference, you will be able to pay off the new loan after 10 years. We read this from *the intersection* between the blue dotted line *"Refinanced loan"* and the solid green line *"Savings agreement"*. Or you can choose to pay both amounts (the new loan and the savings agreement) over the entire period and then have 3.5 million in the account in addition to having paid off the loan in 30 years. We see this where the green dotted savings line stops, and that the blue dotted loan line intersects the zero line in 30 years. Yes, if today's savings and borrowing rates *remain fixed*. But...! They never do. Just below the graph (PgDwn) you will find a tabular overview of the numbers on which the graph is based:

Today's Excisting Annuity Loan:		Refinanced New Annuity Loan:		Savings agreement:		Interest on the savings agreement	
Totalt repayment:		Totalt repayment:		Totalt repayment:		Totalt repayment:	
After 10 years	801 272,60	After 10 years	465 691,80	After 10 years	474 749,10	After 10 years	139 168,30
After 20 Years	#NUM!	After 20 Years	931 383,59	After 20 Years	1 453 221,98	After 20 Years	782 060,37
After 30 Years	#NUM!	After 30 Years	1 397 075,39	After 30 Years	3 469 885,46	After 30 Years	2 463 143,05

The figures have the same premise here as always: *If the conditions do not change.* But the thing is that you don't get a fixed interest rate for such a long period. Nevertheless, it is interesting to look at such assumptions. Cool models? At least it's quite fun and educational, isn't it? Not that it's anything new and revolutionary. Because this is classic financial knowledge based on simple algebra, as I promised. I have only combined models that you have already gotten in previous chapters. And then have made reasonable assumptions. That's all.

But does it work out that way? No, we don't know much about that. What we do know something about is that the loan will cost us so and so much if the interest rate is this or that. Because in the future, the past is historical, so that only today do we know how things really were yesterday. That's the only thing that's certain! It is as certain as the bank wants you to pay back the money you borrowed at today's current interest rate. If you do not choose a fixed-rate loan. Only then will you know exactly what the mortgage will cost. But there is still uncertainty about the savings rate, it is always floating. We know that it can be profitable to save a little. Yes, if we do not get hyperinflation a la what the Germans got in the interwar period in the last century. But we will come back to that in chapter 14.

Now, you will not get test-yourself-questions with summary answers on this chapter. Since you have not got any new and revolutionary models, only combinations of the old ones you already knew, you should have time to digest the insights. And to see how you can solve your own questions. So, one point was to be practical with all the more or less new theory you have ploughed through these previous chapters. Another point was to prepare yourself for a bit high school material in the rest of the book.

I think it's time for you to create some tasks for yourself. Then you can see if you get anything sensible out of it. You have probably faced this type of questions in this chapter. Whether it is about financing a boat or a caravan, or whether it really pays off to borrow more money (a longer loan period naturally costs more money) and then invest the increased liquidity. Isn't it the case that increased income (or liquidity) leads to increased consumption? Well, generally speaking, that's probably the case. *But there are variations here, so maybe you know the answer to this best yourself?*

You can find more information about me and my books here: executivewayto.com or at fireat40.com

Chapter 12. Portfolio Theory and Funds

Since you now have got a model for calculating FV and NV of individual amounts, you can compare values over time yourself. You have also got the loan models as well as the final values of fixed annual savings. I also expect that the lessons learned from the chapter on the opportunity cost have really stuck in the small grey areas in our brains after the review in the previous chapters. Because we take them with us all the time, both the *"alternative costs"*, the *"many small amounts"* and the "*value for money*" principle. The lessons about managing your cash flow from chapter 12 showed that you are making a profit, right? I really hope so, and if not; have you made some radical moves to make a profit?

12.1 Other savings products

In chapter 10 I showed you some theory and algebra behind a bank deposit and final values. We called the formula final value (FV) because the formula calculates the future value of equal annual deposits over a longer period of time, but with a fixed return. We call it arrears probability when we receive the interest on the last day of the term. I have shown you how to combine the models to find answers to somewhat more complex personal finance questions without having to jump from sheet to sheet every time. I did this in the previous chapter so that the knowledge could stick and mature in your brain. Actually, you are now quite well equipped to avoid stepping into the worst financial traps of your financial life. I think that it is time to look at some more advanced material. This is when it really starts to get fun! Therefore, let's start with other savings products than pure bank deposits.

12.2 Confused?

Actually, there is a veritable amount of savings and investment products on offer every day. On a daily basis, we are bombarded by "unique offers" from banks and financial institutions with product names we are barely able to pronounce the name of. We have fresh memories of, for example, the SubPrime scandal 2008-2009 that left millions of Americans homeless, and the entire world financially shaken to its foundations. But the collective memory is short, and bankers also have to live and eat dinner. So those who work in the various financial institutions are constantly coming up with new products and throwing themselves at you whether you are inside the bank premises or online banking. In the past, you got tired of all the hassle and switched to the ATMs or went to the grocery store to withdraw money. But as the banks moved to online banking on the internet, they really got full information about your whereabouts, what you like, think and do, as they monitor you and guide you through the sales pitch. Actually in real time as you navigate their pages. I write much more about this, both what, how and why in my series of Mastering Business Management. It's no more advanced reading than this, but far more terrifying and yet entirely beside the point of this book. If you are interested in what they do with the data hey collects, or other books I have written, you can find more information on our website fireat40.com or executivewayto.com . So, we leave that for now and concentrate on your path to become FIRE@40.

There are almost no limits to the ingenuity of the individual institutions when it comes to the production of financial products to get their hands on your hard-earned money. It is easy for you to get lost, because everyone seems to promise almost gold and diamonds. If you just read the headlines. But now we know better! We do no longer want to let ourselves be fooled into something we don't understand anything of, right? However, a self-respecting bank does have several mutual funds to offer the unsuspecting customer. No wonder, because the bank usually charges both a commission, a purchase fee and a sales fee. So regardless of whether you buy or sell, the bank makes money anyway. This is also the case with stockbrokers. The more people who buy or sell, the more the brokers earn. Nowadays there are not so many brokers anymore, it’s rather stock robots trading. Those who runs the fund, or own the companies behind the funds, are paid in the form of a management commissions and other fees. And they charge at least as many fees and commissions as before all the stockbrokers lost their jobs. This is usually a fixed percentage of your share, and thus the fund's total size. In this sense, both the sellers and the managers make money regardless of whether the stock market i.e. your stocks skyrocket or plummet. But only you lose when everything is racing downhill.

We are daily pumped full of financial news from almost the smallest TV and radio station that wants to update you on what you should and shouldn't do. Chief economists, chief analysts and financial journalists comes forward with their recommendations daily. Some advices are good, while some is downright bad. When you read, hear or see such information, you must never forget that the people behind the information in almost all cases simply have a job to do; make a living from being heard. Foremost to receive their own payroll, not necessarily making you rich in a snap.

How much insight do you really have to assess what is being said? Now the insight is about to become quite good after playing through seven chapters in this book. And your insight and knowledge are constantly increasing, hopefully! Especially since you are now able to do quite a lot of calculations using *"Fireat40.xls"*. Soon we will increase our understanding a notch deeper. In this chapter, you will not get any new models, and therefore no tasks. But in any case, my best advice to you is that you must be both active and selective when reading or listening to such information! Who speaks out about what, and for what purpose? What is actually being said? As the famous Roman lawyer Cicero already 40 years B.C. said, *"Qui Bono?"* (*Who benefits from this?*). In this chapter, we will discuss a couple of new key concepts, but there will be no mathematical deductions. We only take on the theory to better understand the basis of the different products.

12.3 Portfolio theory

We`ll start with some theory at the beginning. A *share* is a security that shows that you have bought a piece or *a share* of a limited company's *total value*. Or put another way: The stock shows not only what value you own in the company, but also what loan the share (your share) you have lent to the company. If the company does well, you will probably get an interest back after the fiscal year has ended and the books are closed, called a *dividend*. Also, you can benefit from the rise of the *stock value*, as the company grows and get wealthier. But if the company perform poorly, your share (value) drops, and if they go bankrupt, you lose all your value in the company.

Perhaps you already have bought a share in a mutual fund? Either way, you can't have avoided hearing about them. As you know, they consist of a fund that you buy a share of. The purpose of the fund is to buy shares, and both secure your money, and get the most return on this money at the same time. The more unitholders, the larger the fund's total investment in equities. Surely the return also increases. But no, that`s not at all true. I will explain in a moment what I mean, and why that is.

The money in the fund is invested by hopefully skilled professional investors who do this for a living. The money is not only invested in a single stock (one company) listed for buying and selling shares on the stock exchange, but a fund is invested in many different stocks. If we have several different stocks, this is called a portfolio, and this is what the fund focuses on. We have several different stocks because we want to spread the risk. This is called *diversification*, and the philosophy is simple: *It is stupid to put all your eggs in one basket when the road to the marketplace is full of bumps, potholes and highway robbers.*

The theory of diversification is true in practice. This can be proven statistically even if we don`t go into that here. The Norwegian professor Jan Mossin at *NHH – Norwegian School of Economics* was one of the sponsors of the development of modern portfolio theory. Central to such portfolio theory is the concept of risk. We have slightly touched this in an earlier chapter. If I ask to borrow $ 100 from you for a year, you will demand a lower interest rate from me if you consider it fairly certain that I am able to repay you, than if you just think it is just quite likely that I am able to repay.

In other words, it is the same mechanism of risk assumptions as on lending. Or when the bank wonders if they dare to lend you any money. The same mindset is used if you choose to spend the $ 100 on buying a single share instead. The greater the risk that you will not get your money back when you want to sell the stock, the greater the return you demand in the first place. No one likes risk, neither as a private individual nor as a professional investor.

You can read more on risk aversion in my book Fire@40!, but you recognize this mechanism. But we all want higher returns, right?

Let's take an example:
Let's imagine that we have a hundred dollars left over at the end of the year. We can't quite decide whether to buy stocks or government bonds or put the money in the bank. But the bank's interest rate is too low. Let's say that government bonds yield an interest rate of 10%. In addition, there is no risk associated with the bond. The government bond is guaranteed to pay both the deposit amount and the interest when the period is over. We call this the risk-free interest rate since we know that there is no risk associated with lending the money to the government, just as we call bank rate risk free too . Let's say that the choice number two we are pondering on is the stock of the company Oilspeculers Ltd. The company needs money to drill for oil in dry wells in the country of Farinstan. The company has a revolutionary technology, but the sale of the shares is slow. The share costs $ 50 each, and the company also promises to pay an annual interest rate of 14% to speed up sales so that oil exploration can start. We call the difference in return between the government bond and the stocks for a risk premium. In this case, it is thus 4% of the 14% . If we only buy government bonds, we get a risk-free return of 10%. But we have become committed capitalists and want more. But we don't want too much risk, because we need the money next year. Therefore, we diversify and buy one share and put the rest in government bonds. The expected return will be 12% (14 + 10) / 2 =12, while the risk will be only half of if we buy shares for all the money. We are sure of the state.

But things tend to go up and down in this world. For some companies, it goes up at the same time as it goes down for others. Ice cream sales plummet if the summer is wet and cold, while sellers of rainwear and umbrellas rejoice. This is called an *unsystematic risk.* We can reduce this unsystematic risk by buying shares in both the rainwear manufacturer and the ice cream manufacturer. Then we have two shares, and the risk is reduced as you well know.

Without going the way of mathematical deductions, we can say that when buying 5 - 6 different stocks, the risk is significantly reduced already! You can also see that in my figure below. We can continue like this until the risk becomes so small that it does not diminish no matter how many more different stocks we put into our portfolio. The remaining risk that we cannot get rid of is called the systematic risk. We show the theory with a graphical representation (again) since these are easy to understand:

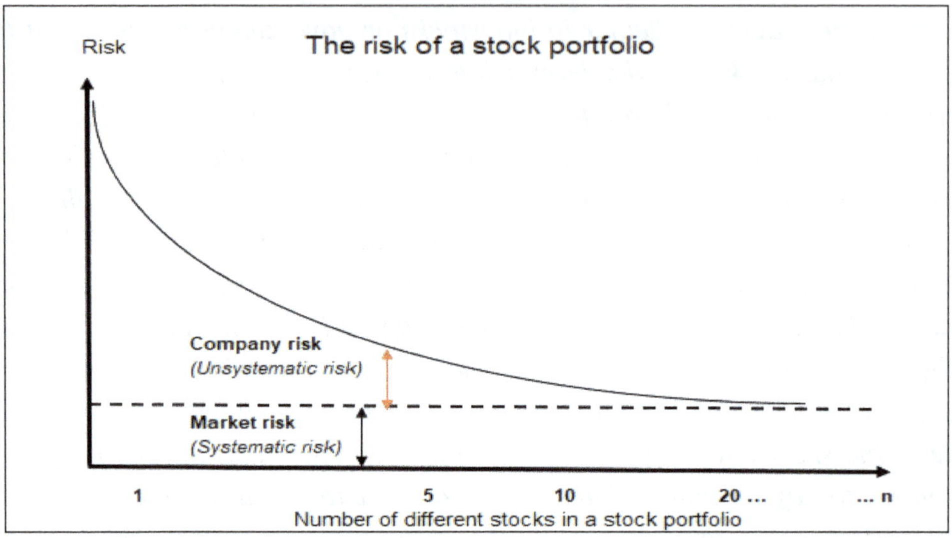

Fig: *The relationships between total risk and the number of different stocks in a stock portfolio. The unsystematic risk decreases quite quickly already at 5-10 different stocks in the portfolio. As you can see, we don't get much done with the market risk, which is expressed as a straight dotted line.*

We can see here that already when investing in only about 5 different stocks, the risk is significantly reduced, while with some 20 stocks, the risk can hardly be reduced any more. We are talking about the diversifiable risk, which is the corporate risk, or the unsystematic risk mentioned. This business risk has to do with the company(s) itself and is affected by, for example, our interest in buying the products, the companies' financial situation, the management's and employees' skills in production and operations. Among other things.

But we do not get rid of all risk when it comes to stocks. The remaining risk will stabilize at a level that we referred to as market risk or systematic risk. This market risk may include changes in electricity prices, changes in oil prices, major interest rate changes governmental politics or perhaps major national or international events such as a pandemic or a major war.

12.4 Totally on the curve!

So far portfolio theory and a little about diversification to reduce the risk on our investments. So, you know that we cannot get rid of all risk. No matter how much we hope and believe, and no matter how much we diversify. Both you and your neighbor and everyone else could decide to sell their shares tomorrow. When everyone wants to sell and no one wants to buy, prices plummet. Anyone who can't sell is left with the sh**bucket and loses everything.

But the stock market is not the only alternative place to the bank where we can invest our savings. During this chapter, you will hopefully understand enough about the relationships between risk and return so you can better look after your own interests. Or your children's if you have any. Don't just blindly rely on "experts" and headlines. Banks are surprisingly good at focusing on how good returns have been. And then they're pretty good at suggesting that it's likely going to be that way in the future as well. Unfortunately, there is not a single person in the world who can look into the future. Therefore we cannot predict the future price of a share, or the share price, with certainty.

It would be easy to answer what is the best fund if someone had calculated all the products the bank or insurance companies offers. This has probably been done at the bank, but it is unlikely that your bankier has done so. So why don't you just ask your bankier what he or she has bought themselves? And then ask why the bankier chose that option? There is a difference in both return and risk between different types of products. You know that risk and expected return are linked.

Bank deposits are so-called risk-free, but they have a floating interest rate. If the interest rate goes up, you get more in return than if the interest rate goes down. At the opposite end of the risk scale, we find individual stocks. If we draw a picture of the different types of products banks offer on a scale that shows the relationship between the products' risk and return, we get something called the risk curve. It will look something like this:

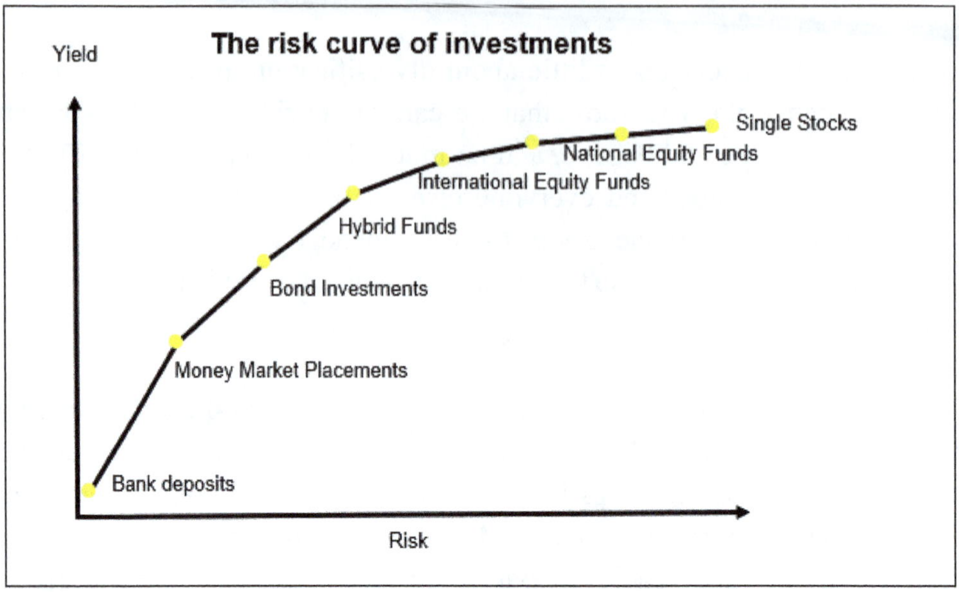

Fig: *This picture explains the context of risk and yield of different investments*

As you can see from the figure, the return does not increase proportionally to the risk we assume! In that case, our graph would have been a straight line at a 45 degree angle from the origo (the zero point, where both scales meet). But it does not. You can also see that the individual stock has a much greater risk than a national equity fund, while the increased return is not proportionate to the increased risk. But you know this, because you read the previous paragraph about portfolio theory, right? If you skipped it, it might be a good idea to read it now while keeping this curve in mind. And then I hope you look at it as you have to deal with the different investment products you have to sniff at. We start with the most speculative first.

12.5 Single stocks

The stronger the upturn, the more people have opinions about different stocks at the stock exchange market. No matter what you say to others, deep down you do not want to have to struggle 12 - 15 hours a day for 365 days a year for your entire life for some boss you might think is a real jerk. Since you are an ordinary student or wage earner, you will at least not have your hard-earned money to just disappear into the blue sky. Let's agree on that, whether you are a hobby socialist or a hobby capitalist. There is nothing wrong with the argument, it is as correct as it gets. We want to spend time with our loved ones, have fun with our hobbies or whatever else. Everyone wants the best possible interest rate conditions, regardless of political background and regardless of the form of savings. In other words, the best possible return.

If you think the interest rate on your loan is too high, you argue with the bank. Or you switch banks. And if you get a lower savings rate than your neighbor, you complain to the bank. Or you switch bank again. At least you should. If you get more out of your savings than you originally intended, you can buy something else or something in addition, save the money or give it to charities. It doesn't matter if you vote outermost red or outermost blue! If you are going to sell your apartment and get twice as much as you gave when you bought it, you naturally accept the money. Because the next apartment you're moving into is so horribly expensive, right?

If you don't know anything about stocks yourself, why do you think an ordinary cashier at your bank knows a whole lot about it? Because it's their job? Well, their job is almost like at the checkout counter at the grocery store around the corner. Even though those in the bank call themselves *advisors*, and even though the bank has renovated the premises and removed the counters. They no longer store large piles of dollars because everyone pays their bills in online banking and otherwise uses credit or debit cards. Their job is like another salespersons, selling different product. And they often have only superficial knowledge of such complex investments products. For such calculations, there are already applications and programs. As I said, you won't get any of me here, because it's a bit too advanced for the points of this book. Here we will first of all present the theories in an understandable way and then enable you to make the most important and common of the interesting calculations yourself. In other words, learn how to tell what' s the sausage and bread in the hot dog, like the MEAs and MBAs do. There are separate associations for members that advise members on stock issues for particularly interested persons. So, I recommend you seek for such associations if you're interested. But the ordinary citizen would rather drive the children to sports, to plant in the garden or to go to church rather than to calculate β-values. If you don't already know what β-values (*beta values)* are,

then just forget the word right away. It is advanced material and is beyond the purpose of this book.
If the risk-free deposit rate in your bank is low, "speculators" like you and me will look for alternatives that provide better returns, or less risk of the same return. But bank savings are risk-free. So, we throw ourselves into the stock market, which offers slightly better returns but much more risk than what the bank provides. But there`s this little thing about risk that we tend to forget. We stare blindly at the percentages, because that is the measure of the return, and we are all greedy. With greed, as a rule, comes carelessness. When everyone invests in stocks, it becomes less likely to pick winning industries or single stocks. In other words, the returns levels off, without the risk being adjusted in the same direction. But all companies can go bankrupt, at least that's true.

What does the concept of return on equity means in this context? We already know that returns in this context are called *dividends*. As owner of one share, you own one part of everything in the company. When the books are closed by the fiscal year, and all taxes and wages are paid in full, the stock owners share a certain part of the profit. This profit is divided into all shares. One share, one part of the profit. The dividend is thus the return the company gives you for borrowing your money (the price of the share) during the period you own the share. More precisely economists call this *the return of invested capital ROI* . The company's *dividend policy* determines how much of the fiscal years profit the stock owners will receive from this year's profit. We can get the return in two ways. Either we can get an annual dividend, or we get a return by the share price rising in value. Most people hope for both. If you are not already an economist, you have probably not heard of Miller and Modigliani. Without going deeper into Miller and Modigliani's *"Dividend irrelevancy Theory"* and an inference about assumptions about efficiency, transaction costs and tax regimes, we can briefly summarize their theory as follows: *Whether the shareholders receive a dollar in interest (dividend) or a dollar in a price increase is irrelevant to the shareholder.*

Of course, there are pros and cons to everything in this world. But right now, it's time for an example of returns and reasons for stock market fever in recent years:

I have a friend who works in a company called Megadeal Ltd. The company has developed a special product for feeding farmed fish. But developing the product has cost blood, sweat and tears for both employees and owners. Yes, not that there is any difference, because the 3 employees own all the shares. But in order to make a living from this, they must have money both for food on the table and money to market their product. From my friend, these other two have heard that I am willing to take risks and have spare money. So, they ask if I want to join the adventure. The shares are not listed on the stock exchange but can be sold freely without clauses or commitments from the owners. The principal price of the share is $ 1,000, - but I have to pay $ 2,000 each. All forecasts show that the firm will make good money since the product will revolutionize the entire aquaculture industry worldwide. The product is ready, sales are next. I say yes, but I don't dare to buy more than five shares.

Those who sell their shares to me (the original owners) have now doubled the value of their shares since they obviously can be sold for at least $ 2,000 each despite the fact that they are not making any money yet. I gamble, or speculate, that they will sell their product and make a good profit, which in turn will give me a dividend next year in return. If I had paid $ 3,000, they would have tripled their value. While I, on the other hand, have not increased my wealth whatsoever, only reduced my liquidity because of this investment. I have also taken on a risk since things can go wrong with the company. I can actually lose all the money I have invested, but that's easy to forget in the midst of all the enthusiasm about getting rich with the company.

*After a couple of years, the company has done well. The company has such a large profit that the accounting value is $ 2,200, - per share. So now I have an unrealized gain of $ 200*5 shares, (11,000-10,000) = $ 1,000, i.e. 10%. It remains unrealized until I can sell the stock to someone else. For now, I don't have realized any profit unless the company starts paying dividends. They do not intend to do this, they need money for marketing, salaries, public taxes and fees, etc. But I have another friend who is willing to take risks. He has heard from me that I own shares in this company. So, he asks me to buy one. But I believe that the stock will rise further since the product will soon be introduced abroad. Besides, I don't need the money right now. Only when my friend offers me $ 3,000 for one share do I say yes and sell. The remaining 4* *shares now have a potential gain of totally $ 4,000. But after my friend brags about the stock and his future prosperity to yet another friend, he sells it for $ 5,000 a month later, that tricker.*

Here lies the seed of the understanding why the *free stock market* goes *"through the roof"* in different periods and then plunges into the abyss in other periods. This is explained by economic bubble theories, the so-called *"Boom-Bust theories"* of both Minsky and Kindleberger. I'm not discussing their theories here, as it falls under more advanced studies. But since I'm at it, I can mention that the Austrian economist Schumpeter almost a hundred years ago described that the economy moves in waves, the so-called *"wave theory"* in his book *"The Theory of Economic Development"* in 1934. So do the movements in the stock markets. I will show you in a minute.

Economics and psychology are two sides of the same coin. This explains a lot about how investors manage risks. The expectation of the stock's price or future return determines whether the price goes up or down today. It is thus the overall belief in the market that determines whether we buy or sell shares making the stock market rise or fall. It is investors' *overall belief in individual stocks* that leads to the movements *in the entire equity markets*. The waves are caused by investors' fear and greed, euphoria and depression. I can show the psychology of the stock market with the help of this graph:

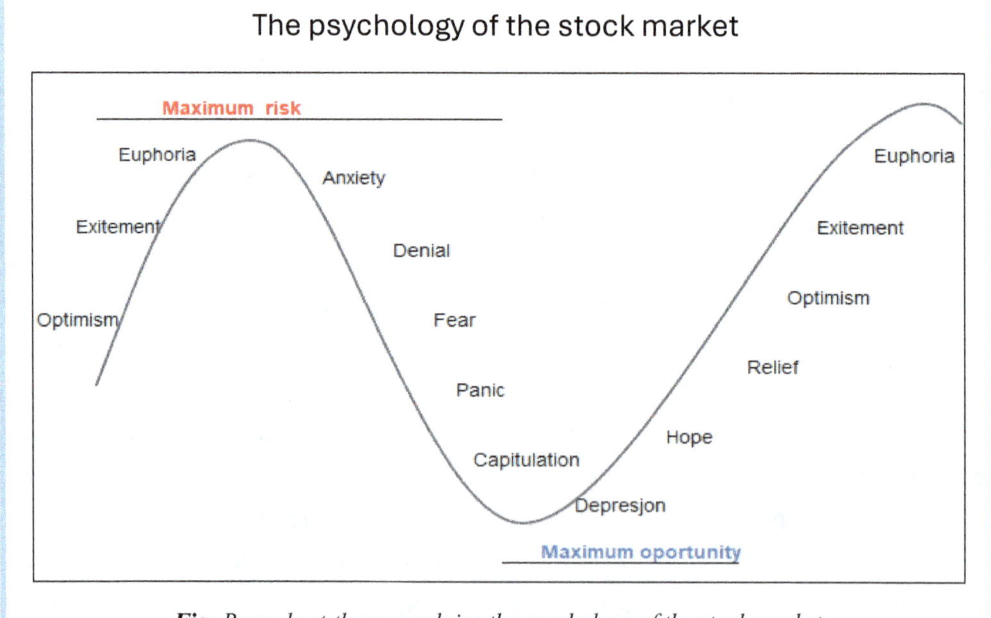

***Fig**: Boom-bust-theory explains the psychology of the stock market*

We call it *stock market fever* when about *"everyone"* jumps into the market in the hope of getting rich overnight. More and more people want to join the upturn, and this pushes the upturn further upwards. Because when prices just rise and rise, the word spreads, not only among investors but in the media. And then further among you and your friends.

Those of us who have survived one, two, and like me three financial crises, are astonished. One would think that people have learned. But the collective memory is very short, and perhaps it is the case that those who should have learned at the time never had participated? I don't know, but I noticed that the slower the price increases, the more people talked about the fantastic returns that *"just have to come soon"*. If the market has decreased, it can just go up again. Because everything grows into heaven, doesn`t it? However that's when you just as well should sell out completely for a period, until the downturn is over.

12.6 This is how to become a stock millionaire! Or…?

However, high risk and low prices seem to attract all hobby speculators, more or less experienced. In this lies a not so little lottery effect. The hope of the big win makes us small savers jump on almost any shares. *"The stock is cheap according to the news; they can surge tomorrow!"*. Even if the company doesn't make money on anything? And never going to produce anything that anyone might be interested in buying? Because if the stock is cheap enough, it can be sold expensively, right? Well, maybe it can, if it's cheap enough. And if you can sell a penny for a dollar to someone you don't know at all. But what is cheap? In any case, it is not a concept of value that is detached from the share's (firm's) intrinsic value in knowledge, technology, production equipment, bank accounts and the like. We will look at this a little later, in the chapter on assessing the stock's price.

So, let's continue with Megadeal Ltd, which "really does do well": My friend who bought one of my shares for $ 3,000 sold it straight on to another friend for $ 5,000. This means that the four shares I have left of the ones I bought for $2,000, now have a potential (and unrealized) gain of 4(5000-2000) = $ 12,000! Yay, I feel rich! Even though, that value is not real until I have* *actually sold my shares. So far, I have only sold one share and had a realized return of 3,000 - 2,000/1,000 =50% on that one stock. And it's much easier to focus on a 50% gain on one stock than 10% on the entire investment. It kind of makes a little better for our self-esteem!*

It is *so* easy to focus on the high price on that *one share* sold at 5 times more than the principal price, because now, this is the actual asking price which all new asking's should *start* at. So, actually this is where I get an itch for more and want to keep my shares for as long as possible hoping for even increased prices. Because the price will probably go straight to the sky. It's "free money" and I would like to have more of that.

*The following year, I found out that several people have sold shares in the autumn. Now for 7,000 each. Despite the fact that sales of the products abroad have not yet materialized, I think that many would be interested in a stock that has had such a fantastic increase in prices. I have now an unrealized gain waiting for me for the whole (7,000 -2,000) = 5,000 * 4 = $ 20,000. That`s twice as much as the investment itself in the first place. If only I had gotten many more shares at the time I bought them, I would be a millionaire today! Yes, if I dared, and if I could have bought 200 shares. This is how to become a stock millionaire! At least on paper. I have now reached the point of euphoria on the figure "Psychology in the stock market" in the previous section.*

That's much better than being an "ordinary" millionaire who has done a honest work and sweated for his money to save in the bank, isn't it? In addition to the thousand dollars I realized last year, the sale of the remaining 4 shares at this price will be an adventurous return. But I need the money for a divorce settlement with my ex-wife, so I look around for buyers. And while I'm doing this, it suddenly comes to light that the product brings with it the unpleasant side effect of the farmed salmon is dying. But I still haven't lost anything. So, I'm offering my shares at a slightly lower price at $ 6,900 each to get rid of them. I'm now in the phase of denial.

But even now, no one is interested. I am therefore quickly offering the shares at $ 5,000 each and know that I still have not lost anything in this bargain. I`m now *in fear* of losing everything. There is still no interest, because now people get the smell of loss. And we`ll do almost anything to avoid a that. No one wants anything but a gain. In my *panic*, I therefore soon *desperately* try to offer the shares at only $ 1,800 each. Without success. Then I suddenly read in the newspaper that the lawsuits for damages are now pouring in against the company. So, no one wants the shares. Finally, I reach rock bottom line in capitulations but meet an opportunist and get to sell 3 of my 4 remaining shares for 10 dollars each.

There is actually a difference between realized and unrealized gains and losses. As long as I don't sell, I have neither lost nor gained. I have only tied up capital. Only when I sell the shares cheaper than when I bought them, or bankruptcy, regardless of the par value of for example, at $ 1,800 or $ 1,500, do I get a realized loss. If the company goes bankrupt, I have lost 100% of the original investment. Not everyone is aware of that fact. Therefore, many amateur speculators sit on stocks until they are worth about zero. They fear a loss more than a win and desperately hope for a miracle that will send the course up to new heights.

*As you can calculate, I have now realized a loss of (2,000-10) = 1990 * 3 = $ 5,970, minus the $ 200 I earned on the first share; a total of 5,770 so far. And then I have a potential unrealized loss in store for $ 2,000 for the last share that I bought for $ 2,000. And when the company is finally declared bankrupt, my realized loss is thus as much as $ 7,770, and that`s no fun!.*

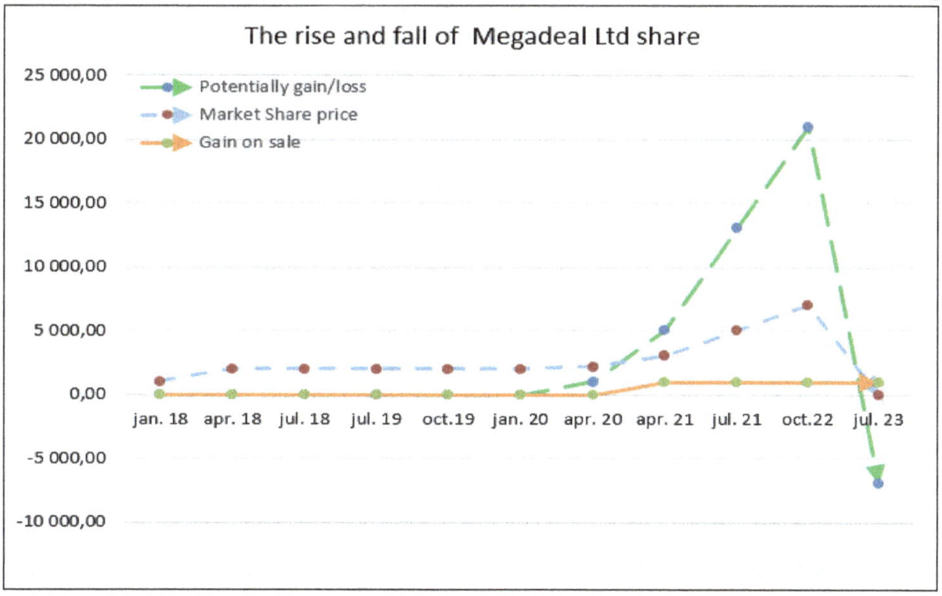

Fig: *The development of my gains and losses on the shares in Megadeal Ltd.*

Actually I know of someone who claims to have *"made millions on the stock market"* despite the fact that both the tax administration and I know that he won money on the lottery! Because in times of stock market upturns, there is naturally more prestige in "winning" on stocks that require a knowledge and insight most people don`t have, than winning the lottery, a game of chance where everyone is on an equal footing. But I actually also know someone who made millions on shares without knowing anything about it. For his own part, he could just as easily have won the lottery. The case was that during a financial crisis and collapse in the markets, he worked in a computer company where the department he worked in was separated from the parent company. The employees who followed over were distributed shares instead of the salary they were owed in the parent company before the company was spun off. But the new, separated company had a product that they eventually made very good money on because a lot of people wanted to buy it. On top it all, the product was neither morally nor ethically reprehensible. And it does not litter the environment either. Which are important points in themselves.

Strangely enough, the closer the price of a listed share gets to 1 dollar, the more amateur speculators come into the field. By the word amateur speculator, I don't mean all of us that don`t spend a lot of our times or have the stock market as their all-consuming and passionate interest. I mean all the rest of us who throw ourselves on the stock exchange in lottery fever, and off again in pure desperation. The reasoning behind such hysteria is as simple as it is wrong: *"I'm buying a share for 1 dollar today, because the price will probably go up to 2 dollars tomorrow since the stock was sold for 5 dollars last month!"*.

So why is this reasoning so deadly wrong? Well, because the amateur speculator has not taken into account the substance of the company (what values are the basis for the price), how liquid both the company and the shares are, etc. You buy a share on the basis of a price today, just because it is cheaper today than yesterday, and you therefore expect it to rise in price tomorrow. But this does not say anything that is *certain* about the price tomorrow. It's not really promising when the price has plummeted from $ 5 to $ 1 in a month, is it? Of course, this does not mean that you cannot make money on such a share, because it can be grossly underpriced for various reasons. Like in the case of a short-term depression in the market, for example, like what we call a market shock. But a glance at the shareholder list (who owns the shares) would probably reveal that all professional investors disappeared when the price was $ 5. Now you may wonder why.

12.7 Assessment of the share's price

Let's say you've now both been a little inspired, but also well warned about how wrong things can go with shares. If you invest in an unlisted market, i.e. in companies that are not traded on the stock exchange, the risk is as described a couple of chapters earlier in the portfolio theory. We have also just been through an example of unlisted shares in *Megadeal Ltd*. What we have not discussed further is how to evaluate the shares on the stock exchange, i.e. the shares in the *listed* stock market. Seems everyone gets rich there these days!

Therefore, despite the warnings about *Megadeal Ltd*., you have considered investing a little on the stock market. You can't blame me if you lose all your savings, remember the precautionary principle. If you are going to enter the stock exchange, you must expect to be able to achieve a better return than the banks' borrowing rate. Your approach to the market can quickly become the example in *Megadeal Ltd*.'s development. That is why the warning comes now, before we go any further. You are hereby warned!

The case is that shares, and the stock market are quite exciting after all. That's why you get financial news and stock market announcements on TV and radio several times a day, whether you're interested or not. Every day. Although some say they don't care, most are either scared or greedy in relation to individual stocks and the stock market. And that's exactly what drives the stock market: Fear and greed!

In any case, it is entirely possible to have a sober view on the stock market, and of the various individual shares. We first started by showing the risk on the various savings products that we are offered by the banks, and then we went on to look at portfolio theory, before I gave you an example of how badly it can go when you are first cautious and then become greedy. And how wrong it can go when you are just greedy. But now to the topic: *Why does the shares cost what they do?* How do you go about assessing the companies' value/shares? And what do all the different abbreviations mean? So, for the record, let's go over some of this now.

Since we do not address accounting analysis, or KPIs in this book, it will not be necessary enter valuation or mergers and acquisitions. For these topics, there are large, good and very thick textbooks reserved for those who have abilities and interests in advanced mathematics. We'll take that to the next level, when and if that book eventually comes out. However, I think it might be a good idea to have an explanation of different abbreviations and what they mean. So, we'll start with the share price in relation to the company's earnings - you've probably heard about the P/E ratio. It is a key performance index (KPI) figure that tells us something about the value of a share i.e. price per share, and therefore the entire company. We use this KPI to compare companies in the same industry, or sector. Therefore, different sectors have different P/E since they operate in different industries. For example, a P/E of 10 means that the stock costs 10 times as much as the company's annual profit. Assuming that the dividend payment is fixed (strictly speaking it never is), we write the formula for P/E as follows:

$$P/E = \frac{\text{Price per share}}{\text{Risk}}$$

If you do not know the price per share but the dividend, you can calculate the P/E as follows:

$$P/E = \frac{\frac{\text{Dividend per share}}{\text{Risk}}}{100}$$

There may be other ways to calculate this. As I have already revealed the dividend per share, which is the return or interest payment you receive for borrowing the share value to the company, is never really fixed in the long run. We can use the previous expression above but include *net interest* from bank interest minus annual growth in the calculation.

We can therefore calculate the P/E of annual growth in the following way:

$$P/E = \frac{1}{\text{((dividend pr share / (risk free interest – yearly growth) x (div.pr share /risk free interest – yearly growth)}} / 100$$

If you want to use pen and paper, or build the model in Excel, you can test the following numbers:

Dividend per share: 10
Risk-free interest rate:7.85%
Annual growth rate: 1%

This should result that the price should be:
Share Price = 145.99 and P/E = 21.31

If the stock is sold at a price other than this, it is either *overpriced* or *underpriced*. In other words, if all else is equal, a high P/E will indicate that the stock price is "cheap" and conversely, a low P/E that point to the stock is too expensive. Still, you have to see this as a *rule of thumb*, because there is no absolute answer when it comes to the stock market and the valuation of companies and their shares. In a business economic sense, we think that value creation occurs when a company uses less of the income they generate, then they create added value. There are a number of key figures to assess both how these values arise, where they come from in operations, and how the company uses the values they create. Such key figures are based on historical data, and all business economists must take various exams on such courses, which are often called something that includes *accounting analysis* or *financial statement analysis*.

In addition, there are a number of more or less mathematical ways of assessing how the company will do in the future, based on how the company performed in the past. As mentioned, there are professional companies that hold advanced courses for private individuals and members. In addition, you can find various online courses of varying difficulty and price that you can complete. For those who already have an academic degree, there are of course various courses in *economic history*, *valuation*, *value creation*, *financial mathematics, finance and investment* and a number of other interesting academic courses that also give credits. Check with your preferred business school.

It is no coincidence that stockbrokers usually had to have both a master's degree in finance, and preferably an additional education as a financial analysist. Today, there are not so many brokers left, they are too slow compared to the stock robots, which trade on the basis of advanced mathematical algorithms in a matter of milliseconds. Nevertheless, it is the case that many professional players fall into the trap of forgetting basic valuations when euphoria arises in the stock market and stock prices rises and rises and the trades must take place at a lightning speed. Today, stockbrokers have been replaced by lightning-fast stock robots. In fact, the battle for the best stock robots is no longer about the fastest servers, but how close *to the wall to the Stock Exchange's server* you can place your stock robot! However, you do not have to compete with the robots, you can manage yourself, being smart and careful.

It is difficult to give a definitive answer to what a good P/E is. The thing is that P/E is used as a "metric" to compare the expectations we have for earnings in an entire sector, or an entire industry that is engaged in the same type of business. Another thing is that we must remember that P/E changes over time, because the dividend, or dividend per share, is in the numerator in the fraction we calculate. Therefore, the P/E can be both above and below average at times. Before we get into this, consider that it may actually *be* that a company with a high P/E is a far better investment than a company with a medium or low P/E. However, we do not dive deeper into the matter here, but end this discussion with some rules of thumb; remembering there is *no definitive answer*:

0 – 13: Lower than expected, the company is not doing so well
13 – 20: Expected level
21 – 28: Above expected, the company is delivering better than expected
28 + : Highly overstated earnings, may indicate bubble tendencies

If you want to be successful with P/E as a helper in valuations, you need to do a thorough analysis of the potential and risks of each stock that you are considering investing in, and P/E alone is never enough. Some may have a strategy of investing in companies with a low P/E because they believe that the stock is underpriced. But this numerical value in P/E can therefore be used by professional investors as a *filter* to find stocks that *do not* fit into their investment strategy. But again: If you are interested, take on a class and join an investor association. If you are moderately interested and do not want to *day-trade,* then buy funds. But anyway: Check the different fund managers' many fees and commissions because they can vary a lot, and that affects your return.

12.8 And then what?

When the market for loans dries up because everyone have invested in shares, the banks have to borrow from the central bank, which does not lend as cheaply from its savings account as you do. Or maybe they lend out cheaper. This depends on what the central bank thinks about everything that has to do with the country's economy, recovery or deterioration, but also on how they want to affect tomorrow's economy. Please refer to my books *"Fire@40!"* or *"Applied economics and Management"* on macroeconomics for more details on this matter But the bank must get money to lend since they make a living on the interest margin. Or, in fact, they live off *the net interest income*, not entirely on the interest margin. And if you are not already a banker, you have probably not heard of *net interest income* before, only about *the interest margin*. So, let's keep it in short:

The interest margin is the difference between the average lending rate and the deposit rate for you and me, i.e. the difference between 1% and 2%. But neither we nor the banks live off percentages. If banks only profited from the interest margin, they would not have had quite as long periods between the times when they correct their interest rate in relation to the central bank. This is because it is *the net interest income* they actually earn money from. At the risk of teasing good bankers, we can explain net interest income as follows: Net interest income (in $) measured as a percentage of average total assets. *This net therefore includes interest expenses and income from other items in the accounts, not just what you and I contribute with.* It is also affected by how the bank hits the market with its interest rate policy. Both in relation to depositors, to borrowers and the rest of the market.

Well, back to stocks and interest rates. When banks have to borrow money expensively from the central bank, they again have to adjust their lending rates to you and me. But when the lending rate from the bank goes up, sooner or later the borrowing rate to the market must also go up. Even if the banks delay the deposit rate to the market (your savings rate) for as long as they can. This is the case until the difference between shares and bank savings is so small that the risk determines whether you would rather put the money in the bank than in shares again. Because now, we are reminded of the specter of risks.

If you have no debt, but a large bank account, you will now get a better return than before on bank savings. If you have a lot of debt to the bank, you now get spanked. Regardless of whether you threw yourself into the stock speculation or not. If you have shares, you may consider selling the ones you may have. When everyone thinks like you and sells their shares around the same time, the result is that the price drops. And when enough people do it at the same time, the prices plummet at the stock exchanges. Or housing market, for that matter. Sad for those who don't pay attention or can't sell at a reasonable price. Please take another look at the *"The psychology of the stock market"* figure explaining the boom-bust theory a couple of pages earlier on. However, it means savings goes straight down the drain! Unless of course you have ice in your stomach, believing that the companies in the portfolio will not go bankrupt, but have a hope that the companies will very soon start making really good money. Or perhaps they already do, and you spot no clouds on the horizon for them. But if you have borrowed money from the bank to invest in shares, you have really swum on a trip out from land. We do not call this speculation, but gambling. Without you even realizing it until you're about to drown. Because you have to pay on the loan that you got to invest in shares. It costs money to pay interest as you well know. In addition, you may lose a lot of money if the share price plummets. You may have to sell them as well because you have to pay the bank. So, then the stock price plummets further.

In simple terms, that's how it all works. At least for you and me. When everyone is doing the same thing at the same time, this affects others who affect us in turn. Hence the phrase that "*there is a lot of psychology*" both in the economy in general, and in the stock market in particular. If you don't already know much about stocks, but would like to know something more about this, the bets tip is that practice makes perfect! There are a number of incredibly talented hobby investors. The "hobbyist" aspect of it is just that these people are not paid by an employer to engage in their investments and speculation. Because their hobby is a passion. You can learn and train yourself by pretending to invest in individual stocks, while in reality you are not spending a penny. You can build spreadsheets and list stocks you believe in and follow the development in a graph. If you have a hobby for many years, you will usually become very skilled after a while. Whether you're hunting or fly fishing or trading shares. As you know, it takes a few years and a little sweat to get "the black belt" of your passion.

By the way, did I tell you that I have a friend who works in the security industry? No? Well, then I'll tell you now. *He called me a couple of years ago in connection with share prices that surged sky high. Interest rates were historically low. He wanted both some general-, but also concrete tips on which individual stocks he should invest in. He spoke excitedly about the "new economy" and the crazy price rises on the shares that rocketed there. He talked about a friend who was already a multi-millionaire on shares in the company he worked for. So, I asked him what this friend did in the company. But he didn't know that, because it had something to do with "the new economy". So, I then asked what this amazing company made. But he didn't know that either and replied a little annoyed that he had already said that "it had something to do with the new economy". But his friend made money like nothing else, because he had just bought a Mercedes for over a hundred thousand dollars. And only after working in the new economy for half a year!*

To make the story short, the tip to my friend was to in general buy shares in two or three mutual *funds* if he could spare the money for eight to ten years. He got a little angry, because he thought about the forty or fifty percent that he hadn't gotten this year, and he figured that it might be over one hundred percent in a couple of years. A reminder that we do not live on percentages naturally fell to the ground. Because when did economists stop talking about percentages? My point is that percentages are a measure of a difference, and the fact economists are able to see the difference between a historical return and a hypothetical possibility of a return. And then we may also remember something about risk. I also told him that we can't all make a living by cutting each other's hair, even if a few people make a very good living from it.

So, what exactly was this "new economy"? Not many people could answer that. But we got the impression that it was an economic revolution. As if all economic thinking had to be discarded and redone. In other words, the principle that *"I have an item that you want, and you have an item that I want, so let's exchange"* was powerless and dead. Although modern man uses money as a medium of exchange. Because money simplifies the valuation between your apples and my oranges. And then we don't have to lug around with a load of apples and oranges every time we need new shoes, a loaf of bread, a handyman's service, a house or other things. Only the youngest and coolest were involved in this new economy. And this had something to do with IT and the internet. On daily basis we could read with wide eyes in the newspapers about crazy stock price increases in this industry. And the media's sensational need to sell column meters and advertising-financed airtime followed up with new economic talk shows, programs and share games on TV. In the IT industry, it became normal to receive shares instead of salary. Stock millionaires were created overnight. To the extent that you were allowed to sell off shares to finance your daily needs for food and shelter. If the share was listed, that was OK. But most were not, and it is difficult to sell unlisted shares to buy a loaf of bread. Some had to go to the bank to borrow money for their living. Of course, the bubble busted.

It's astonishingly easy to pick up trendy words, without necessarily getting any understanding or meaning of it. So, when a 40 year old man trying to look like a teenager in a tired T-shirt and jeans stands on a stage and shouts to the audience that *"I'm going to invest 800 mill in the next few years!"* and in addition, creating a hallelujah atmosphere in the hall, I shy away in horror for several reasons. First of all, it is usually the case that someone who uses the word *mill* hardly has any understanding of the real value of money. It just sounds so cool and fancy! Secondly, any hallelujah mood in an economic context will make all my warning lights as an economist flash brightly right away, it sounds like the first step into a Ponzi pyramid scam. Thirdly, because *"the next few years"* are just as unspecific as a cheap trip to some unspecified banana republic. There is obviously a lack of substance in all corners and edges. At least among the "preacher", and absolutely among the majority of cheering and whistling participants. Fourthly, one should ask oneself where *that* money will come from. And fifth, *the "new economy" was* nothing more than a new market channel. In other words, a new place to market existing products.

Well, if you already havc a small portfolio with high risk, without possessing deeper insight than what you have read in this book, I can put it as briefly and concisely as in I got in trouble to end the conversation with my friend: *"When all police constables throughout the country want to play stock market sharks, you have to sell everything you can. Not buy!".* Immediately I must rush to apologize to absolutely all police forces in any country, because they have done nothing wrong in this respect. I don't have anything against them either, on the contrary. But this was the advice I gave my good friend who was just that, a policeman! Perhaps it is not so strange that he got angry? But he learned an expensive lesson: if you ask for advice, it may be smart to consider it. Even if you don't like it!

In the aftermath, these "stock-based" TV shows was taken off the air when the financial crisis became a fact. And one should of course ask oneself about the role of the press in the bullying of the market that took place. *"Qui bono?"* as Cicero said a couple of thousand years ago. We have all gradually realized that the new economy was nothing more than a new market channel. It was as revolutionary as selling advertising on shopping carts. And that is not a new economy. In fact, industry representatives had to admit that this was not a question of a new economy but a hype for a new market channel.

12.9 Equity funds

Most private individuals investing in the stock market, is buying one or more equity funds, but so do institutional investors to. These funds hold shares in many different companies. After reading the chapter on portfolio theory, we have now understood that it is smarter than buying just one single stock with all our savings. Diversification reduces risk. Therefore, we trust that those whose job it is to manage our savings by investing on the stock exchange know what they are doing. And then we know that the fund has diversified into a portfolio of stocks on the stock exchange. If it is an international fund, it has spread the risk across different stock exchanges around the world, different industries and perhaps in different financial instruments.

We have been told that the *index portfolio* has risen by as much as 18% in the last 5 years. Can we expect them to continue to rise just as much in the future? We have also been told that these are long-term investments that we have to leave be there for the next 5-6 or 10 years if we are to become so rich that we can just lean backwards and take a vacation for the rest of our lives. Unfortunately, this is not the case, as we have now begun to realize during this chapter. There is no reason to trust the fund sellers blindly. As we know, they make a living from trading shares, and they sell even more if prices rise. The fund managers charge every year a management fee (percentage) of the fund's total value, so they make money right down until the last share of the fund is sold at a value almost equal to zero. They also charge a minimum fee every time you buy or sell a share of the fund. This is important to keep in mind because as you know it reduces your return.

As we have learned from both the portfolio curve and the risk curve, national mutual funds have a significantly lower risk than individual shares. We are now aware of this as we know something about risk and diversification. An equity fund has diversified the risk across several or perhaps many individual stocks. We also have two types of funds, depending on the management`s view of the market's *efficiency*. Efficiency means that all information is known to everyone at the same time, as is the case in, for example, the exchange market. One type of fund is called index funds, and the other is called active (managed) funds. The difference is in the name. The actively managed funds buy and sell shares perhaps several times an hour or a day, trying to beat the market. In other words, they realize that the market isn`t fully efficient. The index fund has a somewhat more laid-back strategy since they follow the theory of an efficient market with all relevant information is baked into the prices of all the stocks in the market at all times. In this respect, they are more concerned with securing the return from the total market-, the industry or other sectors in which they have specialized.

To what extent is the market efficient or not has been discussed for a long time. And since they do not completely agree, we do not take on the discussion here. But an index fund will have a broader diversification than an actively managed fund. Therefore, let's just state that there are different types of funds and that you need to think through. Preferably before you do! And either way, you have to be careful, because the likelihood of losing money is regrettably high. An economics journal made a major comparison of equity funds a few years back. The theory behind the survey was that someone has to be the best. And if you are the best, you are best both in upturns and in downturns. The journal thus wanted to see whether the theory was consistent with practice. A statistical comparison was therefore made of all the equity funds in all the stocks between and against the stock exchange's total index. The fact is that many equity funds give a return that is relatively good in boom times (stock market boom). But they often give relatively poorer returns than the upswing would suggest, and they also simply lose relatively much more money in stagnation or downturns than what the market would otherwise suggest as natural. The conclusions was that not everyone can be the best at the same time, and unfortunately most of them are bad regardless of the ups and downs in the market. It is no fun that your equity fund gives a total return over a four or five year period of - 4%! Nor that they manage to land at 2% when the central bank's inflation target is 2.5%. We barely touched on the difference between nominal and real values in chapter 6 but will go into detail about inflation and real interest in the chapter 14. But, if you are going to buy into an equity fund, you must find the two or three best funds that also have the lowest management fees and diversify your investment between them. The tip is that the best are best in both upswings and downswings. The really smart thing is therefore to make such an independent investigation yourself.

Personally, I think there is good reason to treat the individual mutual fund as if it were a single share. By this I do not mean that you should trade (buy and sell the shares) daily or weekly. You must have a long-term perspective, otherwise you can just leave it alone. Diversify in the funds and have an active role in relation to them. Which means that you can have both an index fund and an active fund. And preferably more than one of each. But if the value falls to a limit you have decided on in advance (for example 10, 8 or 5%), you should consider selling and putting the money in a high-interest account instead. The best funds are the best, regardless of whether there are booms or busts.

International equity funds vary considerably in terms of investment profile. Some invest in just one country, others in just one continent, while some invest globally. Some are industry-specific, while some spread further across different industries. Some invest in three, eight, or maybe twelve specific countries. Some may only invest in the Far East, some only in Europe and some only in North America. Some are index funds, and some are actively managed funds. We can see from the risk curve that such funds have lower risk than national equity funds. But here too, it is important to remember that some people are the best regardless of the rise or fall. Things are not necessarily going well in Europe and in the Far East at the same time. So, it is important to find the ones that are suitable for you and your risk profile if you want to invest in such funds. I am therefore referring to what you have already read in the chapter on risk and diversification. And then I appeal to your common sense.

12.10 But...

There are a number of other savings products between extremes such as bank savings and risk-intensive individual stocks on the national market. From combination funds to annuities funds with investment options. We could have gone through all these as well, but then this chapter would undoubtedly have turned into a whole book on its own. It is neither my intention, my goal nor my ambition. My goal is for you to understand diversification and risk so that you will be more able to think for yourself. Without letting yourself be fooled into something you don't understand. Then it's better to stay clear! So that's why we took on the extremes for the sake of illustration.

If you feel that I am saying a whole lot without giving you any clear advice, you are of course absolutely right. It is not my job to give clear advices in the form of buy or sell orders, or about what you should or should not do on financial matters! In addition, I constantly hammer on that when it comes to the future, we must make reasonable assumptions in the absence of exact science. We can calculate until we turn blue over what $ 5,000 a month for 30 years will be if the interest rate is this or that. This is exactly what fund traders do. We can predict until we turn green, and we use fairly advanced statistical methods to find out how likely it is that it will be this way or that way. Because uncertainty means risk, and we don't really like that. We are in nature risk adverse. Alike is the professional investors. If they make an investment, they do so with their eyes wide open and a calculated risk.

I will not make choices for you, although I would like to help you better understand how economists with an MEA or MBA view these issues, to understand the opportunities you have yourself and the consequences of the choices you make in the way they do. It is not for sure it will rain tomorrow just because it rained both yesterday and today, even though meteorologists are trained to do such predictions from very advanced statistical calculations. They fails too. If you buy shares in a failing market, that's of course perfectly fine. You have of course studied my figure of the psychology of the stock market earlier in this chapter.

If you choose to borrow money to buy a car rather than an apartment you need to live in when the real estate market is sky rocketing, that`s fine because it is also your choice. You may be able to live in the car. And it may be that you know more about the country's population growth than everyone else and therefore see that the market will plummet in 10 years because there will be more apartments than need for households. Or that you have a healthy skepticism about the real estate agents' prediction that the price increase in the housing market will increase by 50% in the next five years because they did it in the previous five years, or just because there has been a slight decline in the last two years. It may also be the case that you assume that almost no one learned anything from the different financial crises, stock market crashes, real estate crashes and other financial crisis of the past 40 years. So you now understand that the conditions in the long term are otherwise the same; people have to sell their houses cheaply again because they can't afford both the increase of interests- and living costs. In the meantime, you can rent or stay with Aunt Edna and expect to make a bargain in a few years. Both in the real estate market and on the stock exchange. It is your assessment, your choice and your clear right. But now you have more knowledge than before, hopefully.

You can find more information about me and my books here:
executivewayto.com or at fireat40.com

Chapter 13. Gearing and Tax Effect on Debt

If you haven't noticed, you must be pretty slow. There is nothing that happened in the happy 80s, troubled 90s, or in the 2000s that is not happening today. Just look around you at the car fleet, at the average person's interest in the stock market, the turnover rate in the housing market and not least the prices of both homes, cabins, cars and yachts. One may ask oneself whether this is not the land of milk and honey. And maybe it is just that, at least for those who know how to adapt to the shifting conditions. Like for example you who read this book, so that you will be better equipped in the future.

13.1 Gearing is not necessarily something you only do in the car

It's true, shifting gears isn't necessarily something you do in the car. The expression actually comes from the English word for shifting gearing i.e. the car. This is by the way one of the shorter chapters so far in the book, we will deal with this now. Well, plus we will deal with the tax effect on debt too.

Anyone with respect for themselves have two cars, no matter how many you can drive at the at the same time. And of course you have a cabin. And if you don't own one yourself, you use your parents' cabin and refer to it as if it were your own. You have your self-respect intact, of course. But you just pretend, because of SoMe (Social Media) you think everyone else lives like that, and you don't want to be any less. We are much more afraid of "losing" the race of personal prestige than of winning personal happiness. Especially since the medias every single day is telling us how the economy is skyrocketing these days and that we are so much richer than yesterday. If the neighbor has a car craze and changes cars every two years, then we want to do the same, and if he starts playing golf, then we certainly have to do it that too. Because now everything is going so much better, and we are so rich in this country. Or maybe not.

With the introduction of smartphones, Facebook and other SoMe came a new type of social behavioral competition of posting selfies with a lookalike happy grin, establishing the *"come-to-look-at-my-successful-self"* trends. These influencers turned more than one generation women into unhappy people undergoing all kinds of plastic surgeries whilst ending up in debt. Never really as happy and satisfied as the selfies appeared to be, always looking to peak, being more extreme than the rest. Most of them spent money they didn't have and ended up in deep debt. Because with such a consumption pattern of hair, clothes, travels, parties and restaurant visits, they spent money they did not have but borrowed. Never really happy and satisfied, always looking to be outperforming the rest, being more extreme. One thing is falling into the debt trap; even worse it is when it is on short term consumer debt, as we have seen in chapter 9 in particular. Then personal finances goes really bad really quickly.

But every action has a reaction. The unhappy generation of "Fac`ers, Tiktok`ers and Insta`ers" are now turning around to the need of being in harmony with nature and things that are free, natural and real. Silicone breasts, make-up, fillers and Botox are out. Natural look without it, camping and hiking in the wild nature and growing your own free vegetables are in. But it is just as expensive to remove silicone as to put it in, so these people must take on another consumer loan to do so. This happens almost parallel to the rise of interest rates all over the world. The real value of wages have actually been stagnant or decreased since the early 80s, while all other prices have risen. And now the interest rates have increased rapidly and will stay on this more normal level for a very long time. Perhaps you now understand why I have built up the chapters in my book in the way I have. The previous chapters are leading somewhere. Because now reading this, you remember something from almost all the previous chapters and therefor see connections you probably didn`t earlier. The people with high life living on borrowed money is in a way living life on borrowed time. The personal finances does not add up. Many people all over the western hemisphere have had to take on more jobs because wages do not keep in pace with the cost of living, rising interests and especially the extreme rise of housing prices. *"The working poor"* is a term that`s no longer only an American phenomenon. It`s spreading rapidly throughout the whole Western world. Despite both one and two jobs, you can barely get by.

13.2 Saying what...?

Now let's assume that you live on a nice street with decent neighbors. Not of the overly strenuous kind, but quite OK. Everyone are normal wage earner as you are. You need a new car but feel like you can't afford it. Let's say you simply haven`t been able to save any serious money for the past 10 years. You could say that the 90s were hard, but it hasn't gotten much better since, and the Subprime financial crisis in 2008-2009 led to mass unemployment and a lot of people in the United States having to abandon their farms, land and houses ending up in trailer parks or even worse. Fortunately, economy have gradually picked up again. Over the past couple of years, all of your neighbors have suddenly bought new cars and many of them have started a complete renovation of their bathrooms or other expensive projects. The cars in the parking lots in the street where you live can rival any other street and the craftsmen run back and forth between the houses like frightened chickens. Activity is sky high. When there are so many people in such a short time spending so much money on new cars and are doing heavy renovation projects, not everyone can have won the lottery. The general wage level hasn`t really kept up with inflation in the same period, so this cannot be the reason either.

So, what have they all done? In chapter 10, we learned that many small streams could turn into large rivers over time. But has the interest rate level been so artificially low since the Covid pandemic? In fact, so low that you also feel that you have a little extra in everyday life because the mortgage on the house has become easier to handle. But the explanation cannot lie here, because in terms of age, there is not much variation between you and the neighbors. One does not earn much more or less than the others. It is probably worst with the salary of the newspaper carrier. He is the youngest of all but still has one of the street's most expensive cars. Perhaps in youthful arrogance? No, it must be something your neighbors have noticed, but not you.

Over the past few years since the last financial crises, you and your wife "sat quietly" at home and paid loans and ongoing expenses. Not undertaking any big financial excesses. Your economy has been quite tight despite two good and stable incomes. It has been quite tough to get by, for most people. For the neighbors too. On top of that, the homes were bought at prices that reflected a completely different interest rate than today's. But you have persevered and kept the home, because it has been the first priority for your family. In the media, you could read and hear about those who were forced to leave their real estates. Selling the home because the housing expenses eventually exceeded the salary income. Perhaps one, or both had lost their jobs due to bankruptcy after the bank collapse. Many peoples who owned their homes had to sell it for half the price of what they had bought it for on top of it all! It hurts because they are left with a debt, but without underlying values. The bank that had lent 100% of the real estate value in an overheated housing market just a decade earlier, should naturally have repaid what they had lent out.

It was terrible times! But you still managed, even if you were tired of constantly eating oatmeal for breakfast and spaghetti for dinner. Never treating yourself to either holiday trips or home renovations. Even though the wallpaper in the living room was getting so ugly that it wasn't really nice to stay in the room anymore. But what has happened these years you sat quietly as mice? You saved money of course. Your owned house is what we call your equity. It is just the same with all your bank accounts, cars, boats and cabins as well. That is, if you have any. So, we can say that your equity is everything you own minus the debt you owe. Admittedly, one can call the repayment of debt as "forced saving" if it is encumbered in *real values* that you can sell at a later stage. But what the real value is, may not be easy to determine until these are realized through, for example, a sale. Because you must have a place to sleep and live, and the bank must have repaid the mortgage, otherwise you will be sent straight through the door. It is not very attractive, especially in this cold climate.

13.3 What is the thing about keys and numbers?

When you pay off debt, i.e. the repayments on your debt, you have been "forced to save", so to speak. Let's say the past 10 years. This must hopefully pay off in some way, even if the debt may be expensive. First and foremost, because the debt-to-income ratio is significantly lower now after 10 years than when you started the loan. You know that after going through earlier chapters in this book. You did not only pay interest, but also installments during these 10 years. And the further into the loan period we get, the faster the remaining debt goes down on a loan. The downpayment on debt is saving and increasing your equity, though. We remember this now. In addition, the housing market has recovered and even rosed further on before it continued to skyrocket. The home you bought 10 years ago, and you thought might double in value in these years, now has maybe quadrupled. So, you are now even less leveraged, because the *debt-to-equity ratio* is now far more comfortable. We understand now that leverage has something to do with the debt-to-equity ratio. At least when we talk in economic terms.

We can calculate the debt-ratio according to the formula: Debt/Equity. We call this a key performance figure, or economists terms, KPI. If we say that the household's total debt is $550,000, and that the total equity is $ 1,500,000, then the *debt-to-income* ratio should be 36.67%. The debt is thus just over 1/3 of their total values. It is not at all a bad debt situation as long as your income isn't declining. So we say that you are *low geared*. But as house prices have skyrocketed, banks have adapted to the economic sunshine. In the wake of the *financial crisis* in the transition between 2008-2010, the banks would not lend any money to each other at all if they could avoid it. They didn't trust each other, they didn't trust you, and they didn't trust the market in general. In the aftermath, when the darkest clouds were gone, banks were less restrictive. So, the general recommendation was a key figure of the maximum debt burden or debt ratio should not be more than 2-2.5 times the household's gross income. It has to do with the leverage, even if it is just another way to attack the debt relationship. It means that the debt-to-income ratio is 0.4 - 0.5 to the total income of the combined household.

But the banks are *co-cyclical*, which means that in upturns they shuffle money out for loans to almost anything, whilst in downturns they squeeze the money bag so hard that almost everything in society stops. In other words, the banks exacerbate all problems in the market, it is only when the society floats calmly the bank markets function sensibly. You probably remember the importance of the central bank's goal of keeping inflation stable *«on trend"* i.e. 2%. But the banks make no money if they do not lend out the capital that has been deposited, as I explained earlier. You see, 20 years ago, the banks wouldn`t lend out more than maximum 3 times the total brute income of the household. However, as real estate prices has skyrocketed the past 20 years it is not possible to borrow enough money to buy a house with such restrictions. At the time of writing this, banks have adapted and increased their recommendation of the debt-to-income (DTI) ratio. It is now almost doubled to 5 times the household's disposable income. That is, they have almost doubled the recommendation in 20 years!

It is perhaps not very strange that this key ratio increases when you know that over the course of a decade an apartment could cost 1 million in one year, 1/2 million in the second year and 3 million in the third year. The debt must be repaid regardless of what the home is valued at, at the moment, so the banks have extended the repayment period from 20 to 30 years whether they think you live that long or not. The bank can always claim the house and resell it to someone else and this is the problem from the subprime crises: When the mortgage follows the properties instead of the people, and people lost their jobs, the banks owned the mortgage and the unsellable houses that actually functioned as a lease. So many banks went bankrupt, creating even more unemployment and a malfunctional banking industry at the same time. The fact is that you can hardly buy an apartment for 5 times your income today because the asking prices is often 10 times your disposable income. That tells us a lot about the problems in the property market. People don't have that kind of money, they don't think their able to pay the loan, they can't get big enough a loan, or they don't like the property. Or maybe a combination of all these factors and some more making houses unsellable.

Put in other words, the market price is not linked to the utility value, although we expect that there is a certain connection here. The market determines what the home is worth paying for, not the valuation of the appraiser. Now, there are many reasons why prices have gone through the roof last decade, and it is not just because the appraisers receive a commission on the selling price instead of a fixed salary. Without going through all the details in this context, we can point on increased liquidity in the banks and their increase of liquidity, to an unnaturally low or negative real interest rates (we will treat this in the next chapter), missing or poor housing policy that leads to a low degree of development in which again does not keep up to pace with an ever-growing influx of people to the cities as the most important factor. But don`t forget, there are always some people that have the money, or have parents with that kind of money. Also, when housing prices where low and liquidity high and the Air BnB platform came, a whole lot of people speculated in buying flats for renting out. And for the sake of a simple comparison: If a plane has 500 seats, and 5,000 people want to travel on that particular plane at that particular time, the prices per seat quickly go skyrocketing according to the initial asking price, just like stock in the stock market.

But in any case, it means that the real estate market prices has increased significantly. And in order to be able to give you a loan because banks have to make money too, today they have increased the recommended DTI ratio and at the same time increased the repayment period from 20 years to 30 years. And they have also come up with a new concept, *mortgage credit*, which works like a credit card does but at a better interest. In other words, there is an agreed loan balance within 80-100% of the home's value today, with a mortgage fixed to the house. You can use the granted credit as you wish, and in many cases, there is also a full interest-only period.

There is a warning here, because every action has a reaction. The recoil in the interest rate market occurred at the back of the government's Covid support and the artificially low interest rates from the central banks, which caused all living costs to rise rapidly, i.e. inflation. That in turn caused central banks to raise interest rates to curb inflation, which increased your bond and other loan interest rates. In addition, we now have Russia's attack on Ukraine in February 2022, (actually from 2014!) which again pushes all prices for oil products, iron, technology and not least grain products (Ukraine is one of the world's largest grain exporters) to skyrocket. At the back end of this, loan interest rates have tripled in line with inflation. This means that if you took on a loan around the artificially low covid interest rate and did not stress test for double or triple interest according to the central bank's trend of about 2% inflation, you are now struggling with an interest charge of 7-8% on the mortgage, which may also be "fully financed" a 100%. That hurts! Many people are crossing their fingers and hoping that interest rates will fall back again as inflation slows down and seems to stabilize around "trend". But that hope is futile, one should almost expect a normalized mortgage interest rate of 2.5 - 3 times the central bank's "trend" for a long time. And at least double and perhaps triple this again for current short-term debt such as overdrafts, consumer loans and credit cards as we saw earlier in this book. Until the economy becomes so bad that the central bank has to stimulate the interest rate market due to a poor national economy. More on this in my book *"Fire@40! (Applied Personal Finance)"* or in *"Applied Economics and Management for Business Executives"*.

However, in case that your mortgage interest have been risen by 3 times, and you hardly can cope with the interest alone, you cannot afford to pay instalments any longer. In that case, you are sitting in the debt trap until you can pay installments or sell the house at a better prize than you bought it. That's why a lot of people now must take on another job, a second job to manage all the costs of living. But as all the costs of living, the inflation and the interest to your bank increases more rapidly than your wage(s), it is an open and serious question if you will ever get out of this debt slavery. If so, you have now become one of the middle-class *"Working poor"*.

Whatever the reason, your apartment may not be sold at a price that covers your debts at any given time. Therefore, the bank will hedge in relation to your salary. In other words, we can say that the bank considers both your credibility and your apartment as a project. They look at the likelihood that you will be able to make a profit and pay your debt before they consider whether they will accept you as a client trusted with a loan. It has to do with risk, we know about that. The calculation is made according to the simple formula:
*Total gross income * debt-to-income ratio = maximum recommended debt.*

If you and your wife earn a total of $ 400,000 total, no bank will give you a loan that is so large that your total debt exceeds $ 2,000,000 at maximum. In practice, this factor will vary depending on the type of loan, the type of home you are buying, the location of it, and how secure your jobs are. Because whether you are able to pay your debt or not, it is actually owned by the bank until it's all paid for. If you are unable, the bank have to sell it again at a price that covers their lending plus a little more. When potential buyers smell a foreclosure, they will haggle as hard as they can if they dare to present an offer at all, and that's only going to hurt you. Banks run a shop, not a charity. Be prepared for the fact that the debt-to-income ratio may vary from bank to bank and from state to state if you consider the loan market.

Let's take on an example:

*You are single, and the apartment you want to buy is a sensible one with a bedroom, living room and a kitchen in a more affordable part of the city's residential area. The asking price was $ 800,000 and you earn $ 250,000. Can you fully finance the apartment in the bank? It is both a question of how old you are, how long you can draw on the loan and some other factors. But your debt-to-income ratio here will be 800/250 = 3.20. If the rules of the bank dictate 3.0 (in fear and recession), you will not be given the loan. But if their limit goes to 5.0 (in upturn and excitement), you are within the limit values. Otherwise, it may be good to remember that the bank rarely finances more than 80% of the loan appraisal, even in upturns. So how do you finance the eventual rest anyhow? Not so smart with top loans or consumer loans, regardless of upturns or recession. That is the highway to poverty, I showed you that in chapter 9. So, what do you do? Well, luckily, you had started saving already from your confirmation or bar mitzvah. You have some equity from before, let's say the whole $100.000,- Will the bank finance the remaining $700.000? Maybe, because the $ 700,000 will only be a little more than the bank's magic 80% limit which is (800 *0,8- 640) = $640,000. Your debt load will now be (800,000 - 100,000)/250,000 = 2.8 times gross income. Otherwise, let`s hope your parents are rich and willing.*

Ever closer to the goal, anyway. But certainly not at the finishing line without more savings, more equity or monetary gifts from mom and dad, friend and family. If they can afford to help, that is. This has been the case throughout the Western world. House prices for "normal housing" have increased from approx. 2-3 times gross annual income to 8-10 times! It is completely crazy, and it leads to a housing crisis everywhere. For example, in Rome, it is so expensive nowadays that newlyweds often have to stay at home with their respective parents for many years because they cannot afford to buy their own homes! Neither in up- nor downturns. It is particularly bitter for the young generations who have no responsibility whatsoever for today's housing prices. Or for the generation of their parents who are divorced and newly established on their respective sides. Or who may still be happily married but are at an age where they may never have learned the "lesson of saving" themselves because the conditions were so much better at their age. If they are around 40 years or less, they have never faced a real financial crisis themselves but were perhaps students preoccupied with whatever matters the young generation are. So, they can therefore not impart knowledge or capital to their children in the establishment phase.

Only when the loan market has levelled off and is not rising because no one can buy a home at that price will the banks consider lending 100%. But by then the market has already stagnated, i.e. in a way is "over the top" and you probably recall that behind the top of a bubble there is a downturn. No matter what the smiling real estate agents claims in the media. The banks have to sell a certain amount of loans because they run their shop on what you pay back, and the real estate agents have a certain amount of housing to get food in the stomach tomorrow as well. But some of us have been involved in this before and learned the lesson well because it stung hard in our wallets. There is hardly a better teacher than your wallet. And there is nothing to indicate that the different banks have learned much more than the rest of the population. Unfortunately, the collective memory is just as short here as in the stock market or among politicians! So, when banks advertise 100% financing, maybe it's time for a bit caution?

13.4 Let's gear up!

Let's say you have a mortgage on your house and are considering doing what all the neighbors in the street have done for the past year. You may have almost completely paid off your debt. The neighboring house was sold last week for $ 1,5 million. Your remaining debt is currently only $125,000 and now you pay almost only installments, so the debt deduction in the equation is getting smaller and smaller year after year on your annuity loan. But you still want this gorgeous silver-grey Audi A 6 that I spoke so warmly about in an earlier chapter.

Since you are so low leveraged that your debt-to-income (DTI) ratio is only 0.08 (125/1500 = 0.08), you now receive a letter from the bank stating that you will have your interest rate adjusted *down* by 1% because of this. So, your loan is 1% cheaper in a snap, just because now you are not so dependent on the bank, than when you really needed them. The bank is thus quite desperate to keep its customers, especially you who are able to pay. Because you can be tempted with new loans. But of course, this has to do with the risk. The banks calculates that you and your wife have a debt factor of only (debt/income ratio) 125,000 / 400,000 = 0.31. This is low, your total equity is currently: 1,500,000 -125,000 = 1,250,000,-.

Now, of course, you can get a loan from the bank, which the bank points out in the same letter where they promise to lower the interest rate. *"Do you have a dream you want to realize? Let us do the financing for you!"*, they chant further in the letter, "*Do you have a dream of a cabin, a new car or a yacht? Of course, we will help you!"* They want to earn their money so that they get food in their stomachs tomorrow, too. They know that you are able and willing to pay, you proved that in the hard decade. You have become a *gold customer* with a very little risk. And then you have probably become middle-aged and gray-haired in the meantime.

Now let's gear up the equity a bit for the sake of my example:
*Since you are owning an apartment that the market will give approx. $ 1,5 million for and the debt is vanishingly small, you can realize parts of the value. You can actually borrow up to 80% of the value of this apartment. Because you have security in the apartment. And because there are an upturn and boom times. Otherwise, the apartment would not be so highly priced. But we must remember to deduct the old debt, because it must be settled sooner or later. At the latest is when you refinance your mortgage. You can borrow (1.500 - 125)*0.8 = 1.1 million at the best conditions! For this sum, you can realize an Audi A6 for 150,000 (chapter 6), the cabin in the mountains for 300,000 (chapter 10), and maybe the nicely used sailing yacht for 450,000 (in chapter 11) as well. And then you can give 100,000 to little Ole and little Liza each as a start-up capital for their apartment sometime in the future. Without going beyond the 80% rule that gives you new and pleasant conditions. If you are willing to borrow more...*

You now feel rich, you are probably middle-aged, you may have gray hair and a small "age bump" on your belly. But you're no longer low-geared! If you really borrow 80% to finance these dreams, you are *normally to high geared*! If house prices and all other prices hold up and do not make strange antics, that is. If the economy rises, all the prices of homes, cottages, new cars and new boats will also rise, reducing leverage as your debt does not increase but decreases as you pay it off. Also, the total interest will decrease. It will be easier to handle the loan. Whilst if there is stagnation and recession again, you are suddenly high geared. Because the interest will rise, and you have started on a new loan that will be harder to repay. And which you will not finish until you are well into an retirement age.

To sum it up: If the interest rate *decreases*, it may be okay to be highly leveraged in the first place since the debt then will be lower. Whereas if interest rates rises, it's not quite as fun. What if you or your wife were to suddenly lose your jobs? It would be quite or really high gearing. Uncomfortable and difficult, depending on how long it takes to get a new job. How about if the income drops out due to sickness? Then we can hope that you have an insurance that covers all eventualities. And not an insurance company that tries to avoid its obligations at the end of the day, which can happen. Because of course they do what they can to avoid having to stand up for the promises you think they have made. Also, let`s hope the market doesn`t plummet so that you do not get rid of the cabin at a price that covers its share of your debt.

If your goal is to dispose of such things, then that's perfectly fine. You know how to do the calculations, and you now know something about risk and gearing. You have a budget template in an earlier chapter so that you can quickly fill in the new operating costs and see how these affect your cash flow. You know that both the car and the boat must have both petrol and service, the cabin must have maintenance and perhaps some refurbishment as well. You also know that you must both pay taxes and sacrifice something to achieve something else. If you overhear on the commuting train one day a whispering conversation *"It didn't go so well with our neighbors, they were in such high gearing, the poor people!"*, it might not be you they're talking about. But you know exactly what they are talking about because you have now been thoroughly warned.

13.5 Tax effect on debt

Before we end this chapter, we will take a look at the tax effect on debt. It will be the chapter's only model, because you have already been given the model *"Borrow or save for private investments"* in an earlier chapter. I have previously mentioned that we will come to this model, but I thought that it was natural now. Of course, it also has something to do with what we will go through in the next chapter. But it's also important to get fewer models to begin with so that we become familiar with these, rather than you having to get everything at once and then go completely crazy about what you can use for what, where and when. That's why *"Applied Personal Finance»* packed with everyday examples.

The formula we use is very simple:

*Tax Rate * Interest Amount = Tax Effect on Debt.*

We call this for *Tax Shield*. If you can deduct interests from your tax, the formula is the same regardless of the tax rate and wherever you are in the world. In order for you to benefit from the model, you must therefore find your tax rate. It is not difficult either, but it is required that you find the tax return or salary sheets from last year. So, it's easy to calculate that if you had a tax assessment of $ 28,000 last year, and had a total gross income of $ 100,000, your effective tax rate will be:

*Total tax / total income = (28/100)*100 = 28%.*

It's not more difficult than that. If you are going to take on a loan with your wife on equal terms, you can just merge the items, so to speak. Joint tax is divided by joint income. I can't include all possible constellations of responsibility and ownership of the debt that you and your wife may come up with, but you can probably manage it yourself. Because that doesn't change either the formula or the point. Well, the model you can use looks like this:

Tax Effect on Debt (Tax Shield):			Annual perfomance	-131 360,02
Interest	7,85 %		Tot cost	-3 940 800,56
Annuity loan*	1 500 000,00	* Arrears Annuity	Total Tax Shield:	683 424,16
Duration	30	* Years	Net Cost of Loan:	-3 257 376,40
Tax rate	28,00 %	* Graph showing 30 years, Tot Tax Shield & Net cost of loan after tax at 30		

You can see the graph that comes with this model on the next page.

It looks like this:

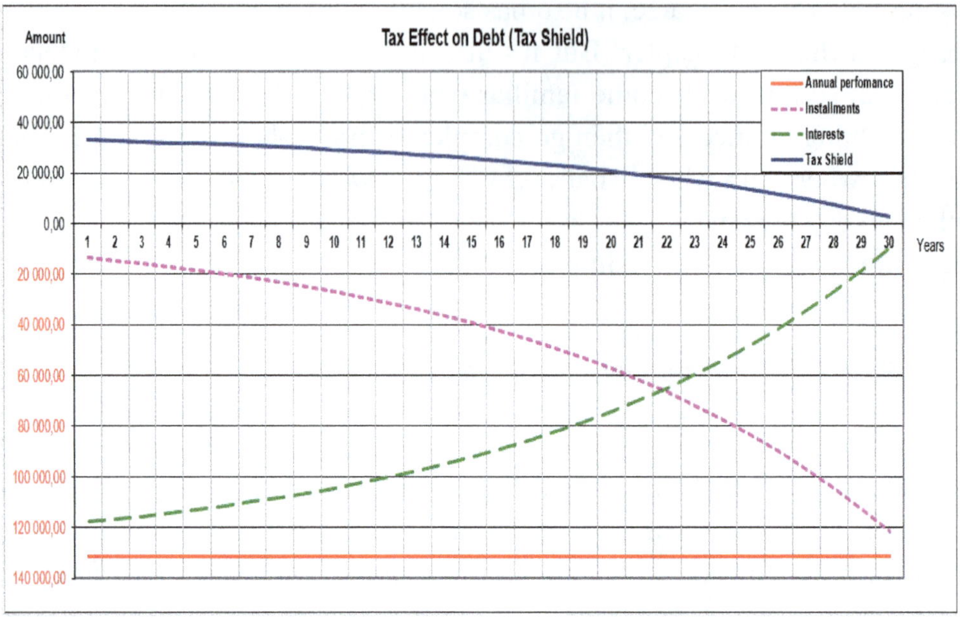

Fig: *This graph shows you the Tax Shield of your debt. It shows 30 Years as usual, but you can point the different graphs for the amount on every year.*

As usual, the graph shows the effect over 30 years. But there is nothing wrong with choosing shorter periods. The numbers are no less accurate because of that.

Of course, you can go in and point to the graph for any year to read off any value in the spreadsheet. Just use your mouse cursor to point the graph on the year you are interested in. But for now, let`s test this ourselves.

You can find more information about me and my books here:
executivewayto.com or at fireat40.com

13 a. Test yourself:

(We assume a fixed interest rate, and we disregard inflation!)

1.

You are considering buying a house that is actually a bit on the expensive side. The loan will be $750,000 after you have included the equity you have after selling the apartment you currently have. You will take on the loan for 30 years so that you will be debt-free the year before you retire. Your job is reasonably secure and all that. You are quite tired of not being low on cash all the time, so you are in a little doubt because of the high cost of borrowing. But the sellers says that the net cost of borrowing will be lower due to the tax effect on their debt. You have a total *tax rate of 33.4%. How much will this tax effect help you:*

***(a)** Every year for the first five years at a rate of 8%?*

***(b)** Total for the entire period if the interest rate and tax level are stable throughout the period?*

2.

How much will the tax effect help you:

***a)** Total for the entire period if the loan interest rate is stable at 10% throughout the loan period?*

***(b)** Total for the entire period if the loan interest rate is stable 6.75% for the entire loan period?*

3.

You suddenly get a pay rise when you are actually on your way to the bank to sign the loan. How much will the tax effect help you if your general tax rate now is at 36%

***(a)** Total for the entire period when the loan interest rate becomes stable 7.35% for the entire period.*

***(b)** Every year for the first 3 years when the loan interest rate remains stable.*

4.

What conclusion do you draw after all these simulations?

13 b. Summary answers

1.

(a) We enter 750,000, 8% interest, 30 years and tax rate 33.40%. We can then Read the graph with the mouse cursor and find the following numbers:

1 year : 20,040.00
2 years: 19,863.10
3 years: 19,672.04
4 years: 19,465.71
5 years: 19,242.86

(b) We read the information in the cell "Total tax asset -417,083, 16"

2.

(a) We just change the loan interest rate to 10% and read the cell Total tax benefit = 546,685.55

(b) We just change the loan interest rate to 6.75% and read the cell Total tax benefit = 339,969.74

3.

(a) We change both the loan rate to 7.35% and the tax rate to 36% and read of value 405,848.52

(b) We use the mouse cursor and read the values:

1 year: 19,485.00
2 years :19,647.78
3 years :19,436.06

4.

The conclusion we draw is that both the interest rate on loans and the tax rate affect the tax effect. We can see this directly from the formula since this is:
*tax rate * interest amount = tax effect on debt.*
The higher the tax rate and the more expensive the loan, the greater the tax effect. That must be the conclusion.

You can find more information about me and my books here:
executivewayto.com or at fireat40.com

Chapter 14. Real- and Nominal Interest Rates

One of the simplest concepts in interest calculations, and most important part of financial economics, is the concept of *real interest*. What is this? This is not a term we hear the news ankers talk much about. But shouldn't they if it is important? By the way, do you remember the linguistic image that the state itself traveled around with a money bag and top hat and distributed money to the dessert generation in the 70s in chapter 14? As I said then, that's actually not how it happened, but the language is also very pictorial. Because it is actually the politicians who decide the tax systems. The state manages it, but the state wasn't that rich, was it? In this short chapter, we will take a look at what happened then, and not least what is happening now.

14.1 Really?

Somewhat simplified, as a rule of thumb, we can say that the *nominal interest rate - inflation = real interest rate*. You know a lot about the nominal interest rate by now. It is the interest bid or the offer of today's loans and mortgages or on savings accounts. And the banks are competing just like the grocery around the corner. Not because there are so many merchants around the corners anymore, they are all franchise managers at somewhat more central areas or malls. Just like the banks.

But it is not the nominal interest you receive, neither as *effective* interest (previous chapter) nor in real interest, which we will deal with in this chapter. Since we have already found out that "numbers and such things" are not as dangerous and difficult as we thought before we started this book, we tackle the strange phenomenon of inflation first. Because even though you've heard of it and hopefully read a bit about it, we may not have much personal experience with it. In any case, not until now, when the much-discussed inflation pushes all interest rates up at high speed. It is because the central bank rules according to an inflation target of "trend" of 2% and uses the interest rate target to slow down inflation.

14.2 Inflation

Let's visit the concept of inflation. If you've read my chapter on macroeconomics, you may remember that inflation is something quite common. This means that the prices of goods and services increase steadily, so that you get less and less for your money with each passing day if wages do not increase at the same rate. This is not good, because prices can run rampant without wages keeping up the pace. When the central bank has an inflation target, i.e. they steer towards steady inflation *on trend* (2%), one of the most important instruments is interest management. In bad times, or in fear of bad times, they lower interest rates to stimulate economic growth. Both business and households (you and me) get to borrow money cheaper from their bank because your bank connection gets cheaper loans from the central bank. This has been happening; we have had an artificially low level of interest in the banks for quite a long time. For example, during the pandemic there were several countries around the world with negative real interest rates. I will explain this term shortly.

But let's say that the nominal interest rate within consists of both an interest rate + expected inflation. We can say that the nominal interest rate should cover the wear and tear of capital (the deterioration of the monetary value) during the period in which money is borrowed or lent, including the lower purchasing power that we might expect to occur in the meantime. We do not know what inflation will be in the future. In other words, there was no point in keeping money in the bank, on the contrary, the economy was stimulated so that you and I would spend money on buying goods and services to keep the wheels of society moving. And in the long term, we cannot have much higher interest rates in our country compared to neighboring countries and our most important trading partners, because then the money will flee over the borders to them instead. The opposite happens when prices rise more or faster than expected, as happened all over the world at the back of the pandemic. Then the central banks raise interest rates to slow down inflation, simply to get us to save more and spend less money, thereby keeping prices in check. We do not want hyperinflation! But both create problems for households. So one can now complain that it is an imported inflation, that is to say that the prices on the world markets for e.g. oil and gas, grain, metals etc. rise sharply due to unforeseen events which in turn affect us negatively. As for example Russia's attack on Ukraine, not only the annexation of Crimea in 2014 but the full innovation itself in February 2022, led to a price explosion of oil and gas (fuel for war machines), steel (war machines, bombs and grenades) and not least of food grains (wheat, rye, oats, corn etc). Europe turned off the oil and gas taps from Russia, while Russian warships blocked the ports so that the world had problems importing food grain from one of the world's largest granary, Ukraine. Another thing about inflation is that it often becomes a self-fulfilling prophecy, at least the part of inflation that is due to domestic conditions: If you believe that " there will be inflation soon", you will demand higher wages yourself or raise the prices of your products or services to stay ahead of the price increase you expect. And so do others you talk to. Then inflation is actually happening, because everyone is demanding more.

Let's sweep further back in history to the equally happy 70s and thus land in the middle. The Peace concept and Flower-power were common property and real wage growth was actually for real. Also, the word inflation. At that time, the tax system was different from today. It was full of patches and holes, just flicked on "a little here and there". So, it was overripe for replacement. The politicians had a fairly firm grip on economic policy in the aftermath of World War 2. And not least on the central bank's banknote press. Because this has to do with the country's money supply. At that time, the unemployment issue was governed by something called the Phillips curve. I'll explain this in the chapters of economics I either the book *"Fire@40!"* or in the *"Applied Economics and Management for Business Executives"*. The theory was that with high inflation, we would have minimal unemployment, and vice versa. Without getting too far into the macroeconomics, I can hopefully explain it briefly this way:

We can imagine that if the salary is relatively high, we will want to work more than if the salary is correspondingly relatively low. If wages rise steadily and constantly, companies will have to make up for this in their prices. If not, they will go bankrupt. And when wages increase, so does consumption. Because increased income leads to increased consumption, we all know that. And with increased consumption, more people may be buying the company's products, so the company may have to expand and hire more workers to meet the demands. Or maybe someone earns so much that they would rather work a little less. But production must be kept up, so the company must take on more employees. So, the effect is that unemployment is falling. At least in the short term.

So, the politicians were steering the country according to the Phillips curve. Nobody wants unemployment, either because it does not lead to anything good for the person who is unemployed, but also because it does not lead to the maximization of gross national product. And maximization of gross national product, *that* is what we want. Because this increases the state's income, which can be used for welfare benefits for the state's residents. In fact, inflation was explained in the following way when I was young: *"Inflation is a strange phenomenon, if you think it will be inflation, it will soon be."* And it's not really strange. You want to be ahead of the curve, so the company doesn't go bankrupt. So, you adjust your prices upwards. But such things spread quickly, so then everyone else raises their prices. But when this happens you have to demand more wages to make life go around. And so do others you talk to. The inflation is on as explained. Then we end up in a situation where the prices of goods and services are constantly increasing, so that you get less and less for your money. Then again, the central banks have to raise their interest rates to slow down inflation. And both weakened purchasing power and increased interest rates create problems for households.

Now, this was a very short and simplified explanation. But more recently it has been acknowledged that the Phillips curve cannot be correct. At least not in the long run. As a rule, we work as much as possible when the salary is relatively high. In that case no more unemployed will be hired, inflation or not. Naturally, but not very social. We are closer to ourselves. Recent research also supports the opposite of the Phillips curve, namely that low inflation means low unemployment in the longer term. Because at low inflation, we get low wage growth and stable conditions for both owners and employees. We can plan for a longer period than for the next quarter or six months, but for years ahead. For example, we have a better indication of the salary level in the next year and then we know that we can pay our loan next year as well as today. And then we can plan for how much we can spend on next year's holiday trip. But this argument naturally opens up for new discussions, such as the question of why real wage growth has not kept in pace with inflation. But we will not have that discussion here.

14.3 Real and nominal interest rates

At the beginning of the last century, the economist Irving Fischer argued that an investor will demand an interest rate that contains both a real required rate of return and compensation for the rise in prices (which we thus call inflation) that may occur in the period between the date of lending and repayment. Let's say that today's interest rate level is 9%. And that the central bank's inflation target is 2.5%. Then we can roughly say that *the real interest rate* is (9 - 2.5) = 6.5%. We can call it a rule of thumb. Naturally, this is most true in periods of low inflation. If we calculate it more accurately, we get 6.34%. This relationship between nominal interest rates, inflation and real interest rates can be written as follows:

$$P_n = P_r * (1+j) + j$$

Here *Pn* stands for nominal interest rate, *Pr* is the real interest rate and *j* of course is an expression of inflation. If we are to find the real interest rate, we can now turn it around a bit, as we have done in previous chapters, and say:

$$P_r = \frac{P_n - j}{1 + j}$$

If inflation is *j* = 2.5%, and banks have a nominal interest rate of Pn = 9%, the real interest rate is now calculated as follows:

$$Pr = \frac{0{,}09 - 0{,}025}{(1+0.025)} = 6.34\%$$

This model can be found in *FIRE@40.xls* under the next tab:

Real- and Nominal interest:	
Nom. Interest (Pn):	9,00 %
Inflation (j) :	2,50 %
Real interest (Pr) :	6,34 %

14.4 Real interest rate after tax and inflation

But this was not the case in the happy yuppie years of the early 80s, when real interest rates were negative. It was even more negative in the happy 70s. Tax has something to do with this. Of course, we must remember to deduct the tax *before* we deduct inflation because the tax is paid on the *actual interest expenses*. Now we want to know what return we achieve after tax on a deposit. The formula we are going to use now looks like this:

$$R_n = P_n * (1 - S)$$

R_n stands for nominal interest rate after tax. In our example, P_n = 9%. Let's say you have a flat tax rate of 28%. Then the nominal interest rate after tax in this case is $R_n = (0.09 * (1 - 0.28))*100 = 6.48\%$.

But since we are so well underway, we want to know what the real interest rate after *both tax and inflation* will be. We fill in the formula for the inflation-adjusted interest rate:

$$R_r = \frac{R_n - j}{1+j} = \frac{0.0648 - 0.025}{(1 + 0.025)} * 100 = 3.88\%$$

So far so well. But now we can also find what the nominal interest rate must be if we are to have a required rate of return after tax and inflation that gives a real interest rate of, for example, 5%. The two formulas can be combined into one that looks like this:

$$R_r = \frac{R_n*(1-s)-j}{1+j}$$

But where does the negative real interest rate come into the picture? Wasn't it the case that it paid to have debt, while it was punishable to save? Was that why so many people had black market money and put their savings in the mattress at the time? No, there are probably completely different reasons for that, because that would even be worse. For the sake of the example, we will do a calculation of real interest rates after tax and inflation from the happy 70s.

Let's say that the nominal interest rate at the time was 12%, the tax-deductible rate was at a flat 60% (it wasn't flat, but the tax system made the tax-deductible interest that large) and inflation was annually at 10%. This makes a real interest rate of -4.73%, compared to today's +4.73! Almost an insane difference of 10%, an actual difference of as much as 9.46% most people would understand.

You can try out your own situation in the workbook. The model in FIRE@40.xIs can be found under the same tab and looks like this:

Real interest after tax and inflation:		
Nom. Interest (Pn):	12,00 %	
Inflation (j) :	10,00 %	
Tax rate (t) :	60,00 %	
Real interest (Pr) :	-4,73 %	

We can easily see that if inflation is high, it does not pay to save. However, your debt becomes much cheaper, it is "eaten up" by inflation in the same way as your salary. The same applies to taxes. It's not a good idea to put the money in the mattress either. In other words, you are left with relatively much less in your savings account than if inflation is low. We get the opposite when inflation and/or taxes are low. Then it pays to save, not to borrow! From the formula, we see that inflation affects the real interest rate relatively much more than the tax rate. Just try it for yourself!

In other words, for every hundred dollars you borrowed, inflation and the tax system ensured that you *earned* 4.73% or 4.73 dollars per 100`s on your loan! Inflation was thus great news to the borrowers. While the savers with a hundred dollars in their account got 4.73% *less* bread for their money just by having them in a savings account in the bank. That's quite a lot of slices of bread over the course of a whole year! Even if no one borrowed a hundred dollars, or a hundred thousand to buy a house, the point should still be quite clear. And if you think this example is taken straight out of thin air, you are of course completely wrong. These are real numbers from when the world was young, at least when I was young. Unfortunately, I was far too young to take on a loan at the time when you could “borrow yourself rich”. But my parents' generation could, and they did so at the expense of those who had saved money in the bank which was my grandparents generation.

To put it a little more to the point, wealth was transferred from a frugal generation of parents who had survived World War II and always paid all their mortgages and also saved money in the bank, handed over, via the tax system and the inflation, to the younger generations who had just bought a house and therefore had mortgages. Now, it is basically nothing strange about parents giving to their children. Especially not when it is handed over directly. But the fact is that many people earned incredible sums for us today, simply by having loans! Because both savings and loans became almost worthless over time. The larger the loan, the greater the transfer of income was, and inflation leads to only one thing on capital goods; they rise. As house prices have done ever since, and as we know, they are rising faster than your salary, which itself barely has kept up with inflation. And when it came to capital owners those days, it was the opposite way, the more frugal you had been and the larger the savings in your bank account, the less it was worth. Those who owned the home themselves already became rich without doing anything other than owning it.

This negative real interest rate disappeared at about the same time as my generation was establishing itself. By then the real interest rate was no longer negative, even if prices reflected the opposite. It just happened a couple of years after I bought my own house. These changes in the tax system came just before the 7th largest financial crisis in world history, the Norwegian Stock Exchange Crash, following Bank Crisis and Subsequent Housing Crisis 1987 - 1993 (Kindleberger & Adliber, 2015). So in the aftermath of the Stock Market crash, people got unemployed and got problems of paying their debt to the faltering banks. The increasing problems made the banks panic as they didn`t trust each other and not their customers, it became a liquidity trap- or drought. So they started to foreclosure houses at large scale, making the housing market crash too. Subsequently, the interest surged. As stated before, the banks are co-cyclical: They enlarge every market imperfections. This in turn forced many families, even with secure government jobs, to sell their homes for as much as 50-75% less than they were bought for just a few years earlier when the sun was shining in the upturn of a financial bubble.

So my generation learned an important lesson in those years that later generations have not. Now you understand the actual effect of Schumpeter's observations in his book *"The Theory of Economic Development"* from 1934, and my figure *"The psychology of the stock market"*, which again explains the essence of economic bubbles, or the boom-bust theories, like Kindleberger and Adliber describes in "*Manias, Panics, and Crashes. A History of Financial Crisis*" (2015). You have been warned.

If someone you know bought a house in the 1960s and then a cabin in the 1970s in addition to a car and then explains that they had to pay an entire year's salary for their house and that it was because they neither smoke nor drank, then that person understands not at all what we are talking about. Not that you don't save money and health by not smoking and drinking. But perhaps they have "forgotten" or did not understand that others paid for large parts of their financial party. And they don't understand that I had to pay three times my annual salary, with inflation at around 7% with tax deductions on only part of the interest due to the new tax system. And then inflation plunged to a normal trend inflation (2-3%) during the 90s, and I myself had a nominal interest rate after tax of a whopping 10.5% for a decade! I wasn't alone in that situation. No wonder people had to sell their houses, and the housing market plummeted as the banks forced people to sell at any price.

That generation would probably never understand the big problems of my sons generation, facing housing prices at 10 times his annual expected salary for the same kind of house! Because my parents' generation simply learned that you could borrow something you hardly had to give back. It's like borrowing a whole cake from your old neighbors, eating as much as you can manage and then handing the plate with a few crumbs back. Such was the relationship between the generations of my parents and grandparents. That's one of the reasons why my parents' generation is called the "dessert generation". Their whole life was a financial upturn. What will my son think of a *real interest rate* of perhaps 5-7% and a house prices that can possibly be 10-12 times more than his normal salary? Well, I'm just asking, because the prices can plummet again. However my son has been asking me the same ever since he was a teenager: *"I wonder how in the world I'll ever be able to afford to buy myself a home, Dad!"* he said. So he has prepared well. And he just finished his MEA with a major in Finance himself.

But, enough about that. Now we are concentrating on the models and our economic understanding again. You probably see that you can first calculate the real interest rate here and then use it in all models where it says, "Nominal interest rate". Just keep in mind that what you put in affects what comes out, so keep your tongue straight in your mouth.

You can find more information about me and my books here:
executivewayto.com or at fireat40.com

14 a. Test yourself:

1.

You and your wife's joint tax rate is 28%, the banks' lending rate is 9.75% and inflation is 1.5%. What will the real interest rate after tax be for you?

2.

If the real interest rate is 7.07% and inflation is 2.5%, what must the nominal interest rate be?

3.

Consider saving a larger amount every year. Your marginal tax rate is 32.3%, the banks' deposit rate is 7.15% and inflation is 4%.

(a) *What will the real interest rate be?*
(b) *What will the real interest rate be if the tax goes down to 25%?*
(c) *What will the real interest rate be if the tax is 25% and inflation is 1.9%?*
(d) *What will be the real interest rate when inflation is 2.5% and your marginal tax rate is 28%?*

4.

Many lobbyist groups speak loudly about "*it is important to reduce taxes*". Why is that, and how should you adapt if you think they are gaining traction?

5.

Who benefits from inflation suddenly rising?

6.

Who benefits from a sudden increase in taxes?

7.

You dream yourself back to the end of the 80s. At the time, you had a pretty well-paid job. But it disappeared with the problems that piled up for the company in the 90s. When the company went bankrupt in 1991, your annual salary was USD 250,000. The real interest rate was 0.5% after your effective tax of 36.7%. But you were one of the lucky ones and got a new job pretty quickly. Since then, both your salary, real interest rate and tax rate have remained stable at this level. Have you lost or increased your purchasing power since then?

8.

We imagine that food prices have fallen in real terms compared to purchasing power in 1991 by 0.5%. When salary, interest and tax conditions are otherwise like the information in the question 7 above, have you increased or decreased your purchasing power?

14 b. Summary answers

1.

We go to the model "Real interest rate after tax and inflation". The real interest rate Rr is now 5.44%. We can also use the Mickey Mouse calculator we've come to love directly on the formula. But remember to use decimal numbers all the way through!

2.

The nominal interest rate is found by experimenting with the model "Real and nominal interest rate" until we find that a Pn of 9.75% and inflation of 2.5% gives a real interest rate of 7.07%

3.

(a) The real interest rate will be 0.81%.
(b) Real interest rate will be 1.31%
(c) Real interest rate will be 3.40%
(d) Real interest rate will be 2.58%

4.

Because they have large deposits in the banks. And partly because they would like to manage more of their money themselves. For example, try reducing the tax in the example above to 25%, and you will see how you should adapt. As you know, this book focuses on personal finances.

5.

When we assume a tax system that includes tax on interest income and deductions for interest on debt, the answer is that it is borrowers and those who do not save will benefit from it. The losers become the savers, or the capital owners as the economic term is.

6.

When we assume a tax system that includes tax on wealth and deductions for debt, the answer is the same as above.

7.

We go to ***«Fireat40.xls»*** spreadsheet chapter 7 and fill in the information of 0.5% interest on $ 250,000 in salary and 10 years in the model for NV and see that your purchasing power has decreased slightly. Your salary is now only worth only 237,836.99 compared to 250,000 in 1991.

8.

As long as you don't spend all your money on food, your purchasing power has decreased. How much depends on how much money you spend on your salary for food.

You can find more information about me and my books here:
executivewayto.com or at fireat40.com

Chapter 15. Finally

Based on a little bit of the algebra that you *had to* learn already in middle school, I think this covers everything you actually need to know if you are not going to become a professional economist but want to be able to have a significantly better financial future regardless of your career choice. The rest is just common sense. This is what economists like me use in our daily lives. It was a shock to me to realize that I already knew all this algebra in middle school. But no one showed me how to use it in practical life. So my point is that you don't need to do a long, expensive and tiring economics degree like an MEA or MBA just to learn these few simple things or be able to become a real *FIRE@40!* It's not your fault that your teachers or parents didn't spend their energy showing you this and letting you practice it. Because no one taught them this either. But now I've done that work! Take good care of this book, it's easy to return to when it's been a little while, and you suddenly realize you have a little book that shows you how professional economists deal with private financial items.

15.1 Too good to be true!

Well, after reading through 14 chapters, there are reasons to ask yourself if all this is not too good to be true. Does 15 chapters in a paperback of a couple of hundred pages provide enough insight for you to become financially sensible? Help you become ***FIRE@40!*** Or at least much better of? What you want to use this insight for is, of course, up to you. Is it not harder to become a millionaire on your own salary? No, not really. It's actually a question of when you start and how determined you are. First of all, remember what I state at our homepage:

"The ability to become «Fire@40», i.e. Financial Independent, Retire Early (F.I.R.E) when you turn 40, depend on three things".

In the section of budgeting, I told you *"creating a proper budget is at least as important as understanding the concept of opportunity cost and the time value of the money! These three things are the very foundation of your financial success*!". Just because it makes you focus on the base of it all: Cost control is the fundament.

However, as true as it is, we also need 4 Basic and Powerful Rules, already accounted for in the very chapter of the Introduction on page 1:

1. It is knowledge,
2. It`s is will,
3. It's savings,
4. It's investment

As a consequence of these 4 basic rules, the insight into how this works leads us back to the concept of what we refer to as *cost control*. How rich, or how wealthy, as we economists say, you will become depends on how determined you are, and what time horizon you have. Because the main point is to convey what all economists know is the algebra you learned in middle school; Math's class could and should have been the most fun lessons in school! As one of the readers of my first book said: *"If only I had this book in junior high school, I would probably get good grades, and the math lessons would have been fun too!"*

The 9 Easy and Powerful Techniques of applied personal finance that I show you and explain here, with completely everyday examples and Q&A's, should be worth its weight in gold to any reader. ***FiRE@40!*** gives you both the toolbox, the knowledge and the foundation you need to get a better insight into some of the things you should have learned to use before you finished high school and consider to enter college or university. It is an excellent starting point for getting both a better overview, and deeper insight into something that absolutely everyone has to deal with in life: Your own personal finances! This is actually what economists use in their everyday lives.

Perhaps you already have such a good overview and control that you can save 2 - 3 - or 400 dollars a month? Well, in that case, you can easily calculate how much it will be over time. Provided that the interest rate is completely fixed throughout the period. But we do not know for sure what the interest rate will be for a long, or a whole period of maybe a decade or two because we know about anything about the future. My models and apps don't show you your future, you have to create it yourself. But I'll give you an idea of how you can manage it financially. Because no calculation gives you more accurate answers than what you put into them! Life itself is not a mathematical formula with definitive answers, nor are the models on which finance is built, they have *prerequisites*. But hopefully you have ideas for how you can steer towards your own economic future goals. Whether you are a true FIRE and plan to drop out of the 9-5 working life and retire at 40 or 50 years old or have long-term financial goals leading up to your 70th birthday. Because maybe you are already a bit older than 20-25 years. Maybe you are in your mid-30s and already have children, and think like me that you want to leave something for those who come behind you, help them get started with their own housing or tuition money? Of course I have models for calculating variable interest rates as well, but that will have to be in the next book on *applied advanced financial economics*. But for now I have shown you what and how you can manage your finances. If conditions in the society around you change along the way, you can react on the basis of your new knowledge. And significantly more qualified than before.

15.2 Now what were we talking about?

Now you know that there is no point in going on strike for a "dollar surcharge per hour", when we on average barely work 2000 hours a year. Because this is not what makes you wealthy, and besides, you have to pay taxes from it too. It's your purchasing power that matters, and that`s affected by more than a dollar surcharge. As we know, purchasing power has to do with inflation. I have explained that both the borrowing rate and the lending rate have to do with the central bank's inflation target but are also governed by the banks' risk assessment of the different types of loans you are applying for. Of course, this is not detached from the nation's economic development and economic policy. And all of this, in turn, has to do with our wage growth and the general labor market, import and export. Also with domestic conditions, but also with our trading partners and the rest of the world. Because we do not live detached from the rest of the world in our globalized economy. To your question about nominal versus effective interest rates, you now know the answer yourself: Namely, that the *effective interest rate* affects your finances, the *nominal interest rate* affects your cash flow and its financing because you pay it every month. When it comes to your private investments, it is *the real interest rate* that matters. Because it says something about the difference in value over time.

Of course, we must never forget the concept of opportunity cost. It is far too basic, and therefore absolutely necessary to keep in mind when considering investments and their financing. Also, don't forget the cost/benefit principle or *"Value for Money"* as we call it. You know that you might be able to achieve about the same thing with an item at a slightly lower price, even if the marketers are paid astronomical sums of money to convince you otherwise. Because when they play with our emotions, we fall short. Marketers have learned this from psychologists. Thus, you must have cost control and budget control to provide a good overview, even if you may have loosened up a little lately. So, if you skipped chapter 8, you have to go through it anyway to get to the finish line. Even if you feel that you have few bills and a full overview. It's easy to create a budget in Excel, where you just fill in new costs and get an overview in an instant. And then you can fill in new changes and also have a basic budget for next year. Maybe the bank has one for you in your online bank as well. They want to sell you all kinds of products all the time. Therefore, of course, I use my own instead.

Even if you know that it is nice to save a few hundred dollars in taxes every year, there will be no big money from it unless you invest it in something. Because otherwise they`re spent on consumption such as a kebab, hamburger, pizza and Coke or iced coffee bought on impulse just *"Because I deserve it!"*. And while it may increase our instant personal well-being, it does not lead to financial well-being in the long run. Nor can you make a living from saving taxes, and we won't remember how much we have saved in taxes after a few years or maybe after thirty.

When Millennials and Gen-X have thrown themselves into this applied finance and turned into the movement we call FIRE - *Financial Independent, Retire Early,* there may be several reasons for this. First and foremost, it is a matter of common sense, and perhaps also a counter-reaction to the consumer society that has lived high on credit and loans that are now becoming difficult to pay as the interest rates are normalizing. But Gen-X and Millennials are nevertheless concerned with exactly what I wrote about in my first book in 2002. There is one thing AI cannot do for you, and that is to think for you, which is why I have created a number of *test-yourself-questions with summary answers* so you can practice how to use this knowledge yourself. Maybe the ambition will change a little along the way. The ambition to be financially independent is of course perfectly fine. But maybe you are ambitious in a different way, have commercial ideas and are considering becoming an entrepreneur and starting your own company(s)? If so, I have written several books for *Mastering Business Management*, perhaps you should start with the book *"Applied Entrepreneurship for Business Executives"*?. At least you will get some ideas about what it takes to establish a viable and successful business and how to develop it and perhaps scale up. In any way, check out executivewayto.com to find a lot of interesting material for visionaries, business managers and leaders!

15.3 A little warning

It goes without saying that the prices of our food products are affected by the prices of the raw materials from which they are made. The fact that food prices in our neighboring countries more or less affect food prices in our country may not be something that many people think about until they have experienced it themselves. But that's the way it is, and the same applies to interest rates and inflation. You do not have to travel across the border to either one country or another to find a product that is cheaper or more expensive there than it is in the domestic market. But in large, they follow each other quite a lot. Even if politicians or individual industry associations or focus groups come forward in the media and claim that everything that is different here at home must be like this. You can read chapter 2 in this book "FIRE@40" to know more about both Adam Smith, Ricardo and the Heckscher-Ohlin theorem.

It doesn't matter what a politician says in the media or how often, it's just rhetorical tricks. But such tricks actually work in the long run if repeated often enough, even if the arguments do not become more correct for that reason. If you don't think about it, you'll more or less believe it after a while. Remember that it may be the same ploy from real estate agents who predict an all-time price increase in the housing market when the decline is obvious to everyone. They live on commission, so they have to sell a certain number of homes at the highest possible prices. This can also be the case when banks on glossy paper predict a "safe" return on their investment products, and about how bright your future will be with their particular products. They know nothing more about the future than you and me. All the financial crises throughout history clearly show us that nothing is for certain, and that the vast majority of investment products are far more speculative than perhaps the sellers themselves understands. A cool job title is no guarantee that they don't have their own agenda. They only sell products that the sales manager has decided, because they in turn have sales figures that they must achieve in order to get their salary. It is this kind of pressure that leads to "creative investment products" that no one understands, but which some are led to sell to those who have no prerequisites to understand anything about what those products are about. That's why we got the Subprime products that led to the 2008-2009 financial crisis.

If I, who have made it through three major financial crises and still have kept both house and family intact can give some basic tips, it would have to be these three:

1. The best tip is the economists' basic tip: "Think logically!".
2. The second tip is Albert Einstein's "Everything is relative!".
3. The third tip is Cicero's "Qui Bono?" (who benefits from this?)!

15.4 Let's play some more

Now that we've been through both summaries and warnings, I thought we'd play a little with numbers. Again. There are a number of other things that could be a good idea to calculate, now that you should be able to use the junior high school's algebra on your own. For the sake of examples, let's assume that you've been inspired by the FIRE movement, even if you don't belong to Gen-X or the Millennials. You will know how much money you need to have in your account to quit your job and live off the interest. For example, how much do you have to win at the Lottery?

Let's say you won the top prize, which this week was a whopping 5,000,000!

*Surprisingly, you won on a purchased ready-made ticket, so you hadn't picked the numbers yourself since you forgot the numbers for your lucky streak at home. And that's not surprising, because the probability of winning is exactly the same. But I do not provide mathematical proof of probability here, because that is far beyond the point of both the book and my example. What we want to know is how you calculate whether you can retire immediately? Let's say the risk-free bank rate is 6%. We can directly see that the actual return on interest would be a whole (5,000,000 * 0.06) = 300,000 each year. Whether that is enough for you to retire immediately, you have to figure it out for yourself. But what if the interest rate is only 3%? And what about the inflation? You can do the math yourself. But keep in mind taxes, so you must include that in your calculation! In addition, you learned something about the time value of money, so you need to keep that in mind too.*

Now let's say you've saved up a lot of money in both cash and housing and are wondering if you should sell the whole Shulamite and move to Spain, Italy, Florida, the Bahamas or maybe Thailand. And you reckon that about $ 300,000 per year should be enough to live the lord's happiest days in exile in a country with a much lower cost of living. How much do you need to have in your bank account when the current nominal interest rate is 6% in a high-interest account that you can draw on free of charge 12 times a year? Well, we saw that from the calculation above. In economics language, this is called an *infinite annuity*. But we have turned the question around and must therefore turn the formula around. The formula we use is this:

$$PV = PMT * \frac{1}{(i)}$$

Here, PV *is the expression* for Present Value, *PMT* stands for *payment* or payout and *i* stands for the interest.

In this example, we get that 300,000/0.06 = 5,000,000. Thus, we get that an annual payment of 300,000 in *perpetuity*, must have interest rate at 6% fixed interest on an amount that is 5,000,000 *in today's money*. But then again we remember after having read chapter on final values that what we really should worry about is the *real value* of the return on our Lotto win. What is the real value of 300,000 in thirty or forty years' worth in today's money, and would that be a decent return to live on? You can now probably calculate how much you need to save and invest to get into a financial position where you can expect to be able to live on the return on your own funds. Or possibly when you can establish a business of your dreams from which you can live and work. I can promise you that`s really, really inspiring!

Now, of course we can simplify the formula and ask ourselves how much we need to win in a Lottery to be able to retire if this, or that. Let's say your need is an *annual annuity* of 300,000 and that is at an interest rate of 5%. It will be the same formula; we know that very well.

But since we are going to use the formula further, we now use other letters:

$$PV = \frac{CF}{i}$$

Here, the cash flow is expressed as Cash Flow (CF). We could just as easily have used PMT, but we will use the expression further on, so we keep it as it is. In our example, we get that *PV = 300,000 / 0.05 = 6,000,000.* In other words, lower interest rates mean that *the basis of return* must increase. In this way, you can easily simulate what a percentage interest rate from, or to, can bring in terms of joys or pains. It pays to keep an open eye!

Let's take another example:
Do you remember the example of the fantastic piece of land you could rent from the farmer in the Western mountains for a lick of nothing? So nice that you might consider to set up a nice little cabin there? Let's say the farmer wants 5,000 a year in rent for as long as you live. Let's say the interest rate is still 6%. But suddenly the farmer changes his mind one day and says that you can buy the land for 50,000 because he thinks that farmers usually tend to rent out too cheaply.

Should you go for it? Well, financially? I would have. Especially if I was already building a cabin there. Because I compare the construction price, or the rental price if you will, with the sale price in today's money. 5,000 /0.06 = 83,333.33. So, the farmer wants 50,000 for something that is worth 83,333.33.33. That`s a real bargain for me!

But what if the farmer changes his mind meanwhile you go to the bank? He does not want to sell the land after all, but wants the rental price index-adjusted by, let's say, 2.5% every year. What now, then?

The farmer wants a payment that covers both the expected interest rate and inflation in order to retain the real value of the property. He wants to regulate this with an eternal growth series or what we economists call an *infinite growth series*. The formula we use is based on the previous one, but with a new element which is the inflation index. We write this formula like this:

$$PV = \frac{CF}{(i - g)}$$

We assume here that the interest rate is higher than the index regulation, otherwise there will be no economic sense in it. In our example, the numbers now become:
PV = 5,000 / (0.06 - 0.025) = 142,857.14.

This is what the property is worth to the farmer in today's monetary value! The question now is whether it is worth it to you or not. Unless you have a lack of liquidity and are not able to buy the land no matter how much you want it. But the price is the same under these conditions. If the interest rate *does not change* in the meantime and the index is fixed *for the entire period*, it will come out the same whether you buy today or rent the land. However, if, for example, the interest rate rises to 8.5% next week, the price of the deal falls to 83,333.33. And if the interest rate drops to 5%, the value of the deal increases to 200,000. You better keep an open eye to these matters!

Other things that might be interesting to calculate a little on are, for example, changes in your income.
Let's say you have a pretty boring job and a poor salary. You don't need a car for work, and since you can walk back and forth, your car is usually parked in the garage. But now you have been offered a job in the neighboring town. Then you have to use your car, because there are a few miles over there. Also, public transport options are pretty poor. Your effective tax rate is 33%, and you calculate that daily driving to the new job will come to a net

$50,000 per year. Or maybe you should calculate on $5,000. It won`t change the point of the example anyway, just the numbers.

What we want to know is how much more *gross* you have to charge so that you don't lose out moneywise by changing jobs. In other words, how to get out at least to zero. We have to take into account increased net costs, since only these are stated. To calculate net salary after tax, we take gross salary and multiply by the tax rate. But if we turn the whole formula upside down, we can say that the formula is like this:

$$\text{Gross salary} = \frac{\text{Net salary}}{(100 - \text{tax rate } (\%))}$$

In this example, the additional salary you claim must be 50,000 /(100 - 33) = $74,626.87 to cover increased travel costs. Or $7,462.87 if you calculated on $5,000 on travels. Note that here we really have to use *the marginal tax rate* in the expression to be completely correct. That is, the tax rate on the last dollar you have to pay income taxes from.

15.5 The end

A lot of formal education without experience is not necessarily better than a lot of experience without formal qualifications. Because there is no guarantee that you will act correctly. There has to be a certain balance. People become interested in different things and acquire informal skills from them, whether it is growing roses, fly fishing, tapestry, diesel engines or predict equity prices. You don't need to have a master's degree in everything you're interested in; it's not at all certain that you need a master's degree at all to succeed in life. There is simply too much focus on master's degrees in today's society, and the problem is not the master's degrees themselves, but that everyone has the same education, and that the education may not fit in tomorrow's society needs. There is too little focus on practical education as I see it. Like you got here in my book.

The ***FiRE@40!*** *(Applied Personal Finance)* is, as you now know, the book for practitioners, regardless of their level of education beyond middle school. The idea is that you should first and foremost know something more about the elementary relationships in the economy which you need to know something about on a daily basis, regardless of what education you choose. But also, you constantly can return to the *test-yourself-tasks* and applications to calculate on things. Here`s dedicated chapters and 38 Q&A's to help you on your practical way to master *Applied Personal Finance*. So, there's just a matter of practice and training until it sticks in your spinal cord, so to speak. It is also my intention that you should visit the book if you suddenly become unsure about something you know you have read about. So that you can give yourself independent advice, instead of acting on advice from someone with an agenda to pick your pockets. That is precisely why this is the book for practitioners! Only when you have reached the last pages of my book do you know what you would have missed if you didn`t read the book! So I sincerely hope you have read all the chapters, or that you do that now.

Well, now. I can't think of anything else you should know more about this time around. At least not as an ordinary salary slave. Then it must be at a far more advanced level. If you think you have learned something, it is nice if you brag about it to others, but I would also like to hear from you! If you have really got a "taste for finance", you can now move on to the books that economists have to take exams on. I have listed some examples of such books I can recommend, in the appendixes at the next chapters. But all of them are written with corporate life in mind. In any case, we now understand much better how to expose ourselves in regard to our own situation and the risks the world otherwise exposes us to. This knowledge free both our minds and resources for more useful things for us, and for our families. Because the thing is that we all learned all the necessary algebra already in junior high school, but we didn't learn to apply it to what we all have to deal with: *Applied Personal Finance.* The problem was that there were no textbooks or teachers who could teach us this, because they didn`t learn it themselves. Otherwise, I would probably have paid more attention to the math lessons myself. Maybe everyone else would too.

So, you have now worked through the whole book on applied personal finance. Now what? I tell you one thing: *Keep this book close at heart!*

Because when you come to think *"Where did I read..."* or *"How was that again?"*, you`ll pick up my book, and look up what could be close to your own situation. Just like your personal encyclopedia.

BEST OF LUCK IN YOUR IMPROVED PERSONAL FINANCIAL LIFE!

You can find more information about me and my books here:
executivewayto.com or at fireat40.com

15 a. Test yourself:

Maybe we should round off the book with some more general questions that summarize some of what I have shown you? On how can you now more easily see how you can adapt to the ever-changing economic situation?

1.

In the news there is a report from a large campsite. The report is mainly about whether the authorities will order the owners to demolish the "cabin tents", extensions of wood, which are highly flammable. These "cabin tents" mainly consist of the caravans being stuck on the site for years and have therefore had both wooden extensions, wooden terraces and fences installed for quite significant amounts. This is an inexpensive way to expand your living space. The commotion in the country's camping community is great, and they are now refusing to comply with orders for demolition from the fire department. The arguments from the owners are summed up by a middle-aged man who says that *"I, as an ordinary wage earner, have never been able to afford to buy a giant cabin for many tens of thousands of dollars".* What do you think about that argument?

2.

On the news, you hear that the interest rate that is now "record high" is expected to continue to rise further despite the fact that inflation is low, and despite the fact that taxes are going down:

a) *Why is the interest rate rising further?*

b) *How should you deal with:*

- ***1)*** *Your mutual fund?*
- ***2)*** *The housing market?*
- ***3)*** *Your loan relationship with the bank ?*

3.

On the news, there is a report about people's strained finances since interest rates are so high. A low-paid woman who says she can't afford to take the bus to visit her parents is interviewed. A brief comment from the Governor comes in between the woman's statements about bad advice. What did he say about not being able to afford a bus ticket because of the high interest rates?

4.

On the news, you hear that food prices in this country are twice as high as in neighboring countries. How does this information affect you?

5.

On the news you hear that "An example of horrible food prices in this country is tomatoes that today cost USD 25 per kilo, compared to USD 8 10 years ago". Is this correct if interest rates have been 8%, inflation 5%, your taxes are 28%, and real wage growth has been 1% in the meantime?

6.

If the tax rate and inflation go up while wages are unchanged, what about your purchasing power?

7.

If interest rates were suddenly lowered, how would it affect most people? If you don't get all the questions right on the fly, you will have to console yourself with the fact that they are complex tasks, and that the book you have now read in many ways needs to "mature a little". If so, don't give up, but give yourself time! Think about both the questions and the answers.

15 b. Summary answers

1.

We understand the tragic fact that both the fortune and the memories are lost and turned into stick wood overnight, without compensation. But economists, and now you, know that this is a question of knowledge, willingness and ability to prioritize. This man did not have that knowledge, will and to save and invest before spending, that we who have read this book now truly know.

2.

(a) The authorities will reduce private consumption, or interest rates will rise in all countries around us, or inflation will rise. Possibly a combination of everything.

b 1) If interest rates are high and inflation and taxes are low; the real interest rate will be high. This will possibly give the business community "breathing problems". You may therefore want to carefully consider whether it will be worthwhile to keep the money in the mutual fund or in a high-interest account, depending on what you think about the interest rate in the long term.

b 2) House prices are likely to fall somewhat in the long term if interest rates are so high that people start to have payment problems. This in turn will affect house prices in the long term. "In the long run" here does not mean "in a couple of weeks" but in a year or two.

b 3) You should carefully consider your expenses and your overall finances if you start to get strained. There may be questions about tougher priorities.

3.

He barked briefly and brutally something about how this is a question of priorities, not a question of interest rates.

4.
You probably stand in an hour-long queue at the border crossing like everyone else to take what you can with you every time. No matter how environmentally friendly it is.

5.
No, this should give a real price increase of 0.72%, compared to a real wage growth of 1%. In other words, there will be 28% more tomatoes per krone.

6.
In that case, purchasing power will be weakened.

7.
Consumption will rise, as debt becomes cheaper, and it does not pay quite as much to save.

If you don't get all the questions right at once, you have to take comfort in the fact that these are complex tasks, and that the book you have now read in many ways needs to "mature a little". But don't give up, give yourself time! Think about both the questions and the answers.

So, you have now worked through the whole book on applied personal finance. Now what? I tell you: Keep the book close at heart. And when you come to think *"Where did I read..."* or *"How was that again?"*, you pick up my book, just as I still do, and look up what you have read could be close to your own situation, like your personal encyclopedia.

"It is impossible for man to learn what they think they already know".
(Epictetus (60-120, e.Kr.) Roman philosopher)

You can find more information about me and my books here:
executivewayto.com or at fireat40.com

Appendix A: References

Awais, M., Aziz S., Usman U., & Bhatti, O.M. (2021). Role of Game Theory in Stock's Investment: Having Loss-Aversion Bias During the Stressed Condition. *International Journal of Management (IJM)* Volume 12, Issue 3, March 2021, pp.872-893.

Cicco, A., (2002). *PRIVATØKONOMEN: Kunnskap for få er makt. Kunnskap for alle er frihet.* 2.nd ed. Ikkyo Publishing

Cicero, M. T. (106-43 B.C). *Selected Political Speeches*. Penguin Books Ltd., London. Bibliography Copyright Michael Grant Publications Ltd (1989)

Kahneman, D., Lovallo, D., Sibony, O. (2011). The Big Idea: Before You Make That Big Decision… *Harvard Business Review.* June 2011.

Kahneman, D., (2011). *Thinking Fast and Slow.* Penguin Books Ltd.

Kindleberger, C. P., Adliber, R. Z. (2015). *Manias, Panics, and Crashes. A History of Financial Crisis.* Palgrave Macmillan, England

Laffer, Arthur B. (2004): The Laffer Curve: Past, Present, and Future. *The Heritage Foundation. No. 1765, June 2004.*

McAfee, A. & Brynjolfsson, E. (2012). Big Data: The Management Revolution. *Harvard Business Review*, 90 (10), 60-68.

Porter, Michael E., (1979) How Competitive Forces Shape Strategy. *Harvard Business Review March - April 1979.*

Porter, Michael E. (1985). *Competitive advantage: Creating and sustaining superior performance.* New York: Free Press.

Schiller, B.R., Hill, C., Wall, S. (2016). *The economy today.* 14th ed. McGraw-Hill

Schwartz, B., (2004) *The Paradox of Choice: Why More Is Less.* Harper Perrenial, 2005.

Thaler, R. H. og Sunstein C. R. (2008). *Nudge. Improving decisions about health, wealth and happiness*. Penguin Books.

Tversky A., Kahneman, D., (1974). Judgment Under Uncertainty: Heuristics and Biases, *Science* [185], 1974, 1124–1131.)

Tversky, A., Kahneman, D. (1992). Advances in prospect theory: Cumulative representation of uncertainty. *J Risk Uncertainty* 5, 297–323

Schumpeter, J. A. (1934). *THE THEORY OF ECONOMIC DEVELOPMENT. An Inquiry into Profits, Capital, Credit, Interest, and the Business Cycle.*

Appendix B: Suggestions for further reading

All of the above mentioned books, plus these three on finance:

Bodie, Z., Kane, A., Marcus, A. J. (2024). *Investments*, 13.th Ed. McGraw Hill, New York

Bowhill, Bruce. (2008). *Business planning and control: integrating accounting, strategy and people.* John Wiley & Sons

Hawawini, G., Viallet, C. (2015, 5.th ed). *Finance for Executives. Managing for Value Creation.* Hampshire, UK. Cengage Learning, EMEA.

Index

A

B

C

D

E

F

U

V

W

X

Y

The Author

P. Leerberg (EMBA, EMM, CPA)

1961 -

Photo: © P. Leerberg

P. Leerberg has two master's degrees in economics and business management, and more than 30 years of experience as a leader and business manager, of which approx. 20 years as senior advisor to more than a hundred other business leaders. He has extensive experience from board positions in business and sports. His professional education and interests are focused on how we can apply research from economics, strategy, management and digitization in real-life business.

His education includes a bachelor's degree in Business Economics, Management and Digitization, following an Executive Master of Management in Applied Economics, Strategic Management and Leadership plus an Executive Master of Business Administration in Innovation Management, Strategic Brand Management, Digitalization and Change Management. He has both an additional specialization as a Certified Public Accountant (CPA) and also an additional specialization in programming and digitalization. Certifications includes topics as Board Management, Business Modeling, Blue Ocean Strategist, PRINCE2 Project Management, and also Data Sciences and Big Data Analytics from MiT.

Other available books from Ikkyo publishing:

Mastering Business Management is a series of books for practitioners, visionaries, entrepreneurs, leaders, and managers. The books are equally suitable for practitioners who do not have higher formal education, and for those who have higher education but want an up-to-date, easy-to-read, research-based refresher. In our publication in progress, *"The Executive Way to **MBA**"*, Mr. Leerberg does not only reveal why business advisors with MBA/EMBA charge so exceptionally well for their services, but he gives you the essence of his own Executive MBA and additional certifications. Appliable but linked to scientific research. As always with all the references and bibliographies. Please visit our website to find all our books on classic managements subjects at www.executivewayto.com:

***Applied Entrepreneurship** for Business Executives*	ISBN 978-82-996199-2-9
***Applied Management and Leadership** for Business Executives*	ISBN 978-82-94176-00-7
***Applied Economics and Management** for Business Executives*	ISBN 978-82-996199-8-1
***Applied Innovation Management** for Business Executives*	ISBN 978-82-996199-4-3
***Applied Strategic Management** for Business Executives*	ISBN 978-82-94176-06-9
***Applied Personal Finance** (What You Just Have to Master!)*	ISBN 978-82-94176-09-0
***Fire @40!** (Applied Personal Finance)*	ISBN 978-82-94176-04-5
***Building a DotCom Business** for Business Executives*	ISBN 978-82-996199-7-4

New book in the pipeline:

*The Executive Way to **MBA***	ISBN 978-82-94176-10-6

Fg 159

www.ingramcontent.com/pod-product-compliance
Lightning Source LLC
Chambersburg PA
CBHW061204240926
51846CB00006B/1108
9788294176045